day trips® from seattle

day trips® series

day trips® from seattle

second edition

getaway ideas for the local traveler

chloë ernst

Globe Pequot
Guilford, Connecticut

All the information in this guidebook is subject to change. We recommend that you call ahead to obtain current information before traveling.

Globe Pequot

An imprint of The Rowman & Littlefield Publishing Group, Inc.
4501 Forbes Blvd., Ste. 200
Lanham, MD 20706
www.rowman.com

Distributed by NATIONAL BOOK NETWORK

British Library Cataloguing in Publication Information available

Library of Congress Cataloging-in-Publication Data available

ISBN 978-1-4930-4412-2 (paper : alk. paper)
ISBN 978-1-4930-4413-9 (electronic)

∞™ The paper used in this publication meets the minimum requirements of American National Standard for Information Sciences—Permanence of Paper for Printed Library Materials, ANSI/NISO Z39.48-1992.

about the author

While ranging through the Pacific Northwest, Chloë Ernst has skied on the slopes overlooking her home in Vancouver, British Columbia, hiked to hot springs in Olympic National Park, been awed by the panoramas of the Gorge Amphitheater on the Columbia River, and followed parts of Ezra Meeker's Oregon Trail. For updates to this guide, she covered more than 2,000 miles of Washington highways, byways, and gravel roads and interviewed more than 150 locals.

Chloë has written more than a dozen travel guides, including titles for FalconGuides, Frommer's, and Fodor's. While she holds a Canadian passport, her affinity with the friendly folk of Washington State has only grown amidst lost wallets, missed turns, and late arrivals in small towns. Find more about the travel journalist's adventures at chloeernst.com.

acknowledgments

Visitor centers, innkeepers, and locals have all provided amazing assistance as I visited new and familiar places around Washington State. All were generous in sharing tips, info, and updates about the beautiful region they call home. Above any destination, travel is first and foremost about people and I appreciate all the contributions.

Thank you also to the many folks who helped along the road to printing, including the editors and staff at Globe Pequot Press. I'm thankful to have the opportunity to explore my Pacific Northwest backyard with the fresh lens of this guide. Happy day-tripping!

contents

southeast

southeast

south

southwest

west

northwest

day trip 01

day trip 02

day trip 03

day trip 04

introduction

From Yakima's 8 inches of annual rainfall to more than 12 feet in the rain forests of the Olympic Peninsula, it's hard to put the Evergreen State in any one category. Wineries, whale sightings, steam-powered railroads, and power-generating dams count amongst the attractions within a 2-hour drive of Seattle.

Three national parks—Olympic, Rainier, and the North Cascades—and one of the nation's most stunning national monuments, Mount St. Helens, all deliver high-altitude, snow-capped scenery. Out on the coast, waterfront and underwater parks venture below sea level. Forests cover about half the state, and the majority of that is government managed. It's no wonder, then, that in this state lassoed by nature, so many people head outdoors to play; there are opportunities for everything from hiking and kayaking to rock climbing, skiing, and stand-up paddleboarding.

Washington takes much of its shape from volcanic activity and the ice age. Heaving plates created the state's volcanoes, many of which remain active to this day. The state shares an international border with Canada at the 49th parallel to the north and is bordered by the states of Idaho to the east and Oregon to the south. The Pacific Ocean lies to the west.

In the northern coastal region, waterfront towns are filled with outdoor art and surrounded by lush farmlands that yield crops of flowers, fruit, and vegetables. Indeed, along the entire tangled coast of Puget Sound, the dense population ensures a mixture of museums, vibrant arts, and busy festivals.

To the east of Seattle lies the imposing Cascade Range. Part of the Pacific Ring of Fire (the stretch of volcanoes and frequent seismic activity that nearly encircles the Pacific), the mountains include the state's tallest peak—Mount Rainier at 14,410 feet—as well as the imposing heights of Mounts Baker, Adams, and St. Helens. Beyond the Cascades to the east, the scenery transforms into the dry but rich agricultural lands of the Columbia Plateau, defined by the grand Columbia River.

The Cascades are the dividing line for the weather in the state. To the west you'll need umbrellas and rain gear to stay dry in a maritime climate that is defined by its mildness, cloud cover, and drizzle. East of the Cascades expect the hottest and coldest extremes in the state. With generally sunny days and clear skies, eastern Washington is a favorite escape from Seattle's low cloud ceiling.

A westward journey ventures into the Olympic Mountains, Kitsap Peninsula, and islands. Rain shadows create hyperlocal climates, which means driving 20 minutes down the road puts you in a new world all together. This is also the region where the Washington State ferry system is most prevalent and provides travelers with access to the San Juan Islands, the far reaches of Kitsap Peninsula, and Canada.

Throughout the state you'll encounter the rich traditions and finely crafted art of Native American nations who have long called the Pacific Northwest their home. Several cities and towns in the state—Snoqualmie, Yakima, Chehalis, Puyallup—bear the names of these Native American nations. Many of the rivers, mountains, and natural features also take names from Coast Salish languages. Not all appear on the map, however, such as Mount Tahoma—the Native American name for Mount Rainier.

Throughout the state, and particularly in the smaller towns, there's an enduring pioneer spirit—one that is preserved in re-created pioneer villages or in community-run museums. Local docents retell the days before and after Washington became a state in 1889.

We can also define the spirit of the state as festive. Faced by many a drizzly day, Washingtonians love nothing more that to get outdoors and celebrate the season. Whether that means catching spring tulips in Skagit Valley, a late-summer fair in Puyallup, the fall grape crush at the wineries, autumn salmon watching in Issaquah, or a winter cowboy gathering in Ellensburg, there's always something to see and do.

Expect traffic in and around Seattle, but a day trip out of the city will take you to places where the roads are open and the horizon beckons. Washington—its mountains, valleys, activities, museums, history, and culture—is truly yours to explore and so much is only a day trip away.

I wrote the first edition of this guide with the help of a Blackberry cell phone and a couple of inch-thick road atlases. The travel world has changed since 2009, and so too has this guide: There are more attractions, more festivals, and more places to stop to give you greater options for your itineraries. Sit back and let these routes do the heavy lifting of planning your next day trip.

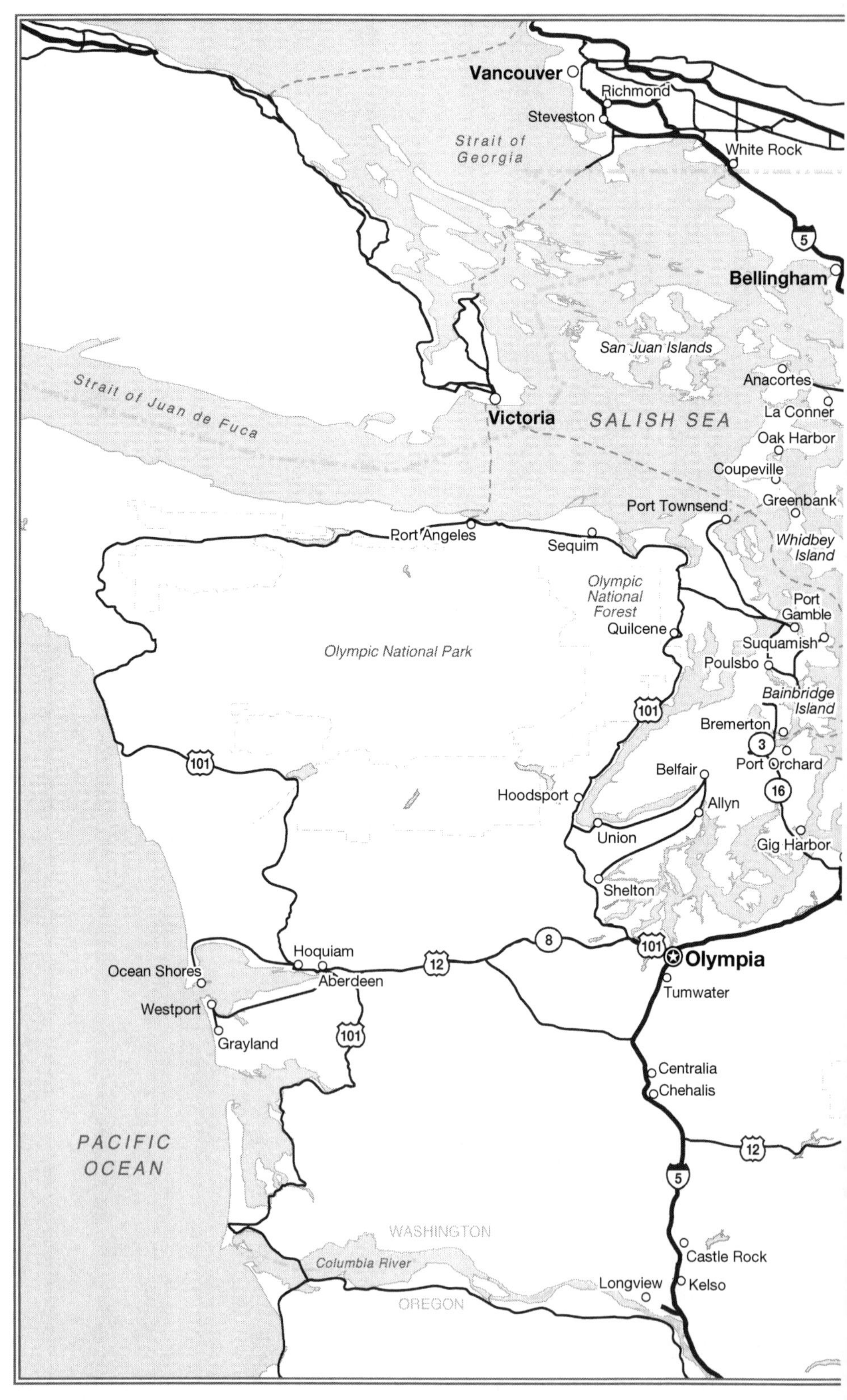
Vancouver
Richmond
Steveston
Strait of Georgia
White Rock
5
Bellingham
San Juan Islands
Anacortes
Strait of Juan de Fuca
Victoria
SALISH SEA
La Conner
Oak Harbor
Coupeville
Greenbank
Port Townsend
Port Angeles
Sequim
Whidbey Island
Olympic National Forest
Port Gamble
Quilcene
Suquamish
Olympic National Park
Poulsbo
Bainbridge Island
101
Bremerton
3
Port Orchard
Belfair
101
16
Hoodsport
Allyn
Union
Gig Harbor
Shelton
8
101
Hoquiam
Olympia
Ocean Shores
Aberdeen
12
Tumwater
Westport
Grayland
101
Centralia
Chehalis
PACIFIC OCEAN
12
5
WASHINGTON
Castle Rock
Columbia River
Longview
Kelso
OREGON

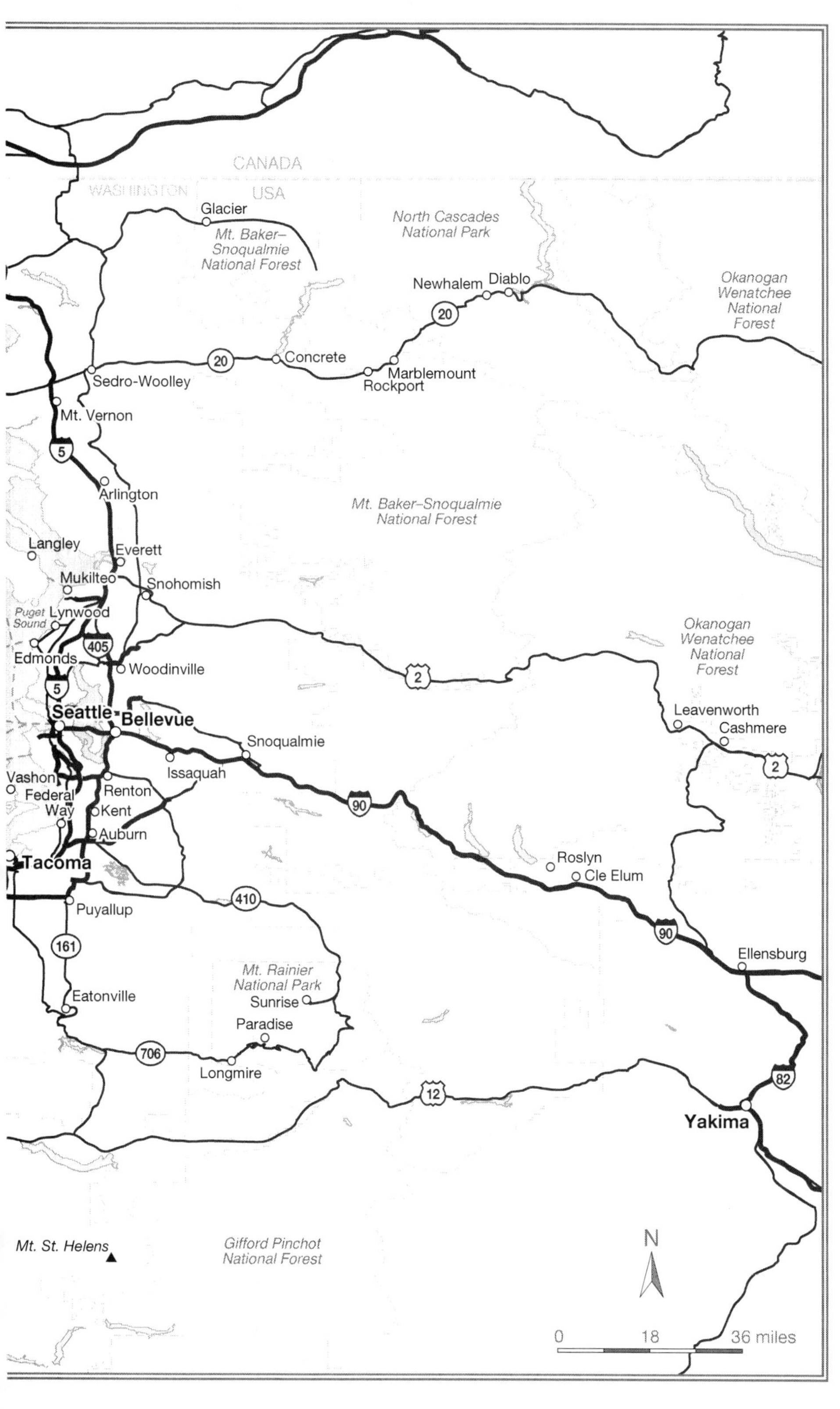

CANADA
WASHINGTON
USA
Glacier
Mt. Baker–Snoqualmie National Forest
North Cascades National Park
Newhalem
Diablo
Okanogan Wenatchee National Forest
20
Concrete
Sedro-Woolley
Marblemount
Rockport
Mt. Vernon
5
Arlington
Mt. Baker–Snoqualmie National Forest
Langley
Everett
Mukilteo
Snohomish
Puget Sound
Lynwood
405
Edmonds
Woodinville
2
Okanogan Wenatchee National Forest
Seattle
Bellevue
Snoqualmie
Leavenworth
Cashmere
Issaquah
Vashon
Federal Way
Renton
Kent
Auburn
90
Tacoma
Roslyn
Cle Elum
Puyallup
410
161
Ellensburg
Mt. Rainier National Park
Sunrise
Eatonville
Paradise
706
Longmire
12
82
Yakima
Mt. St. Helens
Gifford Pinchot National Forest
N
0
18
36 miles

using this guide

This guide is organized as the compass points lie. Deviations from that fall in line with major routes and highways so as not to separate neighboring destinations based on an arbitrary line.

Within each chapter day trips are presented in a nearest-to-furthest order with those closest to Seattle appearing first. Those demanding more travel appear later in the section.

For each day trip we've offered up far more than a day's worth of attractions, activities, and eateries. There are options for family getaways, romantic escapes, independent explorations, outdoor adventures, and historical tours. The intent is to provide diverse options so you can pick and choose from the listings to create an itinerary that suits your own style and interests.

All times and distances are given in relation to downtown Seattle. As you already know—or will quickly discover—being just a few miles outside of the traffic bottleneck will reduce travel time significantly, while hardly impacting the overall distance covered.

hours of operation and prices

We've provided details on hours and pricing as they were at the time of publication. In the interest of accuracy, and because they are subject to continual change, hours of operation in particular are given in general terms. Please always call ahead or check online. If you have specific questions, please use the provided phone numbers and websites to contact the establishments directly—they will be able to provide the most current information.

pricing key

accommodations

The pricing code below reflects the average cost of a double-occupancy room during the peak-price period. Prices do not include state or local sales taxes, occupancy tax, or any other taxes and fees that will be included in a final bill. Always ask about special discounts, which can include AAA, military, senior, or corporate.

- $ less than $90 for a double-occupancy room
- $$ $90 to $140
- $$$ $141 to $199
- $$$$ $200 and up

restaurants

This code prices out the average cost of a main entree. For a full dinner expect to add any drinks, wine, appetizers, desserts, taxes, and tip. In Washington a 15 percent tip is customary, with more for exceptional service. Pricing for lunch and breakfast dishes, where applicable, usually falls in a lower price bracket.

$	less than $10 per entree
$$	$11 to $20
$$$	$21 to $34
$$$$	$35 and up

attractions

This code prices out the average adult entry cost to the listed attractions. Prices do not reflect the total including tax. Family pricing packages and discounts are often available.

$	under $10 for an adult entry ticket
$$	$10 to $19
$$$	$20 and up

driving tips

With ferries, mountain passes, and major highways, a trip along a Washington roadway is no drive in the country. Rockslides, landslides, heavy snow, washed out roads, or ferries with mechanical troubles can all slow down a trip and provide a dose of the unexpected.

An undeniable fact is that it rains and rains a lot in the Northwest. Hydroplaning is a constant danger when the roads are wet. Slow down. Take a byway, not the highway. When roads are slick and water pools, it is easy to lose control of your vehicle.

State patrol is often out, ticketing those who exceed the posted speed limits. Watch your driving speed with particular attention on interstates where speed limits drop, such as the stretch of I-5 south of Bellingham where the limit drops from 70 mph to 60 mph. Fines double in construction zones.

I keep up to date on traffic reports by radio, particularly on I-5, I-90, and I-405 stretches around Seattle. The radio station 97.3 FM reports on traffic conditions every 10 minutes, as does 97.7 FM/1000 AM.

Some highways that traverse mountain passes close in winter. Two such highways are SR 20 between Ross Lake in the North Cascades and Winthrop, and SR 410 from Cayuse Pass near Mount Rainier. Other high elevation roads may be closed or experience dangerous driving conditions such as landslides, rock falls, or washouts. Washington State Department of Transport (WSDOT) provides a traffic information line. Access it by dialing 511 on most phones or (800) 695-7623. Details are also available on the WSDOT website, wsdot.wa.gov/traffic.

Lastly, Washington State Ferries serves as a secondary, floating highway system for the state. But waiting in line patiently and smart planning are all part of the highway code. Ferries are charged with responding to Mayday calls, so journeys occasionally take a detour. Suffice it to say, plan on extra time as you negotiate the system.

highway designations

- Interstates are prefaced by "I" and are generally multilane, divided highways that are also known as freeways or expressways. There are seven in the state: I-5, I-82, I-90, I-182, I-205, I-405, and I-705.
- US highways are mostly two- and three-lane undivided roads and prefaced by "US," although "Highway" is sometimes used locally, as in Highway 2 that runs through Leavenworth.
- State routes are paved and prefaced by "SR," although sometimes they are prefixed by "WA" instead.

highway quirks

State routes are often more commonly known by their destination rather than the number. Thus SR 504, which heads up to Mount St. Helens, is also called Spirit Lake Memorial Highway, and SR 542 is better known as Mount Baker Highway.

The occasional Forest Service road is abbreviated as FSR—you'll mostly find these roads in or near national parks and forests.

Lastly, addresses given by milepost are abbreviated as MP.

travel tips

area codes

Traveling to most of these day trips will put you outside the 206 area code of Seattle, Bainbridge Island, and Vashon Island. Other area codes you'll encounter include:

- 253: Western Washington (Tacoma and area)
- 360: Western Washington (Leavenworth, Ellensburg, Yakima, and east)
- 425: Western Washington (Everett, Bellevue, and east)
- 509: Eastern Washington

- 564: Used throughout the state, as an overlay of other area codes. The area code is available in all of western Washington and switched the state over to ten-digit dialing in 2017.
- For cell phones: Be sure to check with your provider before dialing outside your local calling area—extra charges may apply.

sales tax

Statewide, you'll pay a sales tax on most items save food and prescription medications (6.5 percent in 2020). There can be additional county taxes as well as a hotel occupancy tax. Expect to pay an additional 15 to 20 percent in taxes and fees on hotel rooms.

where to get more information

Day Trips attempts to cover a wide variety of attractions, but those looking for additional material can contact the following agencies by phone or the web. Regarding the latter, there are now incredible volumes of online reviews. Be aware these can be contradictory and conflicting as each person's experience is different.

Each region as well as larger cities and attractions all have their own tourism boards. In addition to these resources (we've listed visitor centers with each of the day trips), a few other helpful sources include:

Amtrak
(800) 872-7245
amtrak.com

National Register of Historic Places
nps.gov/subjects/nationalregister

Washington Independent Inns Network
wainnsiders.com

Washington State Ferries
(206) 464-6400 or (888) 808-7977
wsdot.wa.gov/ferries

Washington State Parks
(360) 902-8844 (information) or (888) 226-7688 (reservations)
infocent@parks.wa.gov (information) or reservations@parks.wa.gov (reservations)
parks.state.wa.us

Washington State Tourism
experiencewa.com

Washington Trails Association
(206) 625-1367
wta.org

best for: itinerary finder

Most day trips have shopping, heritage charm, museums, great dining, beer, local coffee, great parks, scenic views—these are some of the wonderful across-the-state charms of the Pacific Northwest. But beyond that, here's a glance at some of the best aspects of the trips in this guide. And I'll even share my favorites!

	Kids	Beaches	Ferries	Hiking	Biking	Waterfalls	Gardens	Farms	Airplanes	Trains	Art	Wine & beer	My favorites!
Edmonds, Lynnwood, Everett	•	•	•						•		•		
La Conner, Mount Vernon, Chuckanut Drive					•		•	•			•		•
Bellingham, Glacier and Mount Baker	•			•	•	•				•	•	•	•
White Rock, Steveston, Richmond	•	•						•					
Vancouver	•	•		•	•		•				•		•
Woodinville, Snohomish					•		•	•			•	•	
Arlington, Sedro-Woolley, Concrete				•				•	•				
Rockport, Marblemount, Newhalem, North Cascades				•	•	•		•					•
Bellevue, Issaquah, Snoqualmie	•				•	•	•			•	•		
Roslyn, Cle Elum, Ellensburg	•			•	•		•	•			•		•
Leavenworth, Cashmere	•			•	•			•			•	•	•
Renton, Kent, Auburn		•			•			•					
Sunrise, Paradise, Longmire	•			•		•				•			•
Yakima				•	•			•		•		•	•
Federal Way, Puyallup, Eatonville	•			•			•						
Tacoma	•	•			•		•				•		•
Mount St. Helens, Longview and Kelso				•									
Vashon Island, Maury Island		•	•	•			•	•			•	•	•
Olympia, Tumwater, Chehalis	•			•	•	•			•	•			•
Aberdeen and Hoquiam, Ocean Shores, Westport and Grayland	•	•		•	•							•	•
Bremerton, Port Orchard, Gig Harbor	•		•		•		•				•		

	Kids	Beaches	Ferries	Hiking	Biking	Waterfalls	Gardens	Farms	Airplanes	Trains	Art	Wine & beer	My favorites!
Bainbridge Island, Suquamish, Poulsbo	•		•	•	•		•				•		
Shelton, Allyn, Union and Hoodsport, Quilcene	•	•	•	•		•	•	•				•	•
Langley, Greenbank, Coupeville, Oak Harbor	•	•	•	•	•		•	•	•		•		•
Port Gamble, Port Townsend		•	•	•	•				•		•	•	•
Sequim, Port Angeles	•	•	•	•	•	•		•			•		
Victoria			•		•		•				•		

north

day trip 01

trams and planes:
edmonds, lynnwood, everett

North of Seattle you'll find interactive museums, small-town shopping, and waterfront views all just a short drive up the interstate in Edmonds, Lynnwood, and Everett. Amble through Edmonds, along streets lined with trees and independent merchants, where a slow-paced charm insulates visitors from the ever-close Seattle traffic. Then cut back toward I-5 to visit the tiny but historic Heritage Park and a mega shopping center in Lynnwood.

Finally, sea and sky meet in Everett with a lively waterfront district and large marina that boasts a community-on-the-water feel. There's an impressive selection of flight museums (including the must-see Future of Flight Aviation Center and Boeing Tour). Add the special occasion of an AquaSox game or a concert at Angel of the Winds Arena, and the wide streets with historic facades become the ideal place to spend a warm summer evening.

Local events celebrate food, art, music, and so much more.

edmonds

Beyond the charm of the pedestrian-friendly main streets, Edmonds has an enviable position on Puget Sound that offers up picturesque frames of the Olympic Mountains from the city beaches. A central fountain, summer flower boxes, and a historic walking tour—that includes properties on its own Edmonds Register of Historic Places—add an undeniable appeal to a town that also boasts some quirkiness.

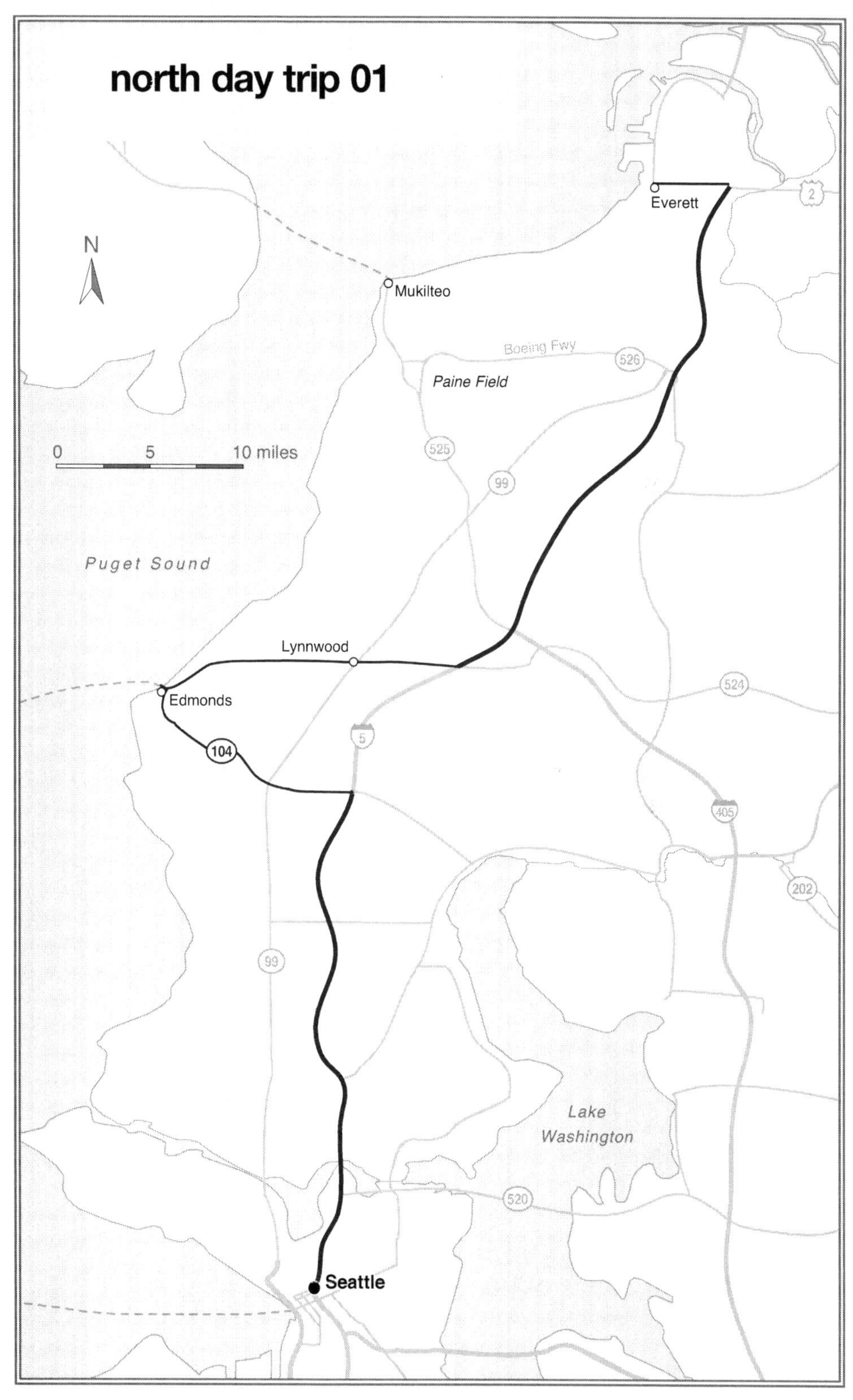
north day trip 01
Everett
2
N
Mukilteo
Boeing Fwy
526
Paine Field
0
5
10 miles
525
99
Puget Sound
Lynnwood
Edmonds
524
5
104
405
202
99
Lake
Washington
520
Seattle

Formerly a mill town, Edmonds now serves as the departure point for daily ferries to Kingston, gateway to Kitsap Peninsula and the Olympics beyond (see Day Trips West 01 and 02, and Northwest 02 for attractions in the area). Near the ferry terminal, venture to an art museum or an underwater marine park off Brackett's Landing Park where sunken boats have become treasure for divers.

getting there

From Seattle, drive 12 miles north on I-5 taking exit 177 to Edmonds. SR 104 zips northwest to Edmonds, becoming Sunset Avenue and intersecting Main Street. The ferry and beaches lie on the shore to the west, while the shopping and museums are to the east. Total travel time is about 25 minutes, not accounting for traffic.

where to go

Edmonds Visitor Bureau. 120 Fifth Ave. North, Edmonds; (425) 776-6711; visitedmonds .com. Housed in the historic Hanley Cabin, the visitor bureau offers area information plus a dose of local history. In its former life this cabin was a home to various local families, the first of who were the Ganahls and the last the Hanleys. Open Mon to Sat.

Cascadia Art Museum. 190 Sunset Ave. Edmonds; (425) 336-4809; cascadiaart museum.org. Exhibits focus on the Pacific Northwest art from around 1860 to 1970. The museum opened in 2015 in a former grocery store and is near the ferry terminal. Open Wed to Sun. $$.

Edmonds Center for the Arts. 410 Fourth Ave. North, Edmonds; (425) 275-9595; edmondscenterforthearts.org. Since hosting its first performance in 2006, the venue has presented a stunning variety of concerts, dance performances, comedy, and film cabarets. The center was once a school auditorium. $$–$$$.

salish sea

In 2009 and 2010 groups named the border-crossing trio of Puget Sound, the Strait of Juan de Fuca, and the Georgia Strait together as the Salish Sea. The name recognizes a shared ecosystem and Coast Salish heritage but doesn't displace any existing names. Common animal residents include orcas, also known as the southern resident killer whales.

Edmonds Historical Museum. 118 Fifth Ave. North, Edmonds; (425) 774-0900; historicedmonds.org. A former library and city hall, the Carnegie Building now houses the Edmonds Historical Museum. Next door to the visitor center, the museum traces the roots of Edmonds back through its incorporation in 1890. Open afternoons Wed to Sun. $.

Edmonds Underwater Park and Brackett's Landing. Foot of Main Street, Edmonds; edmondswa.gov/edmonds-underwater-park-discovery.html. If giant Pacific octopi don't worry you, Edmonds Underwater Park makes a great diving destination. Beneath the waves divers find sunken ships and diverse marine life. Meanwhile for the majority who stay on land, Brackett's Landing has sweeping views of the water and mountains.

Marina Beach Park. 470 Admiral Way, Edmonds. On a windy day thrashing waves beat against the sandy shore. Between a fenced-in dog beach and an impressive marina and boatyard where shelves of boats stack three-high, Marina Beach offers an excellent vantage of the ferries and Puget Sound.

where to eat

Chanterelle. 316 Main St., Edmonds; (425) 774-0650; chanterellewa.com. With a healthy share of well-priced yet creative comfort foods, this eatery will suffice whether you're looking for breakfast, lunch, or dinner. Start with a pear and Brie quesadilla, a medley of mussels and clams, or the famous tomato bisque. Then indulge in a simple meat loaf, fresh salmon, or cioppino stew. Open daily 8 a.m. to 9 p.m.; closes at 1 p.m. on Sun. $$–$$$.

Daphnes. 415½ Main St., Edmonds; no phone. Tiny, intimate, and friendly, Daphnes is one of the most fun spots in Edmonds. With the petite size of the venue (there are just two tables plus the bar), you can't help but meet the locals. Ravenous day-trippers may be best satisfied to make this a before- or after-dinner stop, but do enjoy a little food and a little wine in this lovely little find. Open daily 4 p.m. to midnight. $$.

Red Twig Cafe and Bakery. 117 Fifth Ave. South, Edmonds; (425) 771-1200; redtwig.com. House-roasted coffee, fresh-baked pastries, and Red Twig's own granola are some examples of the pride this eatery takes in what it serves. Hot breakfasts, fresh lunches of salads or power bowls, and shareable fare is also on the menu. Open daily for breakfast, lunch, and light dinner. $$.

The Cheesemonger's Table. 203 Fifth Ave. South, Edmonds; (425) 640-8949; cheesemongerstable.com. This is cheesy heaven. Ripe cheeses, smoky cured meats, and olive-oil-drenched antipasti combine in charcuterie boards, grilled sandwiches, and even dessert. Open daily. $$.

lynnwood

Originally established as the chicken-raising community of Alderwood, Lynnwood has since become a center for commerce. And although in some respects the highways dominate the city (it's at the junction of the state's most heavily trafficked interstates, I-5 and I-405), visitors will find hidden charm amidst the pavement. Discover the time capsule that is Heritage Park, where a telling exhibit on the interurban trolley car, friendly local ambassadors, and an absorbing genealogical society all make the park more than expected. Afterward head out to explore the shopping center at Alderwood Mall, one of the largest shopping complexes in the state. And remember: journeys to Seattle once took two days by wagon!

getting there

Lynnwood lies just 3 miles east, back toward I-5. From Main Street in Edmonds, head northeast on 3rd Avenue North, turn right on Caspers, and continue as it turns into Puget Drive. Follow the twisty route as it becomes 196th Street Southwest and heads into Lynnwood.

Or if heading straight to Lynnwood from Seattle, take I-5 exit 181B.

where to go

Heritage Park. 19921 Poplar Way, Lynnwood; alderwood.org. The historic park offers a few heritage landmarks for a longer-than-expected stop. See the ornate stained glass of the 1909 **Interurban Trolley Car 55,** search family history at the **Sno-Isle Genealogical Society Library** (425-775-6267), or time travel to the now completely transformed community of **Alderwood Manor at Heritage Cottage** (425-775-4694). Mostly run by volunteers, the hours for each park attraction can vary greatly, so call ahead. The park grounds, however, are open daily and parking is free.

on the way to everett

*Stop by the **Mukilteo Light Station** (608 Front St., Mukilteo; 425-513-9602; mukilteohistorical.org) to see the century-old lighthouse with a lens that dates to 1852. There's a park with waterfront access and the vantage overlooks the ferry to Whidbey Island (see Day Trip Northwest 01). Open weekends only from April to September.*

where to shop

Alderwood. 3000 184th St. Southwest, Lynnwood; (425) 771-1121; alderwoodmall.com. Indoor and outdoor shops provide more than 155 shopping and dining experiences at Alderwood Mall. Fashion (including department stores Macy's, JCPenney, and Nordstrom) complements the mix of tasty treats, beauty, accessories, footwear, and other shopping. Open daily.

everett

Air meets the ocean in Everett. The city makes a top destination for flight enthusiasts with a cluster of museums dedicated to flying machines of all kinds. In downtown Everett wide main streets complement the many heritage-fronted commercial properties. Silvertips hockey and concerts at Angel of the Winds Arena and Everett AquaSox games at Funko Field draw crowds into the city. Local festivals harness the young, hip vibe of the city with music concerts, tastings, and more.

The port is a burgeoning area, with summer boat trips to the two-mile-long beach at Jetty Island, great dining with water views, and a Sunday farmers market. Grand Avenue Park Bridge is a connector from the clifftop park to the marina area. Take the journey down to the waterfront, where the impressive marina and requisite excellent sunsets firmly connect the city to its coastal roots.

getting there

I-5 trims the eastern edge of Everett. If your plan includes visiting the flight museums or plane spotting at the airport, take exit 186 to 128th Street Southwest, which becomes Airport Road. Or turn at exit 189, which becomes Boeing Freeway.

If a waterfront stroll and sipping a local brew on a patio are more your speed, follow I-5 to exit 193, leading onto Pacific Avenue and downtown Everett.

where to go

Visitor information. There's no visitor information center in Everett, but local info is available at visiteverett.com.

Flying Heritage & Combat Armor Museum. 3407 109th St. Southwest, Paine Field, Everett; (206) 342-4242; flyingheritage.com. World War II Allied and Axis aircraft form the bulk of this well-restored collection of prop planes, privately owned by Paul G. Allen of Microsoft fame. Be sure to visit on a fly day when you can see the 1935–1945 vintage aircraft outside the hangar, soaring and roaring through the skies above Paine Airfield. Open daily from Memorial Day to Labor Day, closed Mon the rest of the year. $$.

Forest Park. 802 East Mukilteo Blvd., Everett; (425) 257-8300; everettwa.org. Everett's oldest park is a gem encompassing 197 acres of woodland and attractions. A summertime animal farm, forested trails, tennis courts, and indoor swimming pool make the park a perfect low-key day-trip destination. At the very least, take a drive along Mukilteo Boulevard and enjoy the route that winds down through the mossy groves. Open daily.

Funko. 2802 Wetmore Ave., Everett; (425) 783-3616; funko.com. Giant toy figures stand sentinel around this can't-miss-it headquarters, where Funko creates pop culture figures as well as allows visitors to build their own. The store has a playland atmosphere that's worth a visit to witness. Open daily.

Future of Flight Aviation Center and Boeing Tour. 8415 Paine Field Blvd., Mukilteo; (425) 438-8100 or (800) 464-1476; futureofflight.org. By volume the Boeing factory is the largest building in the world. The 90-minute tour takes visitors through the factory, where the majority of Boeing planes are constructed, including the 787 Dreamliner. Extras like a design-your-own-jet program, gallery, and observation deck all add to the experience, making the factory a day trip in itself. There are some hard-and-fast rules: Children must be at least 4 feet tall, and no personal belongings are allowed on the tour (although there are lockers available). Either reserve tickets online or plan to arrive early during the day as tickets sell out quickly, particularly on summer weekends. Open daily except for major holidays with tours starting on the hour. Military and senior discounts available. $$$.

Hibulb Cultural Center & Natural History Preserve. 6410 23rd Ave NE, Tulalip; (360) 716-2600; hibulbculturalcenter.org. The culture of the Tulalip people is introduced through the large gallery of exhibits, a longhouse with story-telling experiences, and a 50-acre nature preserve. Open Tues to Sun.

Historic Flight at Kilo-7. 10719 Bernie Webber Dr., Mukilteo; (425) 348-3200; historic flight.org. Between Paine Field and the Mukilteo Speedway, this working museum restores planes to flying condition and also holds events to show them in motion. The museum focuses on the era beginning with the first cross-Atlantic solo flight through to 1957. Open Tues to Sun. $$.

Imagine Children's Museum. 1502 Wall St., Everett; (425) 258-1006; imaginecm.org. You'll find planes, trains, and automobiles at the Imagine Children's Museum, except these are mini-friendly versions and far less noisy. The museum is like the playroom every kid dreams of: an indoor tree house, pretend downtown Main Street, fire engine, walk-on ferry, and even a mountain. Closed Mon. $$.

Jetty Island. Ferries leave from 10th Street and West Marine View Drive, Everett; (425) 257-8304; everettwa.org/parks. Jetty Island is a human-made slice of sandy shore and a spitting-distance getaway. Free ferries leave every 15–30 minutes from Jetty Landing, by the expansive 10th Street Boat Launch. The summer schedule teems with events, particularly for families. Sunset tours, nature walks, and sand-castle-building contests are all part of the fun. Sitting on dry land in the parking lot is the historic schooner *Equator.* The empty shell of the wooden boat hints at its one-time greatness as a trading ship. Jetty Island is open daily from July through Labor Day. $.

Museum of Flight Restoration Center. 2909 100th St. Southwest, Everett; (425) 745-5150; museumofflight.org. In hangar C-72 there's some work going on: The restoration center refurbishes planes for the ever-popular Museum of Flight in Seattle. A variety of models can be viewed in various states of repair (and disrepair). Open Wed to Sun. $.

Schack Art Center. 2921 Hoyt Ave., Everett; (425) 259-5050; schack.org. The hottest draw here is glassblowing, and the hot shop window is a look into the mesmerizing world of glass artistry. There's also a visual arts gallery, a wide variety of classes for serious students or just the curious, and regularly changing exhibits. Open daily.

where to eat

Lombardi's. 1620 West Marine View Dr., Everett; (425) 252-1886; lombardisitalian.com. On the Everett waterfront sits this sleek restaurant. An outdoor patio complements the interior with lots of natural light—a bright spot to enjoy a rainy day. Head here for a plate of the area's rich ocean bounty: wild salmon or Dungeness crab. Open for lunch and dinner. $$–$$$.

The Vintage Cafe. 1508 Hewitt Ave., Everett; (425) 252-8224; thevintagecafe.net. Serving comfort food, the Vintage Cafe is a charming spot to chow down. Three-course dinners come loaded with extras like soup, a side, veggies, and bread—plus dessert! Open daily for breakfast, lunch, and dinner. $–$$.

where to stay

Inn at Port Gardner. 1700 West Marine View Dr., Everett; (425) 252-6779 or (888) 252-6779; innatportgardner.com. Few better locations exist. The Inn at Port Gardner overlooks the Everett Marina and offers a fun mix of nightlife and comfort. More than thirty rooms all feature queen- or king-size beds, while the harbor-view suites also offer soaking tubs, fireplaces, and decks or patios. Includes breakfast delivered to the room. $$–$$$.

day trip 02

tulips and oysters:
la conner, mount vernon, chuckanut drive

Washington's blooms are on full display in the Skagit Valley each spring. Usually in April—or "governed by Mother Nature" as locals put it—daffodils, irises, and tulips brighten the local fields. But the region offers more than stunning blooms.

A favorite day-trip town, La Conner specializes in quaint—be it the rainbow-shaped bridge or roadside stands of fruit and local vegetables that operate on an honor system. Tucked in the saltwater Swinomish Channel that connects Padilla and Skagit Bays, with a 25 mph speed limit, the village is a place where time slows down.

This route then heads along the coast through farmlands to stop in at tulip central: the nurseries and show gardens of Mount Vernon. Further north, lucky travelers will follow the unrivaled Chuckanut Drive. The route, officially SR 11, connects the Samish farmlands, where hidden eateries are the norm, to cliff-side lookouts, where escarpments tower above the ever-tempestuous ocean. It's a narrow road that was one of Washington's first scenic drives, and it remains an all-time favorite.

la conner

This historic waterfront village warrants an on-foot exploration of quality shops and a walk over the iconic Rainbow Bridge across Swinomish Channel. As La Conner works its charm, stay longer and capture a waterfront vantage from the sculpture-adorned Gilkey Square or from a restaurant patio while you tuck into a seafood feast of fresh Dungeness crab.

north day trip 02

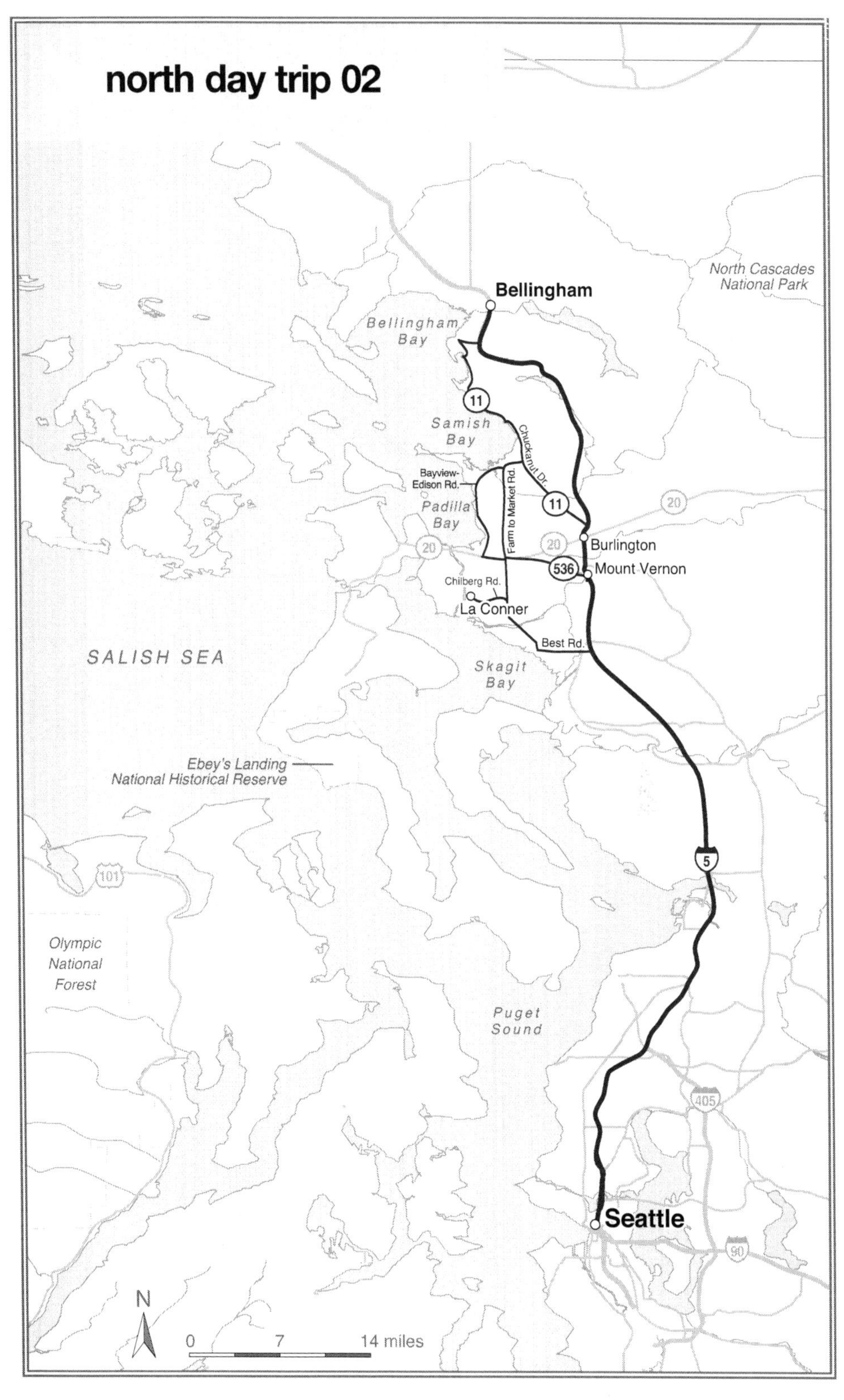

During the Skagit Valley Tulip Festival, La Conner becomes a top destination for enjoying the blooms and the refreshing spring days that accompany the festival.

getting there

To reach La Conner, take I-5 north to exit 221. Head west into Conway, taking Fir Island Road out of town and continuing west. Crossing the north fork of the Skagit River, the road becomes Best Road. Turn left on Chilberg Road and watch for signs for La Conner (not, however, the La Conner–Whitney Road). Circle a roundabout and follow the road as it becomes Morris Street and ends at the waterfront.

where to go

Visitor Information Center. 413 Morris St., La Conner; (360) 466-4778 or (888) 642-9284; lovelaconner.com. Located on the right when heading into town, the Visitor Information Center is open Mon to Sat.

La Conner Volunteer Firefighters' Museum. 611 South First St., La Conner. As you amble along the vibrant stretch of First Street, stop in (if it's open) at the firefighters' museum. Displays trace firefighting back to horse-drawn fire carriages. Open by chance. $.

Museum of Northwest Art. 121 South First St., La Conner; (360) 466-4446; museumofnwart.org. There's a fusion of history and modern polish at the Museum of Northwest Art thanks to the beautiful, cedar-and-hemlock-fronted building. The museum displays contemporary exhibits from Northwest artists. For shoppers the gift shop stocks some of the best goods in town. Open daily.

Pacific Northwest Quilt & Fiber Arts Museum. 703 South Second St., La Conner; (360) 466-4288; qfamuseum.org. Fabrics weave many different stories at this La Conner museum. Housed in the 1891 Gaches Mansion—one of the town's oldest buildings—the exhibits fuse tradition with contemporary art. Open Wed to Sun. $.

Skagit County Historical Museum. 501 South Fourth St., La Conner; (360) 466-3365; skagitcounty.net/museum. A bit tricky to find (Fourth Street only has two access points: Benton and Calhoun Streets that head uphill from Second Street), this county museum features a lovely observation deck looking out from the promontory location. The stories of farm life, Native Americans, and vintage toys all feature in the museum, which is open Tues to Sun. $.

where to shop

In the 1930s and 1940s, La Conner became a haven for artists. Today this creativity lives on and is yours to explore amongst the shopping opportunities on First Street. Including excellent quality crafts, functional pieces, and fine art, this shopping tour represents the diversity you'll find in La Conner:

Earthenworks Gallery. 713 S. First St., La Conner; (360) 466-4422; earthenworksgallery.com. From small jewelry items to larger home decor pieces, this gallery delivers stunning art and functional finds.

Nasty Jack's Antiques. 103 Morris St., La Conner; (360) 466-3209; nastyjacksantiques.com. There's a well-displayed miscellany of antiques, curios, memorabilia, and unusual items at this well-loved store.

La Conner Artists' Gallery. 128 S. First St., La Conner; (360) 399-1660. Local artists come together in this cooperative, with ceramics, jewelry, fiber arts, paintings, and more.

The Wood Merchant. 709 S. First St., La Conner; (360) 466-4741; woodmerchant.com. A diverse selection of beautifully constructed, US-made wood products shows the versatility of this natural material. Endless hours of woodworking create polished pieces that are thoughtful, natural, and appealing. The shop glows with the warm grains of maple, walnut, and pine patiently transformed into children's toys, serving dishes, and furniture.

where to eat

La Conner Brewing Company. 117 S. First St., La Conner; (360) 466-1415; laconnerbrewery.com. The casual and warm atmosphere of this brewery exudes the feel of a local favorite. It's hopping long before any other spot in town and serves a simple but quality selection that hits above the usual deep-fried nature of pub grub. Wood-fired pizzas, a prime-rib dip, warming soups, or local crab cakes strike a lovely complement to a pint of beer brewed mere feet away. Open daily for lunch and dinner. $$.

La Conner Seafood & Prime Rib House. 614 S. First St., La Conner; (360) 466-4014; laconnerseafood.com. With debatably the best deck in town, this restaurant has been serving favorites like slow-roasted prime rib, Dungeness crab, scallops, and clam chowder since 1986. From the Swinomish Channel waterfront, you'll take in views of the Rainbow Bridge and local boat traffic. For less-than-reliable West Coast days, the inside dining room still has excellent views and there's also a lounge with an impressive music history. Open for lunch and dinner daily. $$–$$$$.

where to stay

Hotel Planter. 715 First St., La Conner; (360) 466-4710; hotelplanter.com. The location is unbeatable at this second-floor hotel on La Conner's main street. The views and amenities in all rooms differ: Some include a Jacuzzi tub while others look out over the art-filled, hidden courtyard. $$–$$$.

La Conner Channel Lodge. 205 N. First St., La Conner; (360) 466-1500 or (888) 466-4113; laconnerlodging.com. **La Conner Country Inn.** 107 S. Second St., La Conner; (360) 466-3101. These two sister accommodations are set apart from the bustle of town and each other, but are walking distance from La Conner's excellent restaurants and attractions. The Country Inn is the more economical and dog-friendly. Decor blends a rustic edge with a touch of history and there's excellent on-site dining at The Oyster & Thistle. The Channel Lodge delivers payoff waterfront views from the guest rooms balconies, observation dock, and channel-side deck. Over the two properties, rooms range widely in amenities and size—meaning there are options for most budgets. $$$–$$$$.

mount vernon

This is the heart of the Skagit Valley Tulip Festival, and spring is truly the best (and often busiest) time to visit the area. Mount Vernon also offers rural delights like the iconic Roozengaarde gardens and a lovingly restored Vaudeville-era theater. There's a farmers market on Saturdays in Riverwalk Plaza, along the Skagit River.

Be sure to visit during the **Skagit Valley Tulip Festival,** when the fields fill with tulip, daffodil, and iris blooms on mother nature's schedule.

getting there

From La Conner, head north on La Conner–Whitney Road to SR 20 east. From this stretch of the Cascade Loop Scenic Highway (which connects Puget Sound to the Columbia River Valley via the Cascade Range), head southeast on SR 536 or Memorial Highway to the center of Mount Vernon.

where to go

Mount Vernon Visitor Information Center. 301 W. Kincaid, Mount Vernon; (360) 428-8547; mountvernonchamber.com. Head to downtown for the local scoop on attractions, tickets, accommodations, and dining. Open daily.

Lincoln Theatre. 712 S. First St., Mount Vernon; (360) 336-8955; lincolntheatre.org. The 1920s theater emulates Spanish opulence. Well-preserved and treasured, the historic building is now home to concerts, performances, and movies. The theater's rare Wurlitzer organ gets a spin before most evening movie showings—a tradition retained from the early 1900s when organs added sound effects to silent films. Performances or showings run most evenings. $$–$$$$.

Padilla Bay National Estuarine Research Reserve. 10441 Bayview-Edison Rd. (north of Bay View State Park), Mount Vernon; (360) 428-1558; padillabay.gov. The muddy, flat bottom of Padilla Bay is the rooting ground for an eelgrass meadow that in turn provides a home to herons, eagles, fish, and other wildlife. The large and well-maintained Breazeale Interpretive Center offers information on bird watching as well as access to an observation deck and walking trails. It's just along the road from the beach, camping, and cabins at Bay View State Park (parks.state.wa.us). Trails are open daily. The interpretive center is open Tues to Sat; closed holidays. $.

Roozengaarde. 15867 Beaver Marsh Rd., Mount Vernon; (360) 424-8531; tulips.com. Show gardens bloom each spring with bright-colored flowers from the Washington Bulb Company. Roozengaarde also sells bulbs. Open daily year-round. $.

WSU Discovery Garden. 16650 SR 536, Mount Vernon; (360) 428-4270 ext. 227; extension.wsu.edu/skagit/mg/discovery-garden. With gardens that explore the possibilities for shade, pollinators, low maintenance, the winter season, succulents, and more—this garden offers an unusual and delightful display. Open daily.

where to eat

Calico Cupboard. 121 Freeway Dr., Suite B, Mount Vernon; (360) 336-3107; calicocupboardcafe.com. Visible from I-5, the old granary building sits below the Mount Vernon water tower. Soups, quiches, and sandwiches complement the simple entrees, including burgers, tacos, and potpies. The all-day breakfast is perfect for late starters, and the warm atmosphere will combat any chilly spring morning. Open daily for breakfast and lunch. $$.

The Porterhouse. 416 W. Gates St., Mount Vernon; (360) 336-9989; porterhousepub.net. Celebrate the Northwest's brewing traditions with more than 20 beers on tap at the Porterhouse. The menu has unusual twists, with salmon fish and chips as well as boar and elk burgers. Open daily for lunch and dinner. $–$$$.

chuckanut drive

North of Mount Vernon, the grandeur of Chuckanut Drive twists along the coast, slipping between ocean's edge and mountain peaks. Frequent lookouts and the shoreline of Larrabee State Park provide excellent detours, along with refreshments at roadside eateries. The route connects Skagit Valley to Whatcom County.

getting there

SR 11 officially begins at I-5 exit 231 in the north of Burlington and ends at exit 250 south of Bellingham.

where to go

Larrabee State Park. 245 Chuckanut Dr., Bellingham; (360) 676-2093; parks.state.wa.us. Ocean, lakes, and tide pools create a park with plenty of outdoor appeal. Larrabee was Washington's first state park and is now perhaps one of the best loved. Whether you head there to clam, crab, hike, fish, paddle, train-spot, camp, or bike, the park rates as the best stopping spot on Chuckanut Drive. Open year-round. $.

where to eat

The Oyster Bar. 2578 Chuckanut Dr., Bow; (360) 766-6185; theoysterbar.net. Admiring a sunset over seafood and fine dessert, where the dining area and patio seem to hover over the ocean, may top the beauty of Chuckanut Drive. A seasonal menu of fresh west coast oysters plus mussels, salmon, abalone, halibut, and crab all feature for dinner. Lunch options are more casual, including fish tacos or halibut fish and chips. Reservations are recommended for dinner. Open daily for lunch and dinner. $$$–$$$$.

day trip 03

north

from bay to baker:
bellingham, glacier and mount baker

In Whatcom County a concentration of outdoor sculpture galleries and engaging museums are all located near the soft curve of Bellingham Bay. Follow the shore south along South Bay Trail to reach Fairhaven—a historic district south of downtown, where the weekends are filled with visits to charming shops, community festivals, and jazzy nightlife.

Bellingham also marks the access point for a world-class scenic drive along Mount Baker Highway (SR 542). At 10,781 feet Mount Baker is the northern sentry of the Cascade Range. It's also the snowiest spot in Washington, setting the record in 1998–1999 with a snowfall measuring a whopping 95 feet. Good thing, then, that Mount Baker Highway culminates in winter at a ski hill. (In summer it's the stunning panoramic viewpoint: Artist Point.)

bellingham

The Chuckanut Drive (see North Day Trip 02) scenic highway ends in Fairhaven, a historic district south of Bellingham. There, shops and festivals create a fun atmosphere to explore. Just a short jaunt northward, Bellingham rewards with museums, top-quality restaurants (or cheap burrito stands, depending on your preference), a second downtown, and a university-fueled nightlife.

Spend a summer afternoon on South Bay Trail, which connects Bellingham to Fairhaven via Boulevard Park and a boardwalk, where the ocean laps and shorebirds

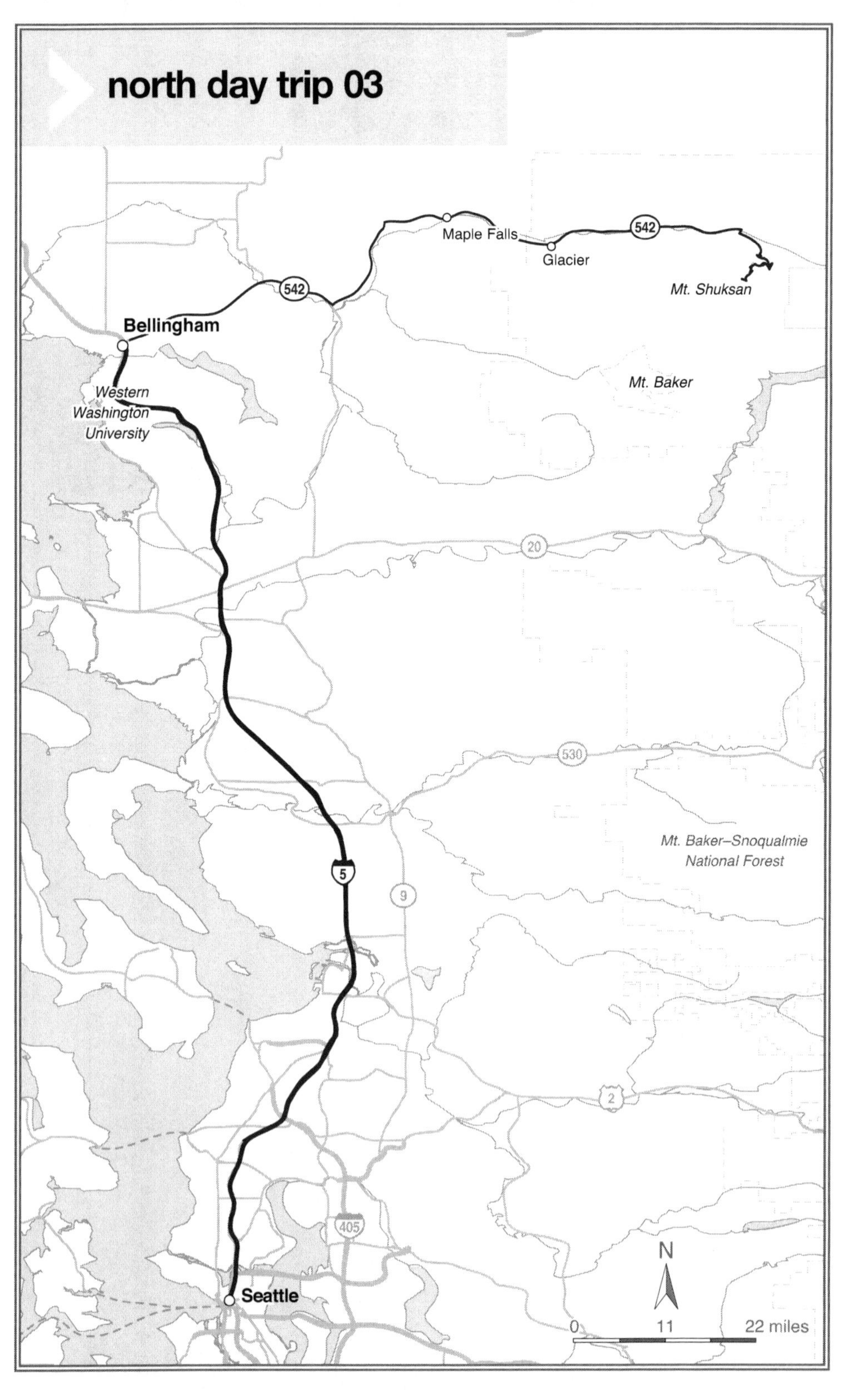
north day trip 03
542
Maple Falls
Glacier
542
Mt. Shuksan
Bellingham
Mt. Baker
Western
Washington
University
20
530
Mt. Baker–Snoqualmie
National Forest
5
9
2
405
Seattle
N
0
11
22 miles

squawk on either side. Another favorite outdoor activity is a visit to the Western Washington University sculpture collection.

Hiking, biking, skiing, and beer take top place in local hearts, and this hub of Whatcom County has also become a base camp for Mount Baker, a volcano in the Cascade Range. It's also a very festive spot, with beer, music, and outdoor adventure celebrated in events such as the epic Ski to Sea relay from Mt. Baker to Bellingham.

getting there

From Seattle, travel north on I-5 for about 90 miles (1.5 hours). Take exit 250 for Fairhaven, exit 252 for Western Washington University, and exit 253 or 254 for downtown Bellingham.

Alternately, opt for a two-hour journey on the Amtrak Cascades train (800-872-7245; amtrak.com). The route is ideal for those spending a weekend.

where to go

Visitor Information Center. 904 Potter St., Bellingham; (360) 671-3990; bellingham.org. This visitor bureau provides information on Whatcom County as well as Bellingham. Open daily.

Bellingham Railway Museum. 1320 Commercial St., Bellingham; (360) 393-7540; bellinghamrailwaymuseum.org. A train simulator takes you on a ride along the rails—and you're in the engineer's seat. Model train and antique railroad items make up the large collection. Open Tues to Sat with a particularly affordable admission option for families. $.

Big Rock Garden Park. 2900 Sylvan St., Bellingham; (360) 778-7000 (Parks & Recreation); cob.org/services/recreation/parks-trails. Bellingham's lesser-known outdoor sculpture garden sits on the outskirts of the city near Lake Whatcom. The permanent collection features more than thirty pieces both large and small. Forested trails twist through the park offering many routes, scultpures, and benches to discover. Open year-round.

Marine Life Center. 1801 Roeder Ave., Bellingham; (360) 671-2431; marinelifecenter.org. This waterfront facility invites you to explore under the water. A touch tank introduces sea stars, snails, and more. Open daily.

Mindport Exhibits. 210 West Holly St., Bellingham; (360) 647-5614; mindport.org. Interactive art exhibits are the highlight of this privately run gallery. Expect to be engaged by works that pique your curiosity and test your mind by blending light, touch, and sound. Open Wed to Sun. $.

SPARK Museum of Electrical Invention. 1312 Bay St., Bellingham; (360) 738-3886; sparkmuseum.org. The museum traces the source of electricity and the story of radio, and on weekends there's a MegaZapper show to demo one of the largest Tesla coils in the US. Open Wed to Sun. $–$$.

Western Washington University's Outdoor Sculpture Collection. WWU Campus, Bellingham; (360) 650-3900; westerngallery.wwu.edu/sculpture. Perhaps the most appealing element of the WWU sculpture collection is how easy it is to engage with the pieces. Of course, standing under Isamu Noguchi's acclaimed *Skyviewing Sculpture* endures as a favorite, but so does an upward gaze to Mark di Suvero's *For Handel* or entering the metal walls of Richard Serra's *Wright's Triangle*. Take a wander through the sculptures on your own schedule, or plan a visit to coincide with a visit to the campus' Western Gallery. Pick up a photo guide to the sculpture collection and be sure to check in with the visitor center at 2001 Bill McDonald Pkwy. for info on campus parking. Accessible year-round.

Whatcom Falls Park. Silver Beach Road (off Lakeway Drive) or 1401 Electric Ave., Bellingham; (360) 778-7000 (Parks & Recreation); cob.org/services/recreation/parks-trails. Flowing from Lake Whatcom to Bellingham Bay, Whatcom Creek is the main vein of the park. The upper falls cascade heavily, and the 1939 sandstone bridge makes an excellent viewing point. A lesser-used fish hatchery, trails, and playground offer a lovely setting. Open daily year-round.

Whatcom Museum. 121 Prospect St., Bellingham; (360) 778-8930; whatcommuseum.org. The 1892 red brick Old City Hall building served as a landmark to sailors for many years, and was the original flagship for this city museum of art and history. The far newer Lightcatcher building (250 Flora St.) opened in late 2009 and offers interactive family exhibits and art displays. Collections reflect the rich culture and spirit-world art of the Northwest. Open Wed to Sun. $$.

where to eat

Bantam 46. 1327 Railroad Ave, Bellingham; (360) 788-4507; bantambellingham.com. This is simple goodness on a plate, with a variety of rotisserie and fried chicken options plus upscale comfort foods like mac & cheese. It's from the same owners as Mallard Ice Cream next door. Open Mon to Sat for dinner.

Boundary Bay Brewery & Bistro. 1107 Railroad Ave., Bellingham; (360) 647-5593; bbay brewery.com. A large selection of house-brewed beers—including seasonal and limited releases—complements a menu inspired by fresh foods. A tasting flight or a recommendation will do the trick. On Saturdays, pair a visit with the nearby farmers' market. Serving lunch and dinner daily. $$–$$$.

Casa Que Pasa. 1415 Railroad Ave., Bellingham; (360) 756-8226; casaquepasarocks .com. Casa Que Pasa's reputation for burritos is international in scope. Casa caters to a younger, thriftier crowd that doesn't worry about the rather basic seating as they emerge (stomachs grumbling) from the slopes of Mount Baker. The potato burrito in particular draws high honors. Open daily for lunch until late. $.

Skylark's Hidden Cafe. 1308 11th St., Bellingham; (360) 715-3642; skylarkshiddencafe .com. Serving breakfast through dinner (with live jazz some evenings), this personality-filled restaurant offers historic style in the Fairhaven district. The menu encompasses both inexpensive and pricier entrees plus a budget menu for lunch and dinner. Open daily. $$–$$$.

where to stay

Fairhaven Village Inn. 1200 10th St., Bellingham; (360) 733-1311 or (877) 733-1100; fair havenvillageinn.com. Adjacent to historic, quaint Fairhaven with views of Bellingham Bay, the Fairhaven Village Inn provides twenty-two contemporary rooms with excellent amenities and a craft cocktail bar that's ideal for a nightcap. Free parking and a beautiful lobby all create a special destination. Choose from the harbor-side rooms with fireplaces and balconies, or the parkside rooms overlooking the lively village green. $$$.

Hotel Bellwether. 1 Bellwether Way, Bellingham; (360) 392-3100 or (877) 411-1200; hotel bellwether.com. Sixty-five guest rooms plus the grand, free-standing lighthouse suite exude luxury and thoughtful presentation. More than half offer waterfront views, and most have balconies or patios, jetted tubs, and fireplaces. There's a spa nearby, room service, and the on-site restaurant provides gorgeous views of the marina—but as the hotel sits on a pier designed for conference guests, there are ample dining choices. For those arriving by boat or even floatplane, the hotel dock provides moorage. For the rest of us, the hotel offers underground parking. $$$$.

glacier and mount baker

Glacier is the feeder town to the volcanic peak and outdoor playground of Mount Baker. Filled with ski-bound traffic, shops, and après-ski eateries, the roadside village is more a departure point than a destination. Heading further east along the highway, the route climbs into Mount Baker–Snoqualmie National Forest and winds along the Nooksack River toward Mount Baker Ski Area and the end of the road at Artist Point.

Annual average snowfall at the ski hill measures about 55 feet; however, in the record-setting season of 1998–1999, the snowfall at Mount Baker topped a jaw-dropping 95 feet.

getting there

At exit 255, take SR 542 that cuts eastward from Bellingham to Mount Baker. The drive to Glacier takes under an hour along Mount Baker Highway, while Artist Point lies another 40 minutes east.

where to go

Mount Baker Visitor Center. 7509 Mount Baker Hwy., Maple Falls; (360) 599-1518; mtbakerchamber.org. At the gateway to the mountain, stop in for friendly help and recommendations. Open daily.

Artist Point. End of Mount Baker Highway, SR 542. This vantage has served as artistic inspiration for decades. Open July to Sept only; closed otherwise due to snow.

Glacier Public Service Center. 10091 Mount Baker Hwy., SR 542; (360) 599-2714; fs.usda.gov. For information on the national forest, stop at this roadside visitor center. Exhibits and information are plentiful. Grab a map and continue along the highway to enter the wilderness. Open daily in summer; weekends only in winter.

Mount Baker Ski Area. SR 542; (360) 671-0211 (snow phone); mtbaker.us. Summer brings hikers and photographers in large numbers to the peak—and Heather Meadows Cafe is open to the public for eats. In winter it's the legendary Mount Baker snowfall that draws skiers, as well as a variety of outdoor enthusiasts to snowshoe, sled, snowmobile, and more in the surrounding recreation areas. Day-pass lift tickets start at about $55. $$$.

where to eat

Graham's Restaurant. 9989 Mount Baker Hwy., Glacier; (360) 599-1933; grahamhistoricalrestaurant.com. Belly-filling eats include chicken, steaks, and burgers. The history of the restaurant goes back to its 1930s days as a general store and self-serve breakfast restaurant. Open for breakfast weekends, and daily for lunch and dinner during peak skiing and hiking seasons. $–$$$.

Rifugio's Country Italian Cuisine. 5415 Mount Baker Hwy., Deming; (360) 592-2888; ilcafferifugio.com. With coffee that rivals any cup in Seattle, this Italy-meets-Northwest eatery is a not-to-miss spot to cap the drive. Seafood, pastas, and daily specials feature on the small menu, and there's also a sculpture garden outside. Open for dinner Thurs to Sun and for brunch Sunday. $$–$$$.

where to stay

Mount Baker Lodging. Glacier; (360) 599-2453 or (800) 709-7669; mtbakerlodging.com. With access to dozens of properties, this rental company provides a huge variety of options for a stay in the Mount Baker area. Ski town chalets, lodge condos, and woodsy cabins sleep anywhere from two to thirteen guests. Depending on the property, you can relax in a private hot tub, cross-country ski outside the door, shoot a game of pool, or barbecue on your own deck. Many options are also pet-friendly. $$–$$$$.

day trip 04

north

canadian fishing villages:
white rock, steveston, richmond

South of Vancouver the cities of White Rock and Richmond blend urban with the historic. Although the White Rock Pier harks back to the city's fishing heritage, a lively waterfront district of packed patios and gelato shops modernizes the city. Yes, there's an impressively sized white rock, but you'll also discover a well-kept museum and perfect views from the promenade.

In Richmond historic Steveston revives its fishing days while the rest of the city embraces an ever-evolving international feel. Here, Olympic venues lie a short distance from Buddhist temples and malls that rival those in Hong Kong.

Celebrations of **Chinese New Year** are particularly impressive—with decorations, costumes, and dancing to mark the lunar new year.

white rock

Just across the US–Canada border, most visitors zip past White Rock on Hwy. 99 to Vancouver without stopping. In all fairness, though, you can't see the city's 5-mile beach, the pier inviting you for an evening stroll, or the walkable waterfront district of shops and restaurants from the highway. White Rock is a seaside getaway so close to the city—plus it sits in Canada's version of the banana belt, rewarding visitors with some Seattle-elusive sunshine.

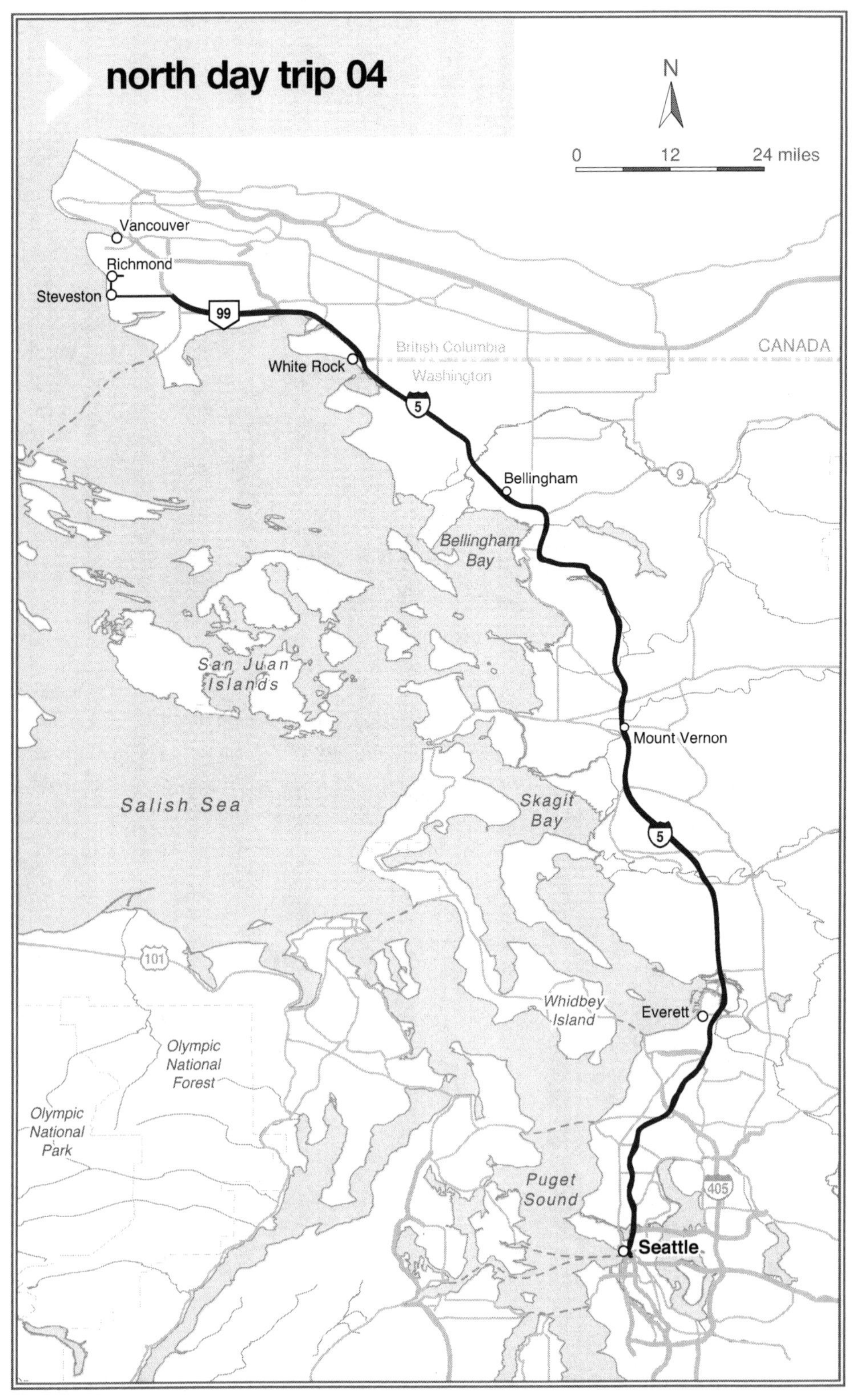
north day trip 04
N
0
12
24 miles
Vancouver
Richmond
Steveston
99
White Rock
British Columbia
Washington
CANADA
5
Bellingham
9
Bellingham Bay
San Juan Islands
Mount Vernon
Salish Sea
Skagit Bay
5
101
Whidbey Island
Everett
Olympic National Forest
Olympic National Park
Puget Sound
405
Seattle

getting there

Simply take I-5 north to the Peace Arch border crossing then continue on the Canadian Hwy. 99. Exit almost immediately at exit 2 to White Rock, heading west on Eighth Avenue. Conveniently, Eighth Avenue turns into Marine Drive and follows the waterfront to the pier.

Waterfront paid parking starts at Finlay Street and continues west. Spots tend to fill up quickly on weekend nights, so grab the first one you see and then walk along the waterfront promenade to reach the beach, pier, and restaurants.

where to go

White Rock Beach, Pier, and Promenade. South of Marine Drive, White Rock; explore whiterock.com. Of course, here is where you'll find the 486-ton white rock that gives the city its name. Although the rock was once bleached by bird guano (another term for excrement), it now sports layers of white paint to cover the graffiti. As dusk settles, walk out under the lighted arches on the historic pier (re-opened in 2019 having been damaged by a storm) and take in the hill of crisp lights that define the shore. The 1.5-mile promenade runs along a significant portion of the beach, connecting parking areas to local restaurants. Benches, safety lighting, and restrooms create a family-friendly destination. Open year-round.

White Rock Museum & Archives. 14970 Marine Dr., White Rock; (604) 541-2221; white rockmuseum.ca. Located on the beach in the old White Rock railroad station, the White Rock Museum features temporary exhibits with a mix of railway, pioneer, First Nations, and local history. See the rails that run right along the water and learn how the railroad helped shape the city. Open daily; closed Mondays Jan to June.

where to eat

The Boathouse Restaurant. 14935 Marine Dr., White Rock; (604) 536-7320; boathouse restaurants.ca. Seafood is the toast of the town at the Boathouse. The restaurant serves seafood in season plus the best of the Pacific Northwest: crab, halibut, salmon, and other feasts. A third-level patio offers a lower-priced menu, younger feel, and the best views, while a glassed-in second level provides a more upscale service and diverse menu. On the ground level the Surfside Grill also serves ocean favorites. Open for weekend brunch and daily for lunch and dinner. $$–$$$$.

Uli's. 15023 Marine Dr., White Rock; (604) 538-9373; ulisrestaurant.com. In a patio standoff Uli's is in the running for its large deck. A diverse menu manages to encompass seafood (daily catch), German cuisine (schnitzel), and pub favorites (burgers). The family-run joint rates as one of the more economical choices on the strip. All this without sacrificing a sliver of view. Open for weekend brunch and daily for lunch and dinner. $$–$$$.

border crossing

US citizens require a valid passport, NEXUS card, US Passport Card, or enhanced driver's license to enter Canada by land. Keep in mind there are restrictions on the goods you can bring into the country—particularly when it comes to fruit, vegetables, dairy, and meat products. As different regulations surround firearms, leave guns in the United States, either at home or in a storage facility.

Taking a detour to the SR 543 border crossing, also known as the truck crossing, can sometimes save minutes. Watch for highway signage giving updated border-crossing times or tune into local radio.

Heaviest weekend traffic is, predictably, from about 9 a.m. to 8 p.m. with the peak around noon.

steveston

Pretty Steveston also has a grounded charm from being an oceanside community built around the fisheries. Fishing boats sell fresh catches from the marina, restaurant patios line the waterfront, and there are parks and historic sites to visit. Although officially part of Richmond, Steveston is set apart as an entirely distinct village.

getting there

From White Rock, return along Marine Drive and Eighth Avenue to Hwy. 99 and cross under the river through the George Massey Tunnel. At exit 32, take the Steveston Highway west toward the village.

Alternately, head north along Johnston Road, which turns into 152nd Street before meeting with Hwy. 99. Cross farmlands and the Fraser River before reaching Richmond and taking the Steveston Highway west.

In Steveston, take a left onto No. 1 Road and head south to the waterfront Bayview Street, for a total travel time of about 35 minutes.

where to go

Britannia Shipyards National Historic Site. 5180 Westwater Dr., Steveston; (604) 238-8050; britanniashipyard.ca. Discover a historic collection of shipyard buildings, including net lofts, old bunkhouses, and a working boat shop. See wooden vessels mid-restoration and birdlife from the shore while you walk the planks of the boardwalk. Open daily.

Garry Point Park. 12011 7th Ave., Steveston; (604) 244-1208 (general parks line); richmond.ca. The park connects a waterfront walk to trails over marsh and dike lands. Summer weekends see the skies filled with kites, including those attached to zippy ground buggies for power kiting.

Gulf of Georgia Cannery National Historic Site. 12138 Fourth Ave., Steveston; (604) 664-9009; gulfofgeorgiacannery.com. The smells of fish oil and engine grease still waft from the floorboards of this historic cannery. For decades the cannery produced herring meal, canned salmon, and was later used as a fish depot and more. Today exhibits re-create the canning process using machinery left behind since a herring reduction plant closed in 1979. Open daily. $$.

London Heritage Farm. 6511 Dyke Rd., Richmond; (604) 271-5220; londonheritagefarm.ca. A farmhouse, gardens, and agricultural equipment take visitors back to the 1880s. Hours vary, but the farmhouse is generally open on weekends in summer. Admission by donation.

Steveston Museum and Post Office. 3811 Moncton St., Richmond; (604) 271-6868; richmond.ca. The 1905 building has had many incarnations over the years: a bank, a doctor's office, and today a post office, visitor center, and museum. Too bad the museum doesn't have talking walls! Regardless, various displays on Steveston life tell the ever-changing tale of this waterfront village. Open daily.

where to eat

Blue Canoe Waterfront Restaurant. 140-3866 Bayview St.; (604) 275-7811; bluecanoerestaurant.com. A step further and you'd be in the ocean. Blue Canoe delivers a hip atmosphere amidst steak and seafood favorites. A bonus: From the patio you can see the docked fishing boats selling the daily fresh catch. Open daily for lunch and dinner. $$–$$$.

Dave's Fish & Chips. 3460 Moncton St., Steveston; (604) 271-7555; davesfishandchips.com. There's an eternal local debate about the best fish-and-chips in town. Dave's chalks up a number of local readers' choice awards after more than four decades of battering. Have your pick of salmon, cod, and halibut. Crab cakes, clams, and oysters are also available. Open daily for lunch and dinner. $$.

Pajo's on the Wharf. The Wharf, Steveston; (604) 272-1588; pajos.com. The other front-runner in the great fish-and-chips debate, Pajo's has four locations with two in Steveston. The dock location is unbeatable, while the Garry Point Park eatery complements a walk in the park with fresh-air dining. The menu features wild cod, halibut, and salmon. Open daily for lunch and dinner in peak season and weather permitting the rest of the year. $$.

richmond

Head north from Steveston (in Vancouver that means driving toward the mountains) and you enter the bustle of a modern Chinatown. Markets, shopping centers, and Olympic venues are all top places to visit in Richmond, but the restaurants are perhaps the pick of the city. Endless varieties of Asian cuisine offer an immersive experience where menus are often written in both English and Chinese.

getting there

The shopping and dining areas of Richmond center around No. 3 Road. Travel east on the Steveston Highway then take the No. 3 Road north into the heart of Richmond—about 10 to 15 minutes from Steveston.

where to go

Iona Beach Regional Park. 900 Ferguson Rd., Richmond; (604) 224-5739 (regional office); metrovancouver.org. The long jetty and beach are both inviting spots for a long stroll and 360-degree views. The park is popular with bird-watchers, having both freshwater and saltwater environments. Open daily.

Richmond Olympic Oval. 6111 River Rd., Richmond; (778) 296-1400; richmondoval.ca. The Richmond Olympic Oval hosted speed-skating events for the 2010 Olympic Winter Games and Paralympics. Its post-Games redesign includes two skating rinks, climbing wall, running track, sport courts, and Olympic exhibits. The building alone is a marvel: The wave-design roof is constructed using wood damaged by the pine beetle. Drop-in day passes available. $$$.

Richmond Summer Night Market. 8351 River Rd., Richmond; (604) 244-8448; richmond nightmarket.com. Enjoy all the bustle of a Hong Kong market without the price of the plane ticket. The market features endless vendors selling gimmicks, gadgetry, and garments. Arrive with lots of time to snack on the creative and varied food stalls. Open Fri to Sun from mid-May to mid-Oct. $.

where to shop

Aberdeen Centre. 4151 Hazelbridge Way, Richmond; (604) 270-1234; aberdeencentre .com. With stores like the legendary Oomomo (a Japanese dollar store, or 100-yen store), Aberdeen Centre makes for an entirely unique shopping experience. A large food court offers many styles of Asian cooking at great value. Open daily.

where to eat

HK BBQ Master. 145-4651 No. 3 Rd., Richmond; (604) 272-6568. Tucked in an unlikely spot beneath a grocery store, head here for mouth-watering barbecue duck, pork, or free-range chicken. Order by the meal or by the bird. $–$$.

Neptune Seafood Restaurant. 100-8171 Ackroyd Rd., Richmond; (604) 207-9888; neptune group.ca. Look for amazing chili prawns and other seafood dishes on the menu. The dim sum draws regulars as does the polished, prompt service. Lots of family seating. Open daily for dim sum, lunch, and dinner. $$–$$$.

where to stay

Fairmont Vancouver Airport. 3111 Grant McConachie Way, Richmond; (604) 207-5200; fairmont.com. Not just for those flying in, this comfortable hotel offers easy access and a fantastic location close to both Richmond and Vancouver. There's dining and a health club with a hot tub and sauna—plus you can easily wander Vancouver International Airport to see many pieces of world-class First Nations art. $$$–$$$$.

day trip 05

olympic city:
vancouver

vancouver

After hosting the 2010 Winter Olympics, Vancouver catapulted into the spotlight as a world-class city for its scenery and facilities. In summer the city's expansive parks and beaches welcome hikers and outdoorsy folk, while in winter it's time to head to the ski hills. Year-round cultural highlights include theaters, concerts, and art galleries, and one of the biggest events is the celebration for Canada Day at Canada Place on July 1.

Each neighborhood is practically a day trip in itself. Shop and people-watch at the beach in Kitsilano before heading to one of the local museums by transit ferry. The University of British Columbia campus gardens, the world-class Museum of Anthropology, and beaches create a lively community. In the downtown district excellent restaurants demonstrate Vancouver's culinary diversity and pair nicely with an amble through historic Gastown or Stanley Park.

getting there

With the fate-decided blessings of a quick border crossing, I-5 followed by Hwy. 99 leads directly to Vancouver in about 2.5 hours (about 140 miles). From there, explore the city's many neighborhoods by ferry, foot, or transit.

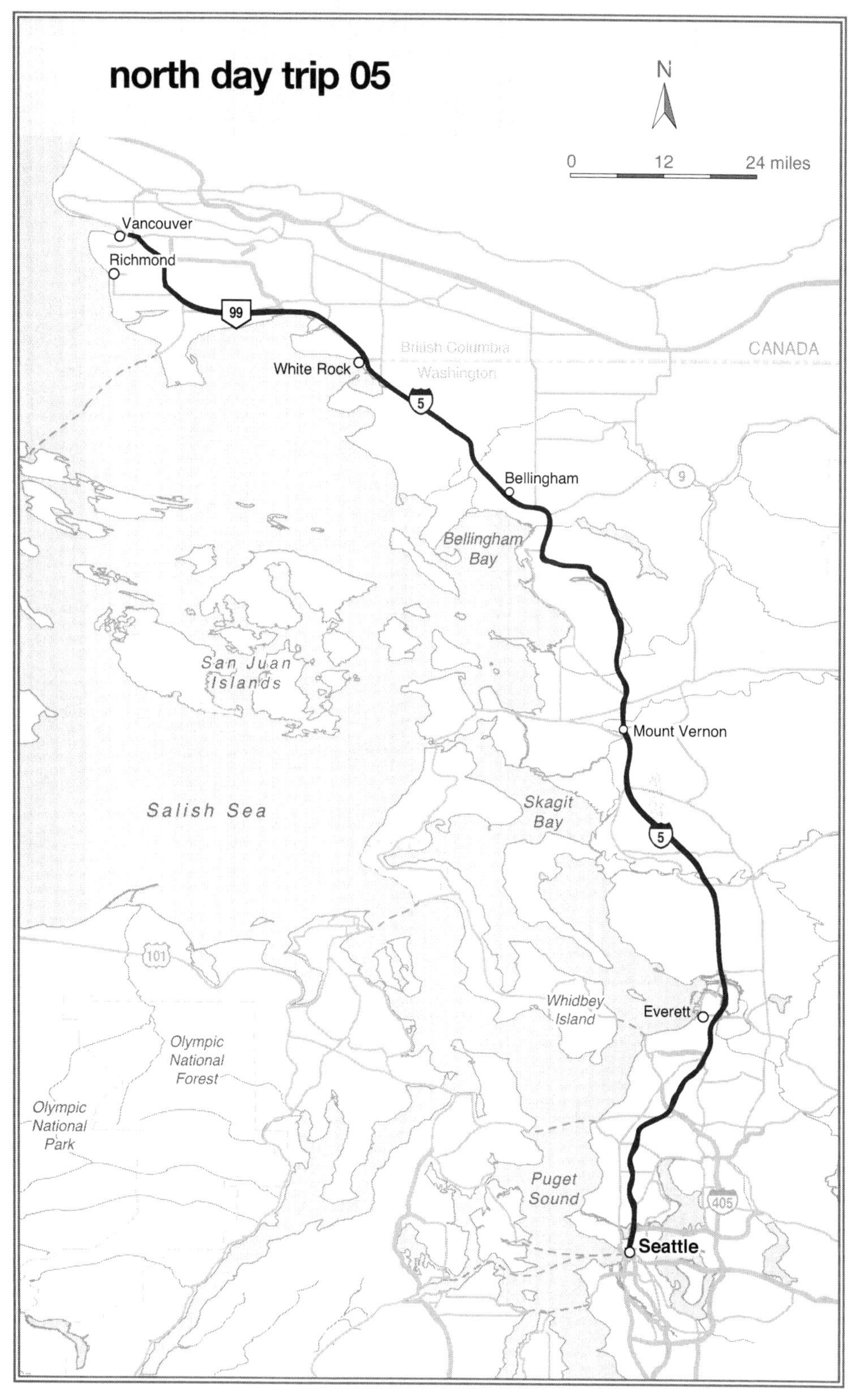
north day trip 05
N
0
12
24 miles
Vancouver
Richmond
99
White Rock
British Columbia
Washington
CANADA
5
Bellingham
9
Bellingham Bay
San Juan Islands
Mount Vernon
Salish Sea
Skagit Bay
5
101
Whidbey Island
Everett
Olympic National Forest
Olympic National Park
Puget Sound
405
Seattle

Alternately, opt for a four-hour journey on the Amtrak Cascades train (800-872-7245; amtrak.com). The route proves easier than driving and is ideal for those spending a weekend in the city without worrying about parking.

where to go

Tourism Vancouver Visitor Centre. Plaza Level, 200 Burrard St., Vancouver; (604) 683-2000; tourismvancouver.com. With lots of staff members, the visitor center is able to assist in directing visitors to attractions, booking accommodations, and providing information. Look for the nearby Tickets Tonight booth that offers great deals on Vancouver-area performances. Open daily.

Granville Island. Anderson St., beneath Granville Street Bridge, Vancouver; granvilleisland.com. This once-industrial district transformed into a center for independent merchants and fine-art studios during the 1970s. Although the cement plant still holds fast to the industrial days, a vibrant, year-round public market (open daily), theater district, public art, and marinas have created a lively atmosphere. Take a ferry from downtown (False Creek Ferries and the rainbow-colored Aquabus both transit to the island) and then explore the alleys of artists, restaurant patios, and kid-friendly parks.

Kitsilano Beach. Arbutus St. at Cornwall St., Vancouver; (604) 257-8400 (City of Vancouver); vancouver.ca. Often named a top city beach, "Kits" is more than sand. With a large outdoor saltwater pool, grassy areas perfect for spreading out a picnic, and a waterfront restaurant with sunset views, Kits is also a haven for those still in touch with their child of summer. The seawall leads from the beach to some of Vancouver's finest museums: Museum of Vancouver (1100 Chestnut St.; 604-736-4431; museumofvancouver.ca); HR MacMillan Space Centre (1100 Chestnut St.; 604-738-7827; spacecentre.ca); and Vancouver Maritime Museum (1905 Ogden Ave.; 604-257-8300; vancouvermaritimemuseum.com)—as well as the summertime Bard on the Beach Shakespeare Festival (604-739-0559; bardonthebeach.org).

Museum of Anthropology. 6393 NW Marine Dr., Vancouver; (604) 822-5087; moa.ubc.ca. Totems stand like trees in a forest at this top-quality museum. Between the carvings, ceramics, and tapestries from around the world, and from the Northwest in particular, large walls of glass occasionally provide forest, mountain, or ocean views. Open daily during summer; closed Mon mid-Oct through mid-May. $$.

Queen Elizabeth Park. W. 33rd and Cambie Sts., Vancouver; vancouver.ca. Attractions in Queen Elizabeth Park include fountains, walking trails, an arboretum, picturesque Quarry Garden, pitch-and-putt golf course, and tropical conservatory. Bloedel Conservatory creates a vastly different ecosystem than the typical Pacific Northwest climate with chattering parrots and cockatoos, concerts by guest artists, and vibrant flowers. Outside a viewpoint is one of the highest spots in the city. Also in the neighborhood are the curling rinks at the Vancouver

Curling Club, baseball diamond at **Nat Bailey Stadium** (4601 Ontario St.; 604-872-5232; milb.com/vancouver), and more plants at VanDusen Botanical Garden (5151 Oak St.; 604-257-8335; vandusengarden.org). Open daily year-round.

Science World. 1455 Quebec St., Vancouver; (604) 443-7440; scienceworld.ca. This alien-looking sphere houses kid- and adult-friendly science exhibits that engage inquiring minds. Despite a hefty admission charge, head inside for many hours of exploring, IMAX films, and experiments. A message to adults: Just remember to let the kids have a turn. Occasionally that is. Open daily. $$$.

Stanley Park. W. Georgia St., Vancouver; vancouver.ca. A 5.5-mile seawall wraps the park, giving walkers, runners, bikers, and in-line skaters access to acres of forest, ocean, and mountain views as well as historic sites and Vancouver's best beaches. Sandy stretches include Third Beach with its sunset views and Second Beach with its outdoor pool and playground. There are many scenic and historic stopping points around the park, such as the totem poles at Brockton Point and Brockton Point Lighthouse. Other park tours and activities include bus rides, horse-drawn carriages, and a miniature train. The Malkin Bowl hosts summer concerts, the rose garden is sweetest in bloom, and the Stanley Park Nature House on Lost Lagoon (stanleyparkecology.ca) provides keen insight into the habitat of this urban park.

Vancouver Aquarium. 845 Avison Way, Vancouver; (604) 659-3474; vanaqua.org. Otters and sea lions are the main attractions at the aquarium, but large tanks of fish, coral, and octopi as well as the tropical zone of butterflies, birds, and a sloth equally mesmerize. Clownfish Cove play area offers great distractions for younger children to make the aquarium a day-long adventure. Located in Stanley Park, the aquarium pioneered the Ocean Wise program to highlight sustainable seafood options at local restaurants—ask for information before heading out to dinner. Open daily. $$$.

Vancouver Art Gallery. 750 Hornby St., Vancouver; (604) 662-4700; vanartgallery.bc.ca. The Vancouver Art Gallery hosts multiple exhibits each year, often featuring works of international fame. Arthur Erickson, one of Vancouver's preeminent architects, transformed the building from a courthouse into the present-day gallery. Open daily. $$$.

Vancouver Police Museum. 240 E. Cordova St., Vancouver; (604) 665-3346; vancouverpolicemuseum.ca. Displays that include confiscated weapons and counterfeit currency are set in a former morgue. The museum has a strangely wide appeal, drawing on a curiosity surrounding death and danger. Open Tues to Sat. $$.

Wreck Beach. Trail 6, Northwest Marine Dr. at University Blvd., Vancouver. The one and only local nudist beach, Wreck Beach endures thanks to its community spirit. Open year-round.

where to shop

Robson Street. From Burrard St. through to Denman St., window-shopping on Robson serves up storefront after storefront of style. From luxury brands to souvenirs, you'll find it all available daily in this top urban shopping district.

West Fourth Avenue. Between Burrard and Vine Sts. Drawing on the hip vibe of Kitsilano, stores such as the first Lululemon, outdoor apparel outfitters, and fantastic shoes at Gravitypope make this street one long but varied shopping excursion.

where to eat

Japadog. 530 Robson St., Vancouver; (604) 569-1158 japadog.com. An inventive take on the humble wiener, these Japanese-style hot dogs come topped with nori, mashed potatoes, noodles, or miso—just to name a few of the eyebrow-raising ingredients. The prices are reasonable and the unique factor unbeatable. This is the brick-and-mortar version of the street-side vendor stands that are located around the city. $.

The Sandbar. 1535 Johnston St., Granville Island, Vancouver; (604) 669-9030; vancouver dine.com. A perfect patio and the glass-walled dining room reveal beautiful views of Yaletown and False Creek. The seafood-focused menu is imbued with an international flair, whether it is the wok squid or seafood hot pot. Open daily for lunch and dinner as well as weekend brunch. $$–$$$$.

Tojo's Restaurant. 1133 W. Bdwy., Vancouver; (604) 872-8050; tojos.com. In Vancouver you have the option of the $8 sushi special (which can be found in almost every city block) or fine-dining sashimi. At Tojo's—one of Vancouver's finest sushi restaurants—you'll find the latter. Opt for *omakase,* where the chef creates your dinner and you simply enjoy. Or choose a selection of sashimi, sushi rolls, and tempura. Open daily for dinner, except closed on Sun. $$$–$$$$.

Vij's Rangoli. 1480 W. 11th Ave., Vancouver; (604) 736-5711; vijs.ca. Vij's has long been lauded by many for its spot-on service and scrumptious Indian-style cuisine. This is an expansion of the popular no-reservations restaurant that's since moved to a larger space (3106 Cambie St; 604-736-6664). Open daily for lunch and dinner. $–$$.

where to stay

The Sylvia Hotel. 1154 Gilford St., Vancouver; (604) 681-9321; sylviahotel.com. Close to Stanley Park and English Bay, this historic hotel rates as one of Vancouver's best for personality and charm. Each room is different—some have kitchens while others are budget options. In any season the creeper on the brick-and-stone exterior creates a color sensation. A restaurant and lounge serve everything from breakfast through to evening cocktails. Kids

vancouver olympics

In 2010 Vancouver hosted the Winter Olympics and Paralympics in conjunction with Whistler. The games showcased the amazing skiing and snowboarding opportunities in the area—including at Cypress Mountain and Whistler Blackcomb Ski Resort—as well as the stunning panoramas of mountains and aqua-blue glacial lakes.

Olympic venues have now transformed into community facilities where you can ski or skate in the same tracks as world-record holders.

For a longer trip, head across the Lions Gate Bridge to North Shore attractions such as Grouse Mountain, Capilano Suspension Bridge, and Lynn Canyon, before venturing further north along the Sea-to-Sky Highway to Whistler. Endless hiking trails, river rafting, wildlife watching, and wilderness cabins deliver the irresistible Pacific Northwest scenery at provincial parks like Garibaldi and Joffre Lakes.

will enjoy the tales of Mr. Got To Go—a stubborn cat who inspired a series of children's books that are available for reading in the lobby. $$–$$$.

The Burrard. 1100 Burrard St., Vancouver; (604) 681-2331; theburrard.com. A 1950s motor inn is now a trendy and central spot in Downtown Vancouver. Borrow a bike, chill out in the garden courtyard, or dine at the street-level restaurant. $$–$$$.

West End Guest House. 1362 Haro St., Vancouver; (604) 681-2889; westendguesthouse .com. Dating to 1905, this century-old house is artfully renovated to offer eight guest rooms and suites with a taste of the original West End neighborhood. Vintage photographs recall the time of the house's first owners. A lavish breakfast is included, as well as free parking. $$$.

northeast

day trip 01

northeast

wine country:
woodinville, snohomish

Fine wines and lovely antiques draw visitors to Woodinville and Snohomish. Wineries and tasting rooms seem to grow at an ever-quickening pace, with a count of well over 100. Each has different hours and different varietals to taste. Venture into the expansive grounds of Chateau Ste. Michelle, a small family winery, or one of the many fine restaurants with stocked cellars and local wines by the glass.

Heading north to Snohomish, hot air balloons rise above SR 9, and mountains linger in view on a clear day. Known as the Antique Capital of the Northwest, Snohomish delivers as promised: a pretty town swept up in the finery of yesteryear.

woodinville

Arriving in the winery heartland of Woodinville, the road curves down to a wooded area and opens up into views of expansive wineries with Mount Rainier behind. Chateau Ste. Michelle started the boom in the wine region, opening the doors to its French-style chateau in 1976. With more than 100 tasting rooms to explore (more than doubling in the last decade!), Woodinville endures as a regional favorite. Tasting fees are about $15 but often waived with purchase.

Catch a series of summer concerts, both at wineries and free community events. From romantic escapes to bicycle rides through the landscape, Woodinville is a spot to take things slowly.

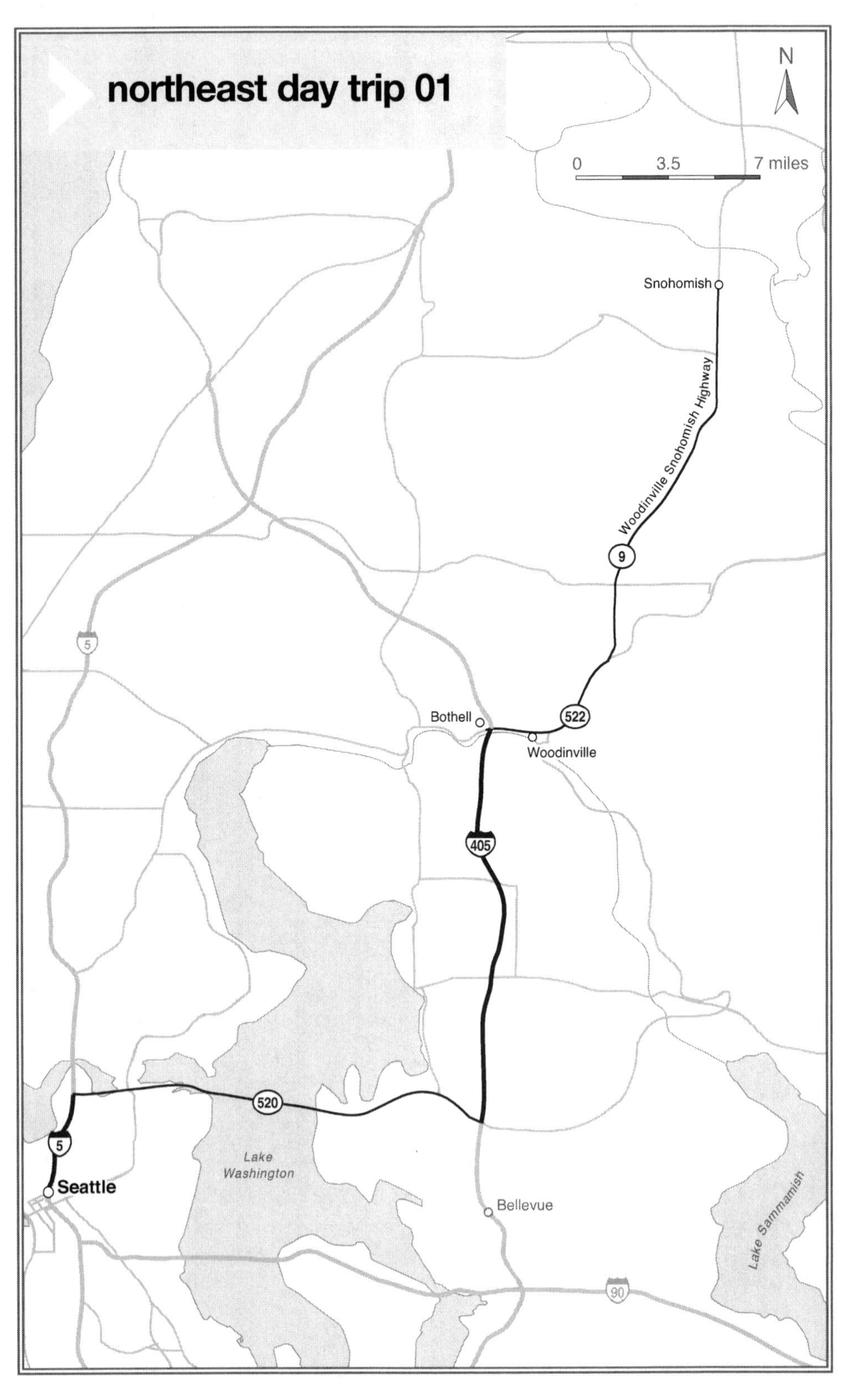

northeast day trip 01
N
0
3.5
7 miles
Snohomish
Woodinville Snohomish Highway
9
5
Bothell
522
Woodinville
405
520
5
Seattle
Lake
Washington
Bellevue
90
Lake Sammamish

getting there

To reach Woodinville, cross Lake Washington then head north on I-405 to the junction with SR 522 at exit 23. Head briefly east on SR 522 then take the exit for SR 202 leading into Woodinville.

To reach Snohomish, the Woodinville-Snohomish Road connects with SR 9, providing a beeline route to Snohomish.

where to go

Woodinville Visitor Center. 14700 E 148th Ave., Woodinville; (425) 287-6820; visitwoodinville.org. Open daily for winery and other local info.

Hollywood Schoolhouse. 14810 NE 145th St., Woodinville; (425) 481-7925; hollywoodschoolhouse.com. This state historical monument is a handsome 1912 brick building that now operates as an event facility and wine-tasting room for **Alexandria Nicole Cellars** (425-487-9463; alexandrianicolecellars.com).

Molbak's Garden & Home. 13625 NE 175th St., Woodinville; (425) 483-5000; molbaks.com. An exceedingly popular nursery and gift shop with plenty for the garden and home. There's also on-site dining at **Russell's Garden Café & Wine Bar** (425-286-6279; russelllowell.com). Open daily.

Sammamish River Trail. Start at Wilmot Gateway Park, 17301 NE 131st Ave., Woodinville. Roughly 10 miles in all, this paved trail travels from Bothell to Redmond, passing through Woodinville on the way.

Teatro ZinZanni. 14300 NE 145th St., Woodinville; (206) 802-0015; zinzanni.com. A wowing spectacle of circus acts combined with dinner theater provides a memorable evening. Reservations recommended. $$$.

Woodinville Wineries. For the most up-to-date and comprehensive listings (without contacting each winery individually), check with **Woodinville Visitor Center** (425-287-6820; visitwoodinville.org). Woodinville is home to more than 100 wineries. Here's a listing of some noteworthy ones that are *regularly open for public tastings.* You can find contact details on additional wineries on the Woodinville Wine Country website, mentioned above.

> **Chateau Ste. Michelle.** 14111 NE 145th St., Woodinville; (425) 488-1133; ste-michelle.com. The largest winery in Woodinville with 105 acres, and in fact the largest in the state, Chateau Ste. Michelle excels at entertaining its visitors. In addition to tasting, visitors can explore the expansive grounds, catch a summer concert, indulge in a special dinner—or engage with wine in new ways through sessions like wine blending. Open daily.

Columbia Winery. 14030 NE 145th St., Woodinville; (425) 482-7490; columbia winery.com. The region's largest tasting room is also a welcoming, spacious option that exudes charm and excellent service. Open daily.

Dusted Valley. 14465 Redmond-Woodinville Rd. NE, Woodinville; (425) 488-7373; dustedvalley.com. The casual, fun atmosphere—with plenty of tasting room neighbors—complements the family-focused winery operations, which are based in the Walla Walla Valley. Open Wed to Sun.

Matthews Winery. 16116 140th Place NE, Woodinville; (425) 487-9810; mat thewswinery.com. With dinners, live music, and social evenings, Matthews becomes a happening spot amidst lovely gardens. Open daily.

Novelty Hill Januik. 14710 Redmond-Woodinville Rd. NE, Woodinville; (425) 481-5502; noveltyhilljanuik.com. Two wineries share an ultra-modern space. On weekends, order a brick oven pizza to complement the wine. Open daily.

Silver Lake Winery. 14701 148th Ave. NE, Woodinville; (425) 486-1900; silver lakewinery.com. A small, friendly spot across from the visitor information center—and there's also a neighboring taproom. Open Wed to Sun.

Woodinville Whiskey Co. 14509 Redmond-Woodinville Rd. NE, Woodinville; (425) 486-1199; woodinvillewhiskeyco.com. Tastings and weekend tours provide insight into this one-time dairy farm turned award-winning distillery.

Woodhouse Wine Estates. 15500 Redmond-Woodinville Rd., Ste. C600, Woodinville; (425) 527-0608; thewoodhousewineestates.com. Woodhouse produces labels such as Dussek, Darighe, and Kennedy Shah. Open Wed to Sun.

For more tasting, and less traveling, head north to Woodinville's Warehouse District. Around the collection of industrial buildings near 19501 NE 144th Ave., you'll find more than a dozen wineries and tasting rooms including **Patterson Cellars/Washington Wine Company** (Ste. D600; 425-483-8600; pattersoncellars.com), Rocky Pond Winery (425-949-9044; rockypondwinery.com), Efesté (425-398-7200; efeste.com), and Pondera Winery (425-486-8500; ponderawinery.com).

where to eat

Barking Frog Restaurant. 14580 NE 145th St., Woodinville; (425) 424-2999; willowslodge .com. Food with a casual Northwest flair complements the great number of local wine offerings at the restaurant. An outdoor deck is open to diners in summer, while an indoor fire pit table keeps the restaurant cozy in winter. Prompt service and a creative menu make dining here a fun experience. Open daily for breakfast, lunch, and dinner. $$–$$$.

washington wine countries

If Washington wine has captured your taste buds, there are a few other regions in the state to swill, taste, and spit the day away. The Washington wine region of the Yakima Valley offers the bulk of winery tours within a day trip (Southeast Day Trip 03), and its rich agricultural lands are also a major source of grapes for wineries around the state. Or, venture to Leavenworth (East Day Trip 03) where more wineries produce fine-quality wines in a Bavarian setting. You'll also find a small selection of wineries on Vashon Island (Southwest Day Trip 01).

The Herbfarm. 14590 NE 145th St., Woodinville; (425) 485-5300; theherbfarm.com. What looks very much like a farmhouse is a world-class destination restaurant. Offering set nine-course menus that are inspired by what's in season, the restaurant has received accolades from endless publications including *National Geographic, Zagat,* and top wine magazines. A local wine pairing accompanies each course, and all the menus draw on fresh local produce and bounty from the restaurant's kitchen garden. Reservations are a must. $$$$.

The Hollywood Tavern. 14508 Redmond-Woodinville Rd. NE, Woodinville; (425) 481-7703; thehollywoodtavern.com. A welcoming patio with a fire pit greets guests to this local institution dating to 1947. But it's the menu that charms from there: be it the gastropub offerings or tender pork ribs with a barbecue sauce spiked with whiskey from the neighboring distillery. Open daily for lunch and dinner. $$–$$$.

where to stay

Willows Lodge. 14580 NE 145th St., Woodinville; (425) 424-3900 or (877) 424-3930; willowslodge.com. With more than eighty rooms, the lodge is perfectly positioned to facilitate a weekend in wine country. Borrow bicycles to explore the Sammamish River Trail, stroll to a neighboring winery (there's even tasting rooms on the doorstep), relax at the spa with its lovely outdoor relaxation pool, or cozy up around an outdoor fire. The staff takes great care to be welcoming to guests and their pets, and there's regular entertainment. $$$$.

snohomish

Known as the Antique Capital of the Northwest, Snohomish rates as a top place to search for rare china, hunt out a bargain, and discover treasures. But the small community with its 26-block historic district also offers lovely park walks, dining on the riverbanks, and a well-maintained community museum. Watch for the community's long-standing street festival, Kla Ha Ya Days, in mid-July.

where to go

Snohomish County Tourism Bureau–East County Visitor Center. 6705 Puget Park Dr., Snohomish; (425) 348-5802 or toll-free (888) 338-0976; seattlenorthcountry.com. There are exhibits here, as well as the usual brochures and info. Open Mon to Fri.

Blackman House Museum. 118 Ave. B, Snohomish; (360) 568-5235; snohomishhistorical society.org. Built in 1878, this museum displays furniture and household items belonging to the house's first owners—Hyrcanus and Ella Blackman—as well as other Snohomish settlers. Open weekends. $.

where to shop

Because Snohomish has long been nicknamed the Antique Capital of the Northwest, it's tough to turn around in town without fixing your gaze on an appealing antique treasure. A walk through downtown—and along First Street in particular—offers the greatest concentration of small dealers as well as other shops and galleries. **Star Center Antique Mall** (829 Second St.; 360-568-2131) opens daily and features 200 dealers in its multiple levels. **Antique Warehouse** (1019 First St.; 360-568-7590) assembles an eclectic mix of antiques, all of which are clearly priced. No doubt you'll discover many other prized spots.

where to eat

Cabbage Patch Restaurant & Catering. 111 Ave. A, Snohomish; (360) 568-9091; cabbage patchrestaurant.com. Set in a single-dwelling home, this restaurant serves all manner of eats. From prime rib and wild salmon to the home-style turkey dinner or meat loaf, the fare is heartwarming. Open daily for breakfast, lunch, and dinner. $$–$$$.

The Repp. 924 First St., Snohomish; (360) 568-3928; therepp.com. Exposed brick, cool-toned wood, and dark beams give an urban feel without losing the olden-times style of the town. The steaks are the prime picks, but booth seating at the Repp also makes it a casual spot for appetizers and a craft cocktail. Open daily for dinner, except closed Mon. $$$.

Snohomish Bakery Cafe. 101 Union Ave., Snohomish; (360) 568-1682; snohomishbakery .com. Fresh pastries are the first, but not the only, draw at the Snohomish Bakery Cafe. Serving hot breakfasts and sandwich lunches, the cozy cafe sits on the main street. Perfect for a quick morning bite or a fuel up before returning home. Open daily for breakfast and lunch. $.

day trip 02

northeast

roos, rails, and rivers:
arlington, sedro-woolley, concrete

From Arlington and Sedro-Woolley, not far from Seattle, to the unromantically named but quaint town of Concrete, which verges on the Cascades, this day trip explores the easy reaches of SR 20, also known as the North Cascades Highway and part of the Cascade Loop Scenic Byway. Logging, railroad, and pioneer history abound amidst the steam engines and stump houses. But just before the region becomes too industrial, you can extend the stay with an escape to state park camping, or enjoy a locally brewed pint at Birdsview Brewery.

It's not the most glamorous of day trips but the raw history, the few gems of attractions, and ever-friendly locals make a visit here a worthwhile trip.

arlington

The lumber town of Arlington serves as a commuter city, but it also retains its history. The main street, Olympic Avenue, parallels railroad tracks, and Arlington is an excellent home base for exploring all points north- and eastward.

Within the area you'll find a kangaroo farm, friendly eateries, and a preserved stump house—a small home fashioned from a giant hollowed-out base of a tree. Plus the summer Arlington Fly-In fills the skies with interesting aircraft.

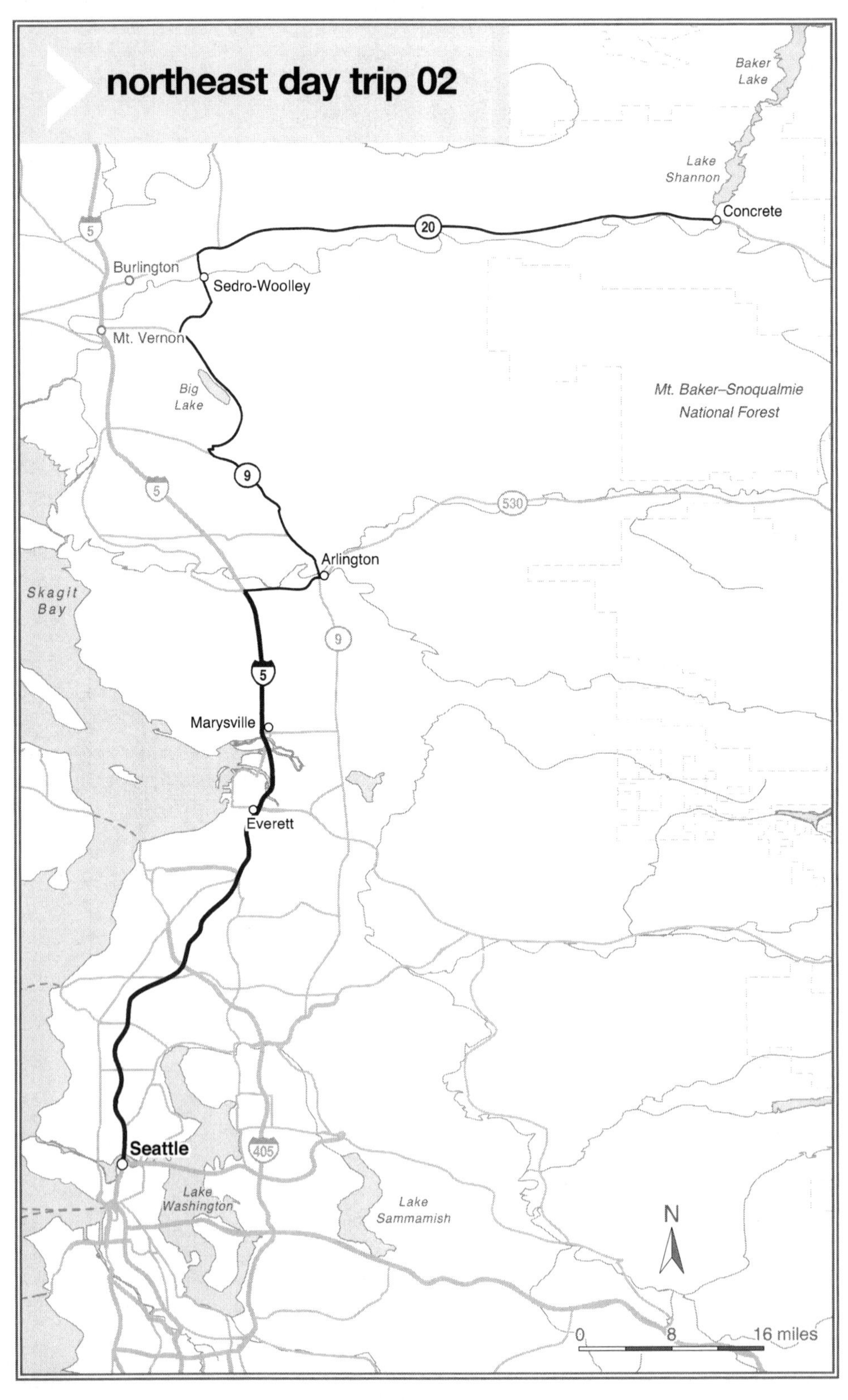

northeast day trip 02
Baker Lake
Lake Shannon
Concrete
20
5
Burlington
Sedro-Woolley
Mt. Vernon
Big Lake
Mt. Baker–Snoqualmie National Forest
9
5
530
Arlington
Skagit Bay
9
5
Marysville
Everett
Seattle
405
Lake Washington
Lake Sammamish
N
0
8
16 miles

getting there

I-5 north provides near-direct access to Arlington. After traveling about 40 miles on I-5, take exit 206 and head east on 172nd Street Northeast, then north on 67th Avenue Northeast. Or take simply take exit 208 off I-5 and follow SR 530.

where to go

Outback Kangaroo Farm. 10030 SR 530 NE, Arlington; (360) 403-7474; wildlifeparkarlingtonwa.com. The farm is home to all manner of marsupials including wallabies, kangaroos, and wallaroos. Forty-minute scheduled tours of the farm also introduce you to the resident lemurs, llamas, donkeys, parrots, and other animals. Open for 'roo tours Thurs to Sun, Mar through Oct. Call ahead to check the schedule. $$.

Stillaguamish Valley Pioneer Museum. 20722 67th Ave. NE, Arlington; (360) 435-7289; stillymuseum.org. Looking out over its namesake river—nicknamed the Stilly—this three-floor pioneer museum harbors a treasure trove of old photos, animal mounts, and artifacts. From music to military items and histories of the dairy and logging industries, the museum captures the past in its displays. Outside, the museum gardens, heritage cabin, and the waterways of Pioneer Park provide more to explore. In November and December, watch the salmon run in the creek. A preserved stump house sits roadside. What's that, you ask? A stump house takes its foundation from a giant tree that's been cut and the remaining stump hollowed-out. This one was once used as a photography studio. The museum opens Wed, Sat, and Sun, although call ahead for hours as it closes Dec and Jan. $.

where to eat

Moe's on Olympic. 434 N. Olympic Ave., Arlington; (360) 322-7604; moesespresso.com. A cheery coffeehouse is popular with the locals, serving freshly roasted brews as well as sandwiches, salads, and pizza. Next door The Lounge has a more curated menu to complement Washington wines, beers on tap, and refreshing cocktails. $.

Nutty's Junkyard Grill. 6717 204th St. NE, Arlington; (360) 403-7538. Set in an old gas station, this very casual and nostalgia-filled burger bar is local-famous for its onion rings and burgers made with homemade patties. The milkshakes are top-notch! Open for lunch and dinner Tues to Sun. $.

sedro-woolley

Proud of its logging heritage, Sedro-Woolley's main street is lined with amber-toned chainsaw carvings from its annual competitions. The local museum and a display steam engine reiterate the area's previous prosperity as a lumber center. And come the Fourth of July, the Loggerodeo brings the industry to life with chainsaw carving and a rodeo.

getting there

From Arlington, SR 9 leads north 27 miles to Sedro-Woolley. Although I-5 is an alternate route, SR 9 passes the shores of McMurray, Big, and Clear Lakes—far more scenic than interstate exits!

where to go

Mount Baker–Snoqualmie National Forest—Mount Baker Office. 810 SR 20, Sedro-Woolley; (360) 856-5700. This office provides thorough and friendly hiking advice for the trails and recreation areas within the national forest. The facility also has an info center for North Cascades National Park (360-854-7200; nps.gov/noca). Hours change with the seasons. Open daily in summer; otherwise only weekdays.

Eagle Haven Winery. 8243 Sims Rd., Sedro-Woolley; (360) 856-6248; eaglehavenwinery.com. A garden, tasting room, and beautiful orchard setting are worth the stop along the way. Watch for summer concerts and events. Open Fri to Sun. $.

Harry Osborne Park and Caboose. SR 20 and West Ferry St., Sedro-Woolley. An old steam-train locomotive and Douglas fir log slice dating to 1102 C.E. are the centerpieces of this quick stop. No admission or set hours, but visitors can explore anyway.

Sedro-Woolley Museum. 725 Murdock St., Sedro-Woolley; (360) 855-2390; sedrowoolleymuseum.org. The museum presents a minitown series of exhibits, including re-creations of a dentist, blacksmith, saloon, and bank. A model-train layout and old autos add interest for rail and car enthusiasts. Open Wed, Thurs, Sat, and Sun. $.

where to eat

Hometown Cafe. 818 Metcalf St., Sedro-Woolley; (360) 855-5012. You'll get a genuine hometown welcome at this classic main-street diner. Pies, coffee refills, and friendly locals fit perfectly with the booths and simple menu. Open daily for breakfast and lunch. $–$$.

the marriage of two towns

*Sedro and Woolley originally stood apart as two independent, and even rival, lumber towns. Sedro is a variation on the Spanish word for cedar (*cedra*), while Woolley is named for town founder Philip Woolley.*

Tough economic times forced the towns to consider merging, which they officially did in 1898. Unable to agree on one name, the towns opted to adopt a hyphenated version incorporating both: Sedro-Woolley.

concrete

Concrete teases you with the Cascades while providing a snapshot of its industrial history. Named for its production of cement, the town is a capsule of the past with many industrial structures still scattering the townscape. There's a summer farmers market on Saturdays, but while the town itself offers limited attractions, the local area includes a quiet state park and local brewery.

getting there

From Sedro-Woolley, head east on SR 20 for 24 miles to reach Concrete.

where to go

Concrete Chamber of Commerce. 45770 Main St., Concrete; (360) 853-8784; concrete-wa.com. Stop by the visitor information center for local recommendations. Open Mon to Sat.

Baker River Hydroelectric Project & Visitor Center. 46110 E. Main St., Concrete; (360) 853-8341; pse.com. Two dams hold in Baker Lake and Lake Shannon to provide energy. Find out about viewpoints, hiking trails, boat launches, and camping here. Open daily in summer; otherwise weekdays only.

Concrete Heritage Museum. 7380 Thompson Ave., Concrete; (360) 853-8347; concreteheritagemuseum.org. Head inside to discover the rich roots of the town, which include logging and, of course, cement. Call ahead for hours. $.

Rasar State Park. 38730 Cape Horn Rd., Concrete; (888) 226-7688 (camping); parks.state.wa.us. An old farm alongside the Skagit River, Rasar State Park offers camping, fishing, and restrooms. Riverside, forest, and field trails provide about 4 miles of hiking in total. But the kid's play area and the picnic area make a nice complement of facilities for families. In fall and winter it's known for eagle watching. Open daily.

Silo Park. 7503 S. Superior Ave., Concrete. The former Superior Portland Cement site is now a town park, but the industrial structures still stand watch—including an impressive bank of silos.

where to eat

5B's Bakery. 45597 Main St., Concrete; (360) 853-8700; 5bsbakery.com. There's loving care to make items that are gluten-free, including pot pies, to-go lunches, and baked goods. Open Wed to Mon for breakfast and lunch.

Birdsview Brewing Company. 38302 SR 20, Concrete; (360) 826-3406; birdsviewbrewingcompany.com. Concrete itself offers little choice in terms of restaurants, but west of town

driving the cascade loop

*The **Cascade Loop Scenic Byway** (cascadeloop.com) is an iconic route that connects some of Washington's best destinations, including North Cascades National Park (Northeast Day Trip 03), Methow Valley, Lake Chelan, Leavenworth (East Day Trip 03), Everett (North Day Trip 01), and Whidbey Island (Northwest Day Trip 01).*

About four nights on the road will allow you to sample the outdoor adventure, cowboy spirit, agricultural richness, and vibrant communities along the drive. Wildflower blooms can start as early as April, and the beauty of Mother Nature continues right through to fall colors. This is one to plan ahead, as Washington Pass closes late Nov to early May due to winter weather.

Birdsview Brewing houses a deli with sandwiches and burgers. You'll find about six beers on tap and the octagonal building is easy to spot with lots of parking. Open daily for lunch and early dinner, except closed Mon. $.

day trip 03

northeast

kerouac country:

rockport, marblemount, newhalem, diablo to north cascades national park

Over just 65 miles this stretch of the North Cascades Highway (SR 20) climbs from barely above sea level to the heights of Washington Pass (5,477 feet). On the way snowy peaks top evergreen forests, farmlands, and recreational lakes. Each season brings something special to this region: the opening of the highway in spring; wildflowers in summer; salmon runs in fall; and eagle watching in winter.

The core of North Cascades National Park is the trio of glacial lakes, each paired with a power-generating dam. Canoe the lakes, hike to the peaks, immerse yourself in an outdoor classroom, hear the hum of the power lines, or lodge at a floating cabin—all within the confines of one of the nation's least-visited national parks.

In these mountains American writer Jack Kerouac spent sixty-three days as a fire watcher in 1956. His experiences on the lookout atop Desolation Peak provided both material and the title for *Desolation Angels,* and he writes about the North Cascades in *The Dharma Bums,* describing the range as "unbelievable jags and twisted rock and snow-covered immensities, enough to make you gulp."

And gulp you will, and not just to pop your ears as the elevation increases.

With the time-warped company towns of Newhalem and Diablo, the panoramas from countless overlooks, and the chilled glacial waters to explore, a visit to the North Cascades effortlessly extends to a weekend or longer. Welcome to the "American Alps."

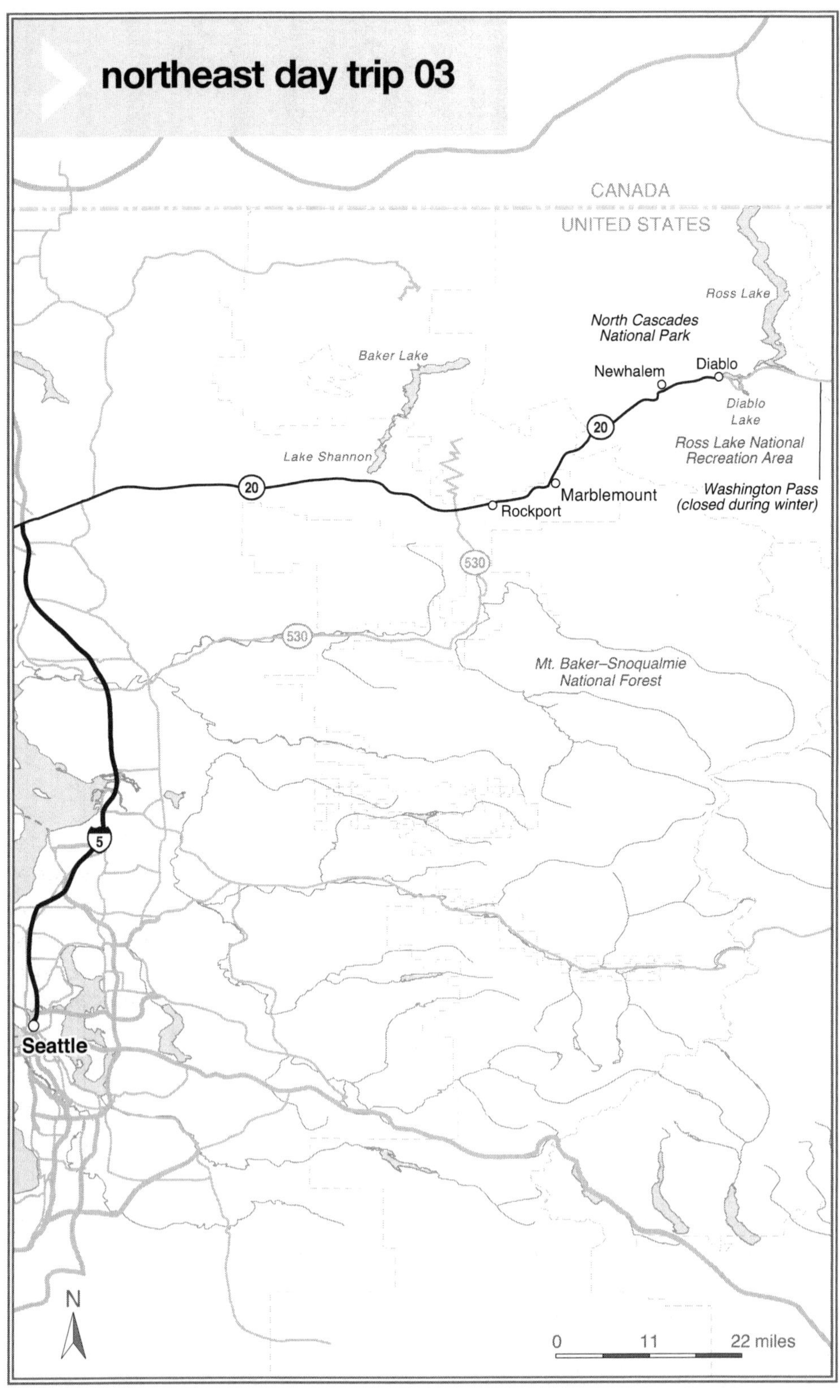
northeast day trip 03
CANADA
UNITED STATES
Ross Lake
North Cascades
National Park
Baker Lake
Newhalem
Diablo
Diablo
Lake
20
Ross Lake National
Recreation Area
Lake Shannon
20
Marblemount
Washington Pass
(closed during winter)
Rockport
530
530
Mt. Baker–Snoqualmie
National Forest
5
Seattle
N
0
11
22 miles

rockport

Rockport is not so much a destination as an address for some of the fantastic farms and parks in the area, and also where the eagles land in January during the Skagit Eagle Festival. The community is a crossroads of sorts: It was once the terminus for the railroad from Anacortes that was essential to constructing the Seattle City Light dams, and it now sits near the intersection of State Routes 20 and 530. The latter leads to Darrington and is an alternate route to Seattle.

getting there

From Seattle, take I-5 north to exit 230 for Burlington/Anacortes. SR 20 heads east from the interstate—just follow signs that lead you through the commercial outskirts of Burlington and then Sedro-Woolley. Once you're steaming along the North Cascades Highway, the directions become simple: Head east through a stretch of farmlands and foothills leading to Rockport (about 100 miles from Seattle), Marblemount, and the park beyond.

where to go

Rockport State Park. 51095 SR 20, Rockport; (360) 853-8461; parks.state.wa.us. This roadside park offers a wooded escape into an old-growth forest. Cross the highway from the parking area and follow the half-mile Sauk Springs Trail, which shelters the largest cedars and Douglas firs in the park. The short loop cuts into a mossy haven where garlands of greenery hang from every branch. Open daily.

Sauk Mountain Trail. 7 miles on Sauk Mountain Rd., Rockport; (360) 856-5700. A zigzag of switchbacks heads up the mountain to a hiking trailhead. Over a total hiking distance of 4 miles out and back, the trail gains nice elevation to provide views of the twisting Skagit River and the North Cascades. If you're lucky, there may be some hang gliders launching from the slopes. An important word of warning: While the views are worth the trip, a hunter accidentally shot a woman on this trail in 2008, mistaking her for a bear. Wear bright colors, preferably hunters' orange, when walking the trail.

Skagit River Bald Eagle Interpretive Center. 52809 Rockport Park Rd., Rockport; (360) 853-8808; skagiteagle.org. In Howard Miller Steelhead Park, this seasonal attraction is open only when the eagles gather: in winter. Educational and guided programs are available. Open weekends Dec and Jan.

Wildwood Chapel. 58468 Clark Cabin Rd., Rockport. Part of Glacier Peak Resort (located across the highway; 360-873-2250), this tiny chapel has room for only a handful of people. But Wildwood Chapel still hosts an occasional wedding and provides a token of quiet for travelers. Generally open daily.

where to eat

Cascadian Farm. 55931 SR 20, Rockport; (360) 853-8173; cascadianfarm.com. Feasts of fresh blueberries and raspberries, in season, as well as homemade ice cream are the reward for stopping at this roadside fruit stand. Cascadian organic products and produce make a great choice for those planning to camp in the national park. Stock up on granola, jam, and the tantalizing berries, and then perk up with an espresso in the pretty gardenside seating area. There are restrooms and lots of parking. Open daily from May to Oct. $.

marblemount

Once a gold rush town and base for prospectors, Marblemount now welcomes rushes of outdoor enthusiasts. Eight miles east of Rockport, the town offers the greatest concentration of services whether you're headed out on the Pacific Crest Trail, on a quest for Kerouac, or simply enjoying the views of the craggy mountains at Washington Pass. Stop in Marblemount to gas up, rest up, and feed up before heading east into the national park.

getting there

From Rockport, drive east along the North Cascades Highway (SR 20) for 8 miles (about 10 minutes).

where to go

Wilderness Information Center. 7280 Ranger Station Rd. (MP 105.3), Marblemount; (360) 854-7245; nps.gov/noca. One of seven information centers for North Cascades National Park and surrounding national forests, this visitor center is geared toward those headed into the backcountry. Registration services and parking passes are available, as well as a few exhibits on the ecology of the park. A raised-relief map provides a hint of the dams, lakes, rivers, valleys, and mountains you'll see on your journey. Open daily May to Sept.

where to eat

Marblemount Diner. 60147 SR 20, Marblemount; (360) 873-4503. Homemade flourishes make the simple diner menu standout, from the inventive burgers to the towering house-specialty pies. Battered seafood, fresh salads, and friendly service all add to lunch in the Cascades. Open Fri to Sun for lunch and dinner as well as weekend breakfast. $$.

where to stay

Buffalo Run Inn. 60117 SR 20, Marblemount; (360) 873-2103 or (877) 828-6652; buffaloruninn.com. Cozy rooms range from economical units to those with extra amenities in this historic 1898 roadhouse. Basic rooms share immaculately clean bathrooms and a comfy common area, while the regular rooms have private baths, coffeemakers, microwaves, and refrigerators. $–$$.

newhalem

There's a buzz about Newhalem—and it's the humming electric wires that run overhead from the dams and power stations upstream to Seattle on the coast. Established as a Seattle City Light company town, Newhalem was built just below the first of the three dams. The community has seized on the appeal of the area, providing walking trails that abut the main street and superb services. A visitor center, restrooms, parking, public benches, and outdoor sculptures all invite you to stop.

Seattle City Light's boat tours on Diablo Lake also depart from Newhalem.

getting there

Drive northeast from Marblemount to reach the small community of Newhalem. The journey covers 15 miles and takes 20 minutes.

where to go

North Cascades Visitor Center. MP 120, Newhalem; (206) 386-4495; nps.gov/noca. Just west of Newhalem, a large visitor center offers exhibits revealing the park in many seasons. A large raised-relief map uses lightbulbs to identify park features. It's an excellent way to become familiar with the peaks of the park. Look, too, for a binder containing ranger trip reports for the season. You'll find great tips on worthwhile hikes and corners of the park. Open daily mid-May to Sept.

Gorge Dam. MP 123, Newhalem. A short, accessible trail leads to an overlook above the first dam. The oldest of the three, Gorge Dam demanded some creative construction techniques. Because the glacial sediment beneath the river was so prone to slides, engineers used refrigeration tubes to stabilize the ground while building progressed. Nearby is Gorge Creek Falls, one of the many cascading streams of water for which the national park was named. Open year-round.

Ladder Creek Falls. MP 120, Gorge Dam Powerhouse, Newhalem. The falls rate as a favorite with many visitors, especially the after-dark light show. Follow the trail beside the powerhouse over a suspension bridge, up steps of wide paving stones, and past pretty gardens to the headliner—the tiered Ladder Creek Falls. Light show runs daily from dusk until 11 p.m. from April/May through Oct.

Skagit Information Center. MP 120, Newhalem; (206) 684-3030. The information center is the departure point for trips on Diablo Lake with Skagit Tours (tour info 360-854-2589;

skagittours.com), which are run by Seattle City Light. Lunch and afternoon cruises set a course across the aqua waters of Diablo Lake. You'll also see Diablo Dam, which was the world's highest dam when it was completed in 1930 (although it didn't generate power until 1936). Adult prices start at $30 for summer cruises running from Fri to Sun; lunch tours run more frequently, Thurs to Mon. Make advanced reservations to secure a spot. $$$.

Trail of the Cedars. South of the main street, MP 120, Newhalem. A swaying suspension bridge leads to the trail. First winding along the edge of the Skagit River, the trail then loops through old-growth forest. A half-mile loop trail, the Trail of the Cedars makes a quick addition to a stop for restrooms and homemade fudge. Open year-round.

where to eat

Skagit General Store. 502 Newhalem St., Newhalem; (206) 386-4489. The general store is not so much a dinner option as a source for picnic supplies, but it's the lone option in Newhalem. Here you can grab a few sandwich items or hot soup and a coffee to enjoy on the store's veranda. For dessert, try a slice of homemade fudge—a Newhalem favorite. Open daily during summer, weekdays only in the off-season. $.

diablo to north cascades national park

A quick drive into the community of Diablo itself yields little to see beyond the shingled homes built for Seattle City Light employees. A few are boarded up, but most house current employees of the electric company.

Instead, continue on the North Cascades Highway, stopping in at each of the dams and lookouts. Feel the gusting winds over Diablo Lake, rent a canoe at the floating Ross Lake Resort, or photograph the big skies and big mountains at Washington Pass. En route, forests, trails, and falls line either side of the road, and all are well signposted.

getting there

Reach Diablo in just 10 minutes from Newhalem. The much longer journey to Washington Pass adds another 45 minutes (one way) to the road trip.

where to go

Diablo Dam. MP 127.5, Diablo. The second of the park's dams, Diablo Dam was once the world's largest. When traveling east, a left turn near MP 127.5 takes a steep, narrow route down across the dam. There's no stopping allowed but continue to the far side and visit the environmental learning center or simply admire the scenery from the lakeshore.

Diablo Lake Overlook. MP 132. Far below this viewpoint lies a reservoir, held in by Diablo Dam. From the roadside overlook the lake's turquoise hue cuts against the evergreen slopes and pencil line of the dam. Easy and stunning photo opportunities abound.

North Cascades Environmental Learning Center. MP 127.5, north shore of Diablo Lake; (360) 854-2599; ncascades.org. A modern, cedar-planked complex becomes the nerve center for adult and children's programs tackling everything from ecology to visual arts to relaxation. The center provides meals, lodging, and lessons to participants—review the list of seminars in advance. This is also the destination for Diablo Lake lunch tours. $$$.

Ross Dam and Overlook. MP 134 and MP 135, Ross Lake. In addition to the roadside overlook (MP 135) where the panoramas include Kerouac's Desolation Peak, there's the well-graded, mile-long Ross Dam Trail down to the reservoir from MP 134. En route, gaps in the evergreens reveal frames of the lake, the floating Ross Lake Resort, and the largest of the dams: Ross Dam.

where to stay

Colonial Creek Campground. MP 130. An arm of Diablo Lake provides a sheltered area for camping, picnics, and fishing in the national recreation area. Be cautious with watercraft: The levels of the lake rise and fall as water is held and released through the dams. Don't be left high and dry! $.

Ross Lake Resort. Ross Lake; (206) 486-3751; rosslakeresort.com. This floating lodge dating to the 1950s is accessible only by a short hike and boat ride, or a long hike. Floating cabins range from simple to expansive, sleeping up to 10, and families will be particularly entertained thanks to on-site boat rentals. The canoes, kayaks, stand-up paddleboards, and

desolation peak

A fire-watching station on Desolation Peak has become a pilgrimage of sorts for modern followers of the Beat Generation. A fire lookout on the peak served as home to many writers over the years, including Jack Kerouac, who served as a fire watcher in 1956. The On the Road *author penned* Desolation Angels *and* The Dharma Bums *based on the experience.*

Beat Generation poets and figures in the San Francisco Renaissance Philip Whalen and Gary Snyder also served at fire-watching posts in the North Cascades. A Pulitzer Prize winner, Snyder was Kerouac's inspiration for the character Japhy Ryder in The Dharma Bums.

motorboats are also available to day-trippers on a per-hour or daily basis. No restaurant or groceries available on-site. The resort is a truly hidden find, and its limited accessibility means it will remain so. Open mid-June to Oct—reservations taken a year in advance. $$$–$$$$.

worth more time

Washington Pass. MP 162, 42 miles from Newhalem. At 5,477 feet a rocky overlook provides panoramic views from the highest point of the highway. Look down and see the brake-light-burner road snake down the mountain face. Heading further east will take you to the Wild West town of Winthrop. This portion of the highway (from Ross Lake at MP 134 through to MP 177) is open only May to October because of heavy snowfalls. Check with the Washington State Department of Transportation for highway updates (wsdot.wa.gov).

east

day trip 01

fish ladders and waterfalls:
bellevue, issaquah, snoqualmie

This easy jaunt east is all about luxury. Well, with a few fishy bits thrown in for interest. From the gold-paved streets of Bellevue to the tranquility of the Salish Lodge at Snoqualmie Falls, the attractions along the western portion of this nationwide highway (I-90) are diverse, popular, and engaging. A huge variety of festivals range from fashion to music to the holidays.

Cheer on the spawning salmon as they climb the fish ladder at the salmon hatchery in Issaquah, hear the white noise of the power-generating Snoqualmie Falls, and wander amid the lushness of Bellevue Botanical Garden—all within a half-hour drive from downtown Seattle.

bellevue

Across Lake Washington from Seattle, Bellevue is synonymous with money: Locals include tech workers at Microsoft and Expedia, head offices pack the city, and you'll find some of the best high-end shopping in the state. Skybridge walkways connect shopping to hotels to dining to entertainment. There's lots of free parking and a pedestrian corridor along Northeast 6th Street to link key areas of the city.

The city is young, having been incorporated in 1953, but there's also Old Bellevue centered on Main Street, where small storefronts are a more traditional slice of Washington. City festivals are family-friendly and offer lots more to explore.

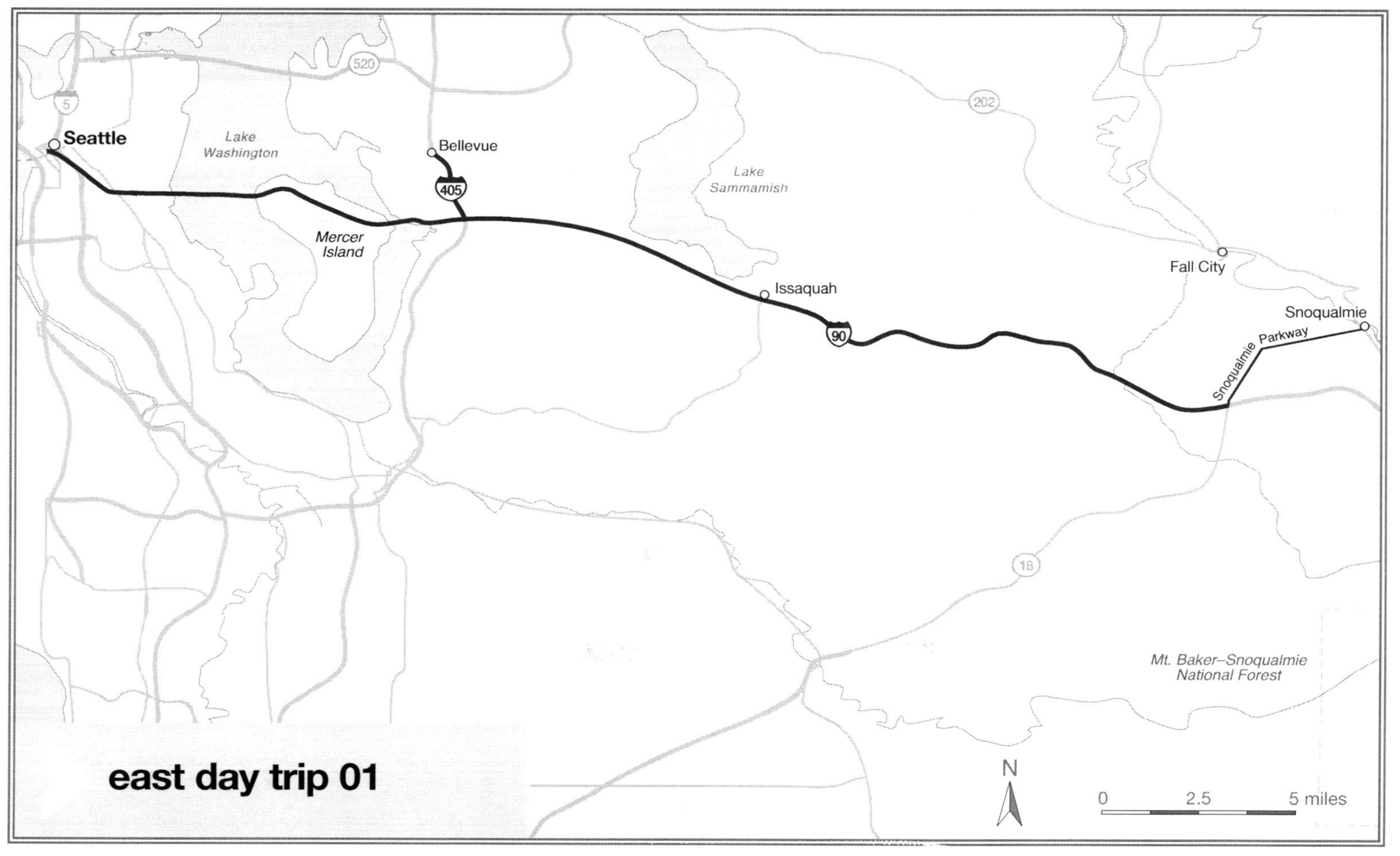

east day trip 01
Seattle
5
520
Lake Washington
Mercer Island
Bellevue
405
Lake Sammamish
Issaquah
90
202
Fall City
Snoqualmie
Snoqualmie Parkway
18
Mt. Baker–Snoqualmie National Forest
N
0
2.5
5 miles

getting there

I-90 runs east from Seattle, providing access in minutes to Bellevue (10 miles, 15 minutes), Issaquah (17 miles, 20 minutes), and Snoqualmie (29 miles, 35 minutes). Allow plenty of extra time in traffic. Or follow SR 520 east and cross Lake Washington on Evergreen Point Floating Bridge, the world's longest and widest floating bridge when it was replaced in 2016, then head south on I-405.

where to go

Bellevue Arts Museum. 510 Bellevue Way NE, Bellevue; (425) 519-0770; bellevuearts.org. The beautiful vibrant brick-red building designed by Steven Holl provides a polished exterior for the museum's exhibits, which focus on craft and design. Past exhibits have ranged from quilts and tapestries to ceramics and glass. There's an outdoor rooftop sculpture garden with a display of changing works. Open Wed to Sun. $$.

Bellevue Botanical Garden. 12001 Main St., Bellevue; (425) 452-2750; bellevuebotanical .org. This hilltop garden eschews the bustle and traffic of Bellevue to offer a green oasis of twisting paths, creative gardens, and educational exhibits. The Waterwise and Rock Gardens are particularly commendable for their Northwest elements, while the Rhododendron Glen celebrates the state flower. Bellevue Botanical Garden neighbors Wilburton Hill Park, a favorite spot for picnics. Open daily with free admission.

Downtown Park. 10201 NE 4th St., Bellevue; (425) 452-6885; bellevuewa.gov. This impressive and newer park is dominated by the circular promenade alongside a canal. There's also a large playground, waterfall feature, and regular events. Open daily.

KidsQuest Children's Museum. 1116 NE 108th Ave., Bellevue; (425) 637-8100; kids questmuseum.org. Climbing, transportation, and story time are some of the experiences for kids up to eight years old. Open Tues to Sun. $$.

where to shop

The Shops at the Bravern. 11111 NE Eighth St., Bellevue; (425) 456-8780; thebravern .com. With a long list of luxury—from Neiman Marcus to Prada and Louis Vuitton—this shopping destination boasts a well-heeled clientele. Valet parking shows the Bravern is no regular shopping experience. Open daily.

The Bellevue Collection: Another favorite Bellevue shopping experience clusters around Bellevue Way at Northeast Eighth Street. The downtown destination includes **Lincoln Square, Lincoln Square South, Bellevue Place,** and the largest center, **Bellevue Square.** The latter features a Macy's and Nordstrom, plus two levels of boutiques, shops, art galleries, and services. Watch for art works such as blown glass by Dale Chihuly. The Hyatt Regency Bellevue anchors Bellevue Place where you'll also find art galleries, restaurants, and services. Sharing a corner with the Bellevue Arts Museum, Lincoln Square includes dining favorites such as **Pearl Seafood & Oyster Bar** (425-455-0181; pearlbelle vue.com) and **Maggiano's Little Italy** (425-519-6476; maggianos.com), plus a bowling alley, arcade, movie theater, and spa. All properties are open to shoppers daily.

issaquah

Issaquah is where the wilderness of the east begins. Despite being just 20 minutes from Seattle, it retains its small-town charm and connection to the outdoors. Parks edge the outskirts of the city, with Cougar Mountain Wildland Park, Squak Mountain State Park, Tiger Mountain State Forest, and Lake Sammamish State Park on the doorstep.

Volunteers create wonders at the local salmon hatchery. The city's grand event is October's Salmon Days Festival, when thousands visit Issaquah to watch as volunteers capture salmon from the river and harvest the roe. Other wild encounters include the cougar sanctuary and wandering the many trails at local parks.

getting there

Follow I-90 east from Seattle or Bellevue. From exit 13 a drive east along Newport Way directs you to Cougar Mountain Zoo, while exits 17 and 18 lead more directly into the downtown.

where to go

Cougar Mountain Zoo. 19525 SE 54th St., Issaquah; (425) 391-5508; cougarmountain zoo.org. Besides the cougars the zoo is also home to macaws, reindeer, and tigers. Extra-fee "close encounters" experiences allow you to feed reindeer or come face-to-face with a tiger—through safety glass that is. Open Wed to Sun from Jan to Nov and daily in Dec for the Issaquah Reindeer Festival. $$.

Gilman Town Hall Museum. 165 SE Andrews St., Issaquah; (425) 392-3500; issaquah history.org. Besides exhibits in the town hall that include a kitchen and a dynamite blaster, there's a 1914 jail in back with iron bars and thick concrete walls. Open Thurs to Sat. $.

Issaquah Depot Museum. 78 First Ave. NE, Issaquah; (425) 392-3500; issaquahhistory .org. All-aboard exhibits allow visitors to see a variety of railroad cars and equipment, including a caboose once used in the Weyerhaeuser logging railroad. Inside the restored train station, which dates to 1889, you'll discover a telegraph station and lots of interpretive displays. The Issaquah Valley Trolley makes 20-minute rides through town from mid-May to Sept. Open Fri to Sun. $.

Issaquah Salmon Hatchery. 125 W. Sunset Way, Issaquah; (425) 392-1118 (tour info) or (425) 391-9094 (hatchery); issaquahfish.org. Visit the hatchery to follow the life cycle of the salmon that return to Issaquah Creek each fall to spawn. Trace the salmon's journey from the weir that prevents the adult fish from heading further upstream and directs them into the hatchery where volunteers collect the roe. Underwater holding tanks show salmon beneath the surface. A note for families: The spawning salmon are at the end of their life cycle and are killed before the eggs are harvested—it could be upsetting, but most kids tend to be intrigued. The non-profit Friends of the Issaquah Salmon Hatchery runs the volunteer programs and tours. Open daily with free admission, although donations are accepted. $.

Village Theatre, Issaquah. Francis J. Gaudette Theatre, 303 Front St. North, Issaquah; (425) 392-2202; villagetheatre.org. Issaquah's Village Theatre specializes in family theater and musicals, including some they've commissioned. Five shows each season. Full-price tickets start at about $60. $$$.

where to eat

Levitate Gastropub. 185 Front St. North, Issaquah; (425) 677-8497; levitategastropub .com. With two patios this main-street eatery basks in the delight of local sights, bounty, and friendliness. There's a tasty menu of pub favorites, plus seafood, vegan options, and weekend brunch. Open daily for lunch and dinner.

snoqualmie

Meaning "moon" in Salish—the language spoken by the Native American people of the same name—Snoqualmie has long endured as a popular destination. Travelers flock to see the spectacular 270-foot waterfall, which is nearly 100-feet taller than Niagara Falls, and to bask in the fine mist and excellent views.

But besides the namesake falls, the town boasts a luxury lodge where spa treatments, intimate dinners, and hearty breakfasts make for a true escape. Railroad enthusiasts can wander a street-long depot featuring rail cars, cabooses, and engines. And if you haven't sated your appetite for waterfalls, venture further to the cascades at Olallie State Park.

getting there

I-90 provides easy access to Snoqualmie. Take exit 25 then head along Snoqualmie Parkway to the falls and downtown—a quick journey from both Issaquah (12 miles, 20 minutes) and Seattle (29 miles, 35 minutes).

where to go

Northwest Railway Museum. 38625 SE King St., Snoqualmie; (425) 888-3030; trainmuseum.org. The Northwest Railway Museum is an added favorite. A wonderfully restored Victorian depot reveals snapshots of the former grandeur of the rail age, and at times you can also tour the museum's massive train shed on Stone Quarry Road. The Snoqualmie

Valley Railroad embarks on 5-mile journeys in antique coaches. The railroad runs on weekends Apr to Oct only, as well as special holiday-season trips. The depot is open daily with no admission charge. Train fares: $$.

Snoqualmie Falls. 6501 Railroad Ave. SE, Snoqualmie; (425) 831-6525 (gift shop); sno qualmiefalls.com. The 270-foot waterfall serves many a purpose. It generates power for Puget Sound Energy, remains a spiritual place for the Snoqualmie tribe, and is a sight to behold for more than 1.5 million annual visitors. Viewing platforms provide vistas of the falls, which are 100-feet higher than Niagara Falls. There are a gift shop, coffee bar, restrooms, and large free parking lot on the opposite side of Railroad Avenue with an overhead walkway to reach the observation areas. Open daily.

Snoqualmie Falls Hydroelectric Museum. SE 69th Pl., Snoqualmie; (425) 831-4445; pse.com. On the opposite side of the river, this small museum gives insight into the history behind harnessing the power of the falls to produce power. Open Wed to Sun from Memorial Day weekend to Labor Day.

where to eat

The Attic at Salish Lodge. 6501 Railroad Ave., 4th Fl., Snoqualmie; (425) 888-2556 or (800) 272-5474; salishlodge.com/attic.php. Proximity to the falls, smaller plates, and a relaxed atmosphere are just a few reasons the Attic is my preferred yet lesser-discovered dining option at Salish Lodge. The salads with Dungeness crab, stone-fired pizzas, and Washington wine list keep the focus on what's fresh in the Northwest. Open weekends for breakfast and daily for lunch and dinner. $$–$$$.

Woodman Lodge. 38601 SE King St., Snoqualmie; (425) 888-4441; woodmanlodge.com. A classic steakhouse with an edge of modern Wild West and strong historical roots dating to 1902, the Woodman Lodge bridges casual and fine polish. Grill options range from elk to pork chops to filet mignon, but the lighter fare is equally exceptional. Burgers offer a more moderately priced option. Unfortunately for vegetarians, meat-free options are as rare as the beef despite some seafood. Open Tues to Sun for dinner; closed Mon. $$$–$$$$.

where to stay

Salish Lodge. 6501 Railroad Ave., Snoqualmie; (425) 888-2556 or (800) 272-5474; salish lodge.com. A historical lodge dating back to 1916, the Salish Lodge can well be called a long-time favorite. Fireplaces and deluxe showers or soaker tubs grace each of the rooms. It is arrestingly easy to slip away into an escape at the lodge. Great dining, an on-site spa with soaking pools, and being walking distance to Snoqualmie Falls offer many reasons to stay. But do at least make it to breakfast, where the traditional "honey from heaven" christens a freshly baked biscuit. $$$$.

worth more time

Olallie State Park. 51350 SE Homestead Valley Rd., North Bend; (425) 455-7010; parks.state.wa.us. Best known for its waterfalls, this day-use park takes its name from the Chinook word for salmonberry. Twin Falls is the largest of the cascades, but there are more to see including Weeks Falls. Other park activities include hiking, mountain biking, fishing, and rock climbing. Open daily. $.

day trip 02

east

cowboys and northern exposure:
roslyn, cle elum, ellensburg

Venturing from the Roslyn streets that formed the backdrop for *Northern Exposure* to lovely, historic downtown Ellensburg, this day trip rates as a personal favorite. Plus, the region has undiscovered scenic drives in every direction.

Roslyn is the living spirit of the Wild West, with Washington's oldest bar—The Brick Saloon—and its unusual segregated cemeteries. In nearby Cle Elum, railroad history and a busy main street retain the feel of travelers arriving by horseback or on the Burlington Northern Railroad.

Further east along I-90, Ellensburg delivers attraction after attraction. A bustling university campus, art and historical museums, plus beautiful natural surroundings make the town an excellent getaway with a more modern western charm.

roslyn

Founded as a coal mining town in the 1880s, Roslyn once produced up to two million tons of the black stuff a year. Much later the city (yes, really!) gained fame as the setting for television's favorite fictional Alaskan town—*Northern Exposure*'s Cicely. Fans of the television show still visit the state's oldest bar The Brick Saloon, enjoy a coffee on the community patio, and explore the town museum to read production sides.

A visit is best approached with patience, especially on summer weekends and during the Sunday farmers market. You'll see many folks ambling about town, soaking in the

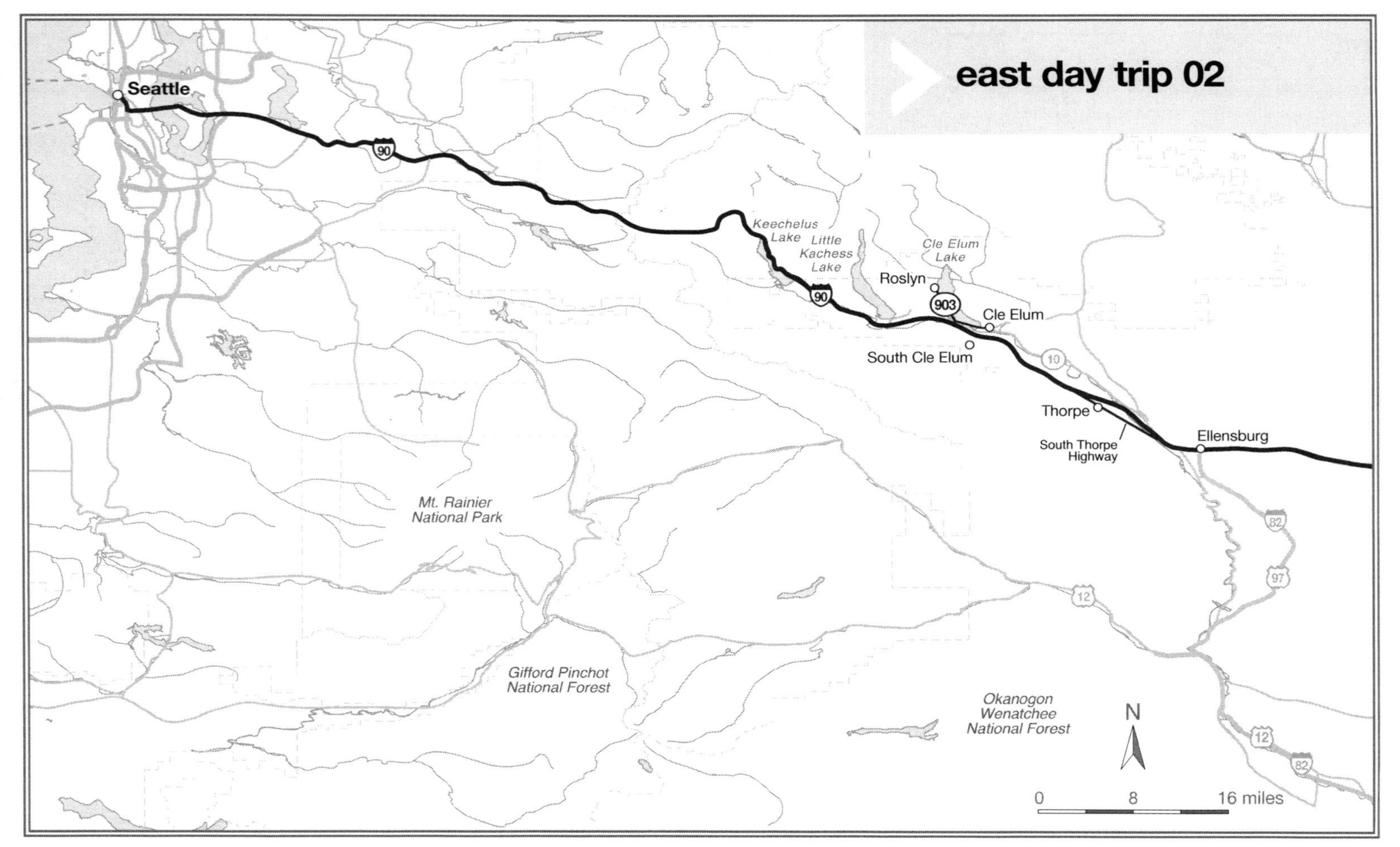

east day trip 02
Seattle
90
Keechelus Lake
Little Kachess Lake
Cle Elum Lake
Roslyn
903
Cle Elum
South Cle Elum
10
Thorpe
South Thorpe Highway
Ellensburg
82
97
12
Mt. Rainier National Park
Gifford Pinchot National Forest
Okanogon Wenatchee National Forest
N
0
8
16 miles

atmosphere and visiting shops, cafes, and art galleries. And while the history of the coal-mining era lives on in museums and trails around town, it can truly be remembered in a visit to the twenty-five cemeteries.

getting there

I-90 provides quick and direct access to the area. Take exit 80 for Roslyn (83 miles, 90 minutes from Seattle) then follow Bullfrog Road past Suncadia to First Street, which leads into town.

where to go

The Brick Saloon. 100 W. Pennsylvania Ave., Roslyn; (509) 649-2643; bricksaloon.com. A staple exterior shot in *Northern Exposure,* the Brick is a favorite place for fans of the show to visit. Add to that it's reputed to be one of the state's oldest bars (dating to 1889) with a running-water trough for the olden-days delight of tobacco spitting, and it rates as a place you'll not find the likes of anywhere else. Open daily.

Roslyn Cemeteries. Memorial Road, Roslyn; ci.roslyn.wa.us. It's not often that a cemetery is an attraction, unless there's a famous grave to be found. But the draw here is the division of graves into ethnicities and lodges—more than two dozen in all. It's a testament to the city's eclectic mining history. Open daily.

Roslyn Museum. 203 W. Pennsylvania Ave., Roslyn; (509) 649-2355; roslynmuseum.com. The coal industry once drew many new residents to this now-small city. In fact the population during the 1920s was greater than today. Museum exhibits touch on coal-mining history, the diverse ethnic groups who came to work in the mines, and its television alter-ego on *Northern Exposure.* Most items have been donated by local community members, making the slightly odd-ball collection easier to appreciate as one that is both about and from a community. This by-donation museum is open daily in summer. Sat only in winter. $.

Suncadia. 3600 Suncadia Trl., Cle Elum; (509) 649-6400; destinationhotels.com/suncadia-resort. Three golf courses, miles of trails, restaurants, and spas—this resort is jam packed with amenities and activities. It's hidden in a forest grove, where a drive through the scenic grounds can be interesting to get a feel for this escape.

where to eat

Basecamp Books and Bites. 110 W. Pennsylvania Ave., Roslyn; (509) 649-3821; basecampbooks.com. Small-town businesses often wear many hats, and Basecamp does this extremely well—as bookstore, bar, and restaurant. Grab some hearty fare (sandwiches, burgers, big salads) and take a relaxing seat in the neighboring community space **The Yard.** Open daily for breakfast, lunch, and dinner. $$.

coal mines trail

A 4.7-mile trail connects Cle Elum to Roslyn and Ronald, near the shores of Cle Elum Lake. The route follows the bed of the now-dismantled Northern Pacific Railroad and is popular with bicyclists and walkers. Twenty points of interest are described in a local guide (available from the Cle Elem Visitor Center). Although the scenery isn't exceptional, the exercise and excellent interpretive booklet make it a worthwhile journey. Check with ***Ride Roslyn*** *(109 West Pennsylvania Ave.; 509-649-5300; rideroslyn.com) for maps and bike rentals.*

Roslyn Cafe. 201 W. Pennsylvania Ave., Roslyn; (509) 649-2763; theroslyncafe.com. Another familiar site for *Northern Exposure* fans, the cafe appeared in the TV series as the only slightly rebranded Roslyn's Cafe. A sunny outdoor patio and cozy indoor dining area serve up excellent options to share, plus full meals like hearty salads and burgers. Open Thurs to Sat for breakfast, lunch, and dinner; Sun and Mon for breakfast and lunch; closed Tues and Wed. $$–$$$.

cle elum

Although trafficked First Street means the town doesn't offer the best options for a weekend stroll at first glance, venture off the main drag to find an excellent museum, freshly made treats, and locally roasted coffee that all make the mining and logging town worth including in a day trip. Then the scenic drive between Cle Elem and Ellensburg will take you past Kittitas Valley Wind Farm, Thorp Grist Mill, and a couple of barn quilts.

getting there

From Roslyn, follow SR 903 east to Cle Elum (2 miles, 5 minutes from Roslyn).

where to go

Cle Elum Visitor Center. 312 W. First St., Cle Elum; (509) 674-6880; discovercleelum.com. With details on the Coal Mines Trail and local museums, the visitor center is conveniently located in the west end of Cle Elum. Open Mon to Sat.

Carpenter Museum. 302 W. Third St. (at Billings Ave.), Cle Elum; nkcmuseums.org. This may perhaps be Washington's best community-run museum for its simplicity and community spirit. It's a collective operation between Cle Elum artists, who staff the museum and will most likely be painting on-site when you visit, and the local historical society. The airy, regal rooms of the 1914 Carpenter family home are filled with antiques, intricate quilts, and local art. Hidden staircases and the freedom to explore the home extend a warm welcome. Open Fri to Sun.

Cle Elum Historical Telephone Museum. 221 E. First St., Cle Elum; nkcmuseums.org. The museum sits in the old offices of the Pacific Northwest Bell Telephone Company, and puts the changes of telephone technology into context. Open Memorial Day to Labor Day.

South Cle Elum Depot. 801 Milwaukee Ave., South Cle Elum; (509) 674-2006 (restaurant); milwelectric.org. The South Cle Elum Depot once served as a stop for trains running between Chicago and Tacoma. Now the restored 1909 railroad station is home to a small museum, historical rail yard trail, and restaurant. Exhibits open Sat, while the restaurant is open Tues to Sun. $.

where to eat

Cle Elum Bakery. 501 E. First St., Cle Elum; (509) 674-2233. This street-front bakery has been in operation since 1906. Fresh loaves and treats, lunch sandwiches, and picnic items are available. Open daily. $.

El Caporal. 105 W. First St., Cle Elum; (509) 674-4284. The hanging flower baskets that surround this location in summer create a welcoming vibe for this cantina. A spacious dining room and attentive waitstaff round out a usual Mexican food menu. Open daily for lunch and dinner. $–$$.

where to stay

Flying Horseshoe Ranch. 3190 Red Bridge Rd., Cle Elum; (509) 674-2366; flyinghorseshoeranch.com. Travelers once arrived by stagecoach to this family-run horse ranch. A variety of lodging ranges from tents and bunkhouses to cute cabins and a log house that can sleep six. There are large shared kitchen facilities, a fire pit, and unending grassy fields for games. Horseback riding is available and there are about thirty horses on the lush property, where access to trails is on the ranch doorstep. $$–$$$.

ellensburg

Ellensburg combines one of the state's most charming historical districts with the youthful energy of Central Washington University. An 1889 fire leveled the city, dashing hopes for it to become the state capital, but for visitors it means much of the architecture dates to the same late-Victorian period.

Ellensburg is full of surprises: a quirky creative's house and art-filled yard, university gardens and galleries, a February cowboy festival, and summertime rodeo. Go explore: You'll find character-filled restaurants beside century-old roadhouses and university pubs.

i-90 recreation corridor

Palouse to Cascades State Park Trail *(previously Iron Horse State Park Trail) now stretches more than 100 miles along I-90 following old railroad beds that connect North Bend to Vantage on the Columbia River. One neat feature is that the trail route heads through railroad tunnels, the safe traverse of mountain passes. Mountain biking through the tunnels with good lights and rain gear makes for a popular and unique adventure. Check the state parks website (parks .state.wa.us) for updates on tunnel closures or dangerous conditions before heading out.*

The trail covers similar territory to the ***Mountains to Sound Greenway*** *(206-382-5565; mtsgreenway.org). Providing a recreation route over Snoqualmie Pass, the greenway includes many miles of trail and recreation opportunities between Seattle and Ellensburg.*

Historic barns are a treasured local feature, with century-old agricultural buildings being adorned with "barn quilts"—paintings of traditional designs. These are mapped as a self-guided driving tour.

getting there

Both SR 10 and I-90 provide a quick, roughly 25-mile journey (30 minutes) from Cle Elum to Ellensburg. The city lies at exit 106, 110 miles (or 1 hour and 45 minutes) east of Seattle.

where to go

Ellensburg Chamber of Commerce. 609 N. Main St., Ellensburg; (509) 925-2002 or (888) 925-2204; myellensburg.com. Centrally located, the chamber runs a visitor center that is open Mon to Sat.

Central Washington University. 400 E. University Way, Ellensburg; (509) 963-1111; cwu .edu. The sprawling campus between University Way and Wildcat Way abuts downtown. Although the once-excellent chimpanzee institute has closed, the campus includes a variety of attractions including Japanese gardens, an open-air butterfly garden, a gallery of student artwork, and the free Museum of Culture & Environment that's also a student classroom.

Clymer Museum of Art. 416 N. Pearl St., Ellensburg; (509) 962-6416; clymermuseum.org. The western-focused work of John Ford Clymer, much of which was created for US and Canadian magazines, forms the foundation of this museum. The subjects are diverse, but the spirit and humor of the Northwest persist throughout. Ellensburg Rodeo Hall of Fame also operates from the same spot. Open Mon to Sat. $.

Dick and Jane's Spot. 101 N. Pearl St., Ellensburg; reflectorart.com/spot. Whether you visit by night or day, this house is a treat to behold. A fence of reflectors wraps a house and yard filled with whimsical art. While the house is certainly a must-see, it is also a private home, so sign the guest book and admire respectfully. Street viewing welcomed year-round.

Kittitas County Historical Museum. 114 E. Third Ave., Ellensburg; (509) 925-3778; kchm.org. Extensive geology exhibits, including the state's official gemstone—petrified wood—as well as stunning Ellensburg blue agates, which can only be found in this region, create a nice departure from a pioneer focus. Car exhibits and Native American artifacts also feature in the handsome Cadwell building, dating to 1889. Open Mon to Sat.

Olmstead Place State Park. 921 N. Ferguson Rd., Ellensburg; (509) 925-1943; parks.state.wa.us. The pioneer homestead gives a slice of late-1800s life through old cabins, farm equipment, and a heritage barn. Open daily. $.

Wild Horse Renewable Energy Center. 25905 Vantage Hwy., Ellensburg; (509) 964-7815; pse.com. Look out over the churning turbines that harness the wind to create energy. Mountain views and guided tours (which require closed-toe shoes) make the extra distance worthwhile. Open daily from Apr to Nov.

where to eat

Rodeo City Bar-B-Q. 204 N. Main St., Ellensburg; (509) 962-2727. Not the best place for vegetarians, but for lovers of ribs and steak, this restaurant is a Main Street institution. Open daily for lunch and dinner, except closed Mon. $$–$$$.

Yellow Church Café. 111 S. Pearl St., Ellensburg; (509) 933-2233; theyellowchurchcafe.com. Intimate and cozy, the Yellow Church Café presents comfort food with a modern flair. Planked salmon, veggie burgers, pastas, and steak create an eclectic yet simple menu. The old Lutheran church, dating to 1923, makes a romantic and historic background for a quiet dinner. Open for weekend breakfast and daily for lunch and dinner. $$–$$$.

where to stay

Ellensburg KOA. 32 Thorp Hwy. South, Ellensburg; (509) 925-9319 or (800) 562-7616; koa.com/campgrounds/ellensburg. As Ellensburg enjoys a much warmer and drier climate than Seattle, the camping season is a little more reliable here. Pitch a tent beside the Yakima River at this clean campground. Season runs approximately Apr through Sept. $.

columbia river gorge

Winding through much of the state, the grand Columbia River offers superb recreational activities, from windsurfing to fishing and hiking. The river is truly the main artery of the Pacific Northwest, and it's also a surprisingly fantastic place to catch a concert.

Music fans make annual pilgrimages to see performances at one of the world's most spectacular music venues: the ***Gorge Amphitheatre.*** *With the plummeting gorge as the stunning backdrop and desert sunsets as lighting, the music just sounds better. Tickets to events and festivals can go quickly, despite the 150-mile journey from Seattle to the Gorge, located between Quincy and George (georgeamphitheatre.com).*

Hotel Windrow. 502 N. Main St., Ellensburg; (509) 962-8000; hotelwindrow.com. Incorporating historic architecture with all the charm of a modern boutique hotel, Hotel Windrow offers something unusual in Ellensburg including a rooftop deck, restaurant, and ballroom. $$–$$$.

day trip 03

east

bavaria and apple country:
leavenworth, cashmere

Two rival high-school-sports towns pair to create an engaging getaway to Bavaria and apple country. Although best known for its transformation into a slice of Bavaria, Leavenworth also rates as one of best places in the state to experience the outdoors, having received mentions for top rock climbing, rafting, and hiking. In-town oddities include a nutcracker museum, morning alpenhorn serenade, and mountain goats grazing on a putting course. Add outdoor sculptures that include a piece by famed glass artist Dale Chihuly, local wineries, great beer, and lively festivals, and Leavenworth will soon be on your list of annual-tradition day trips.

Further east on US 2 (called Highway 2 locally), Cashmere offers a more subtle charm. With a main thoroughfare called Cottage Avenue, the town's well-kept detached homes create an idyllic Pleasantville feel. Visit the pioneer village or candy factory for engaging and easy-to-enjoy family activities.

leavenworth

Best known as a Bavarian-themed town, Leavenworth also reveals itself as a haven for wineries, the arts, and the outdoors. A day trip satisfies only a taste. Start at the Front Street Park where events take place like concerts, the Christmas Tree Lighting, and Village Art in the Park (villageartinthepark.org), an outdoor gallery of sorts on weekends May to October.

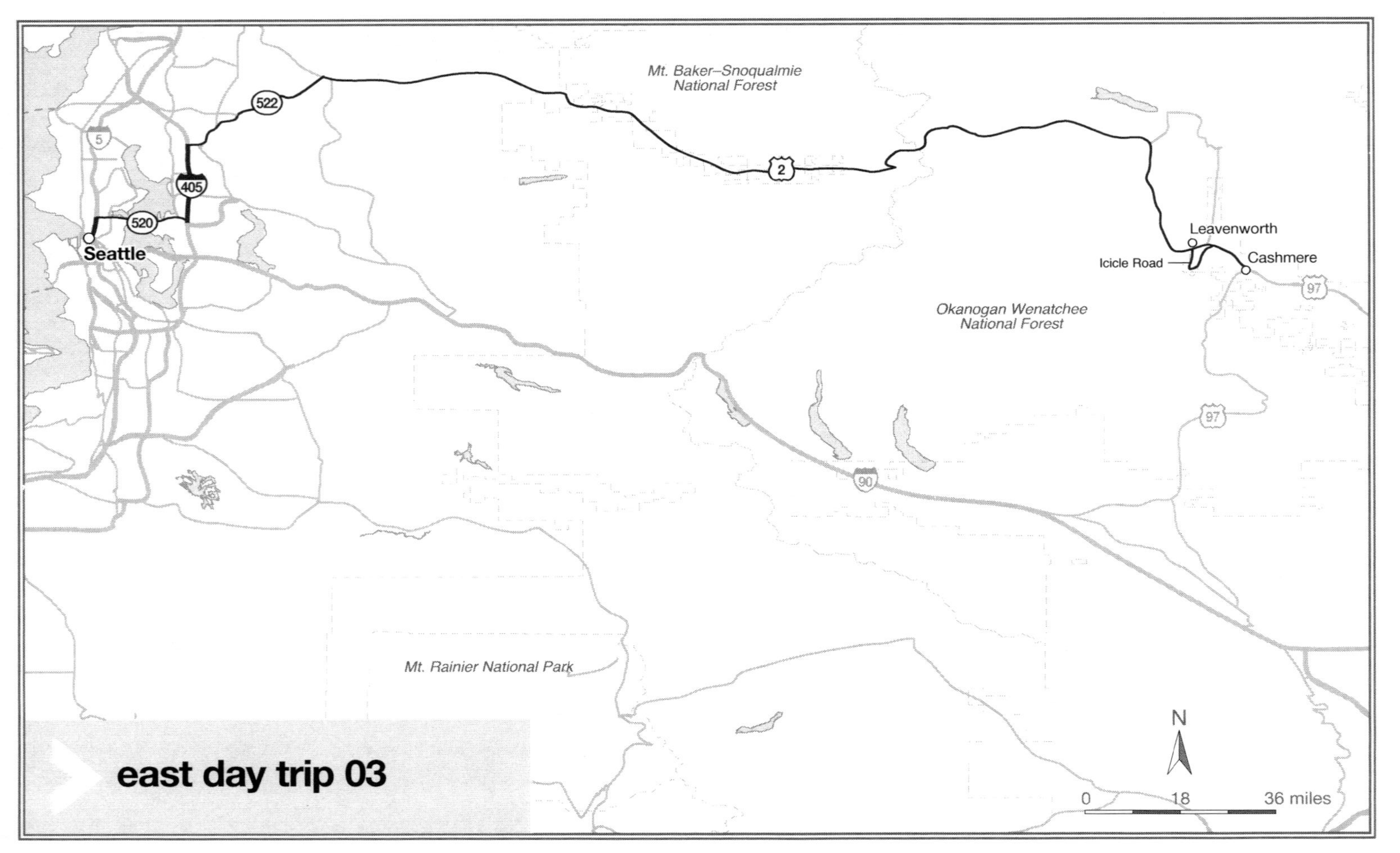
east day trip 03
Mt. Baker–Snoqualmie National Forest
Okanogan Wenatchee National Forest
Mt. Rainier National Park
Seattle
Leavenworth
Cashmere
Icicle Road
5
405
520
522
2
90
97
97
N
0
18
36 miles

In the mid-1960s the community underwent a transformation from a lumber town to a stylized Bavarian village. Holding strongly to the theme, even major corporations have redesigned their signs in preapproved scripts. Oh, and don't be surprised to see lederhosen and alpine hats about town—locals have fully embraced the German spirit.

Besides shopping and admiring the quirky Bavarian vibe, linger longer to explore the outdoors from skiing to hiking to river rafting to walking the trails of Waterfront Park.

getting there

Head north on I-405 to the junction with SR 522. The route leads northeast to US 2 (Highway 2) heading east. Winding through small towns and mountain passes, US 2 emerges on the sunny side of Washington and leads directly through downtown Leavenworth (about 2 hours).

where to go

Leavenworth Visitor Center. 940 Hwy. 2, Leavenworth; (509) 548-5807; leavenworth.org. Unable to snag that hard-to-find room? Head to this central visitor center for attentive assistance. Open daily, with later hours on Fri and Sat.

Wenatchee River Ranger District. 600 Sherbourne, Leavenworth; (509) 548-2550; fs.usda.gov/recarea/okawen. Find trail, camping, and other recreation info about Okanogan-Wenatchee National Forest. Open Mon to Sat in mid-May to Oct; Mon to Fri only in winter.

Greater Leavenworth Museum. 735 Front St., Leavenworth; (509) 548-0728; leavenworthmuseum.org. This museum traces the town's history from logging bust to tourism boom. $.

Icicle Creek Center for the Arts. 7409 Icicle Rd., Leavenworth; (509) 548-6347 or toll-free (877) 265-6026; icicle.org. This performance center hosts everything from films to concerts, as well as runs a series of arts camps and workshops. A neighboring property, Sleep Lady Mountain Resort (7375 Icicle Rd., Leavenworth; 509-548-6344; sleepinglady.com) is a silent sanctuary for arts, fine cuisine, and nature. See the rare Dale Chihuly outdoor installation *Icicles* (which is made of more than 1,000 pieces of handblown glass), the fabulous riverside salmon sculptures, and other spectacular outdoor artworks. The art walk is open daily, although it may be closed for special events.

Leavenworth National Fish Hatchery. 12790 Fish Hatchery Rd., Leavenworth; (509) 548-7641; fws.gov/leavenworth. This large hatchery welcomes those looking to learn about the Chinook salmon that return annually to the river. Large holding tanks, fish ladders, and the salmon life cycle will interest all ages. Informative brochures allow for self-guided tours. The government-run hatchery is open daily.

Leavenworth Nutcracker Museum. 735 Front St., Leavenworth; (509) 548-4573; nutcrackermuseum.com. It's all in how you crack it at the Leavenworth Nutcracker Museum. Thousands of nutcrackers on display demonstrate a real passion for the often-overlooked ornament, symbol of the holidays, and kitchen implement. Open daily. $.

Leavenworth Reindeer Farm. 10395 Chumstick Hwy., Leavenworth; (509) 885-3021; leavenworthreindeer.com. Farm tours introduce a series of animals, including ponies, pigs, chickens, and yes—the majestic reindeer themselves. There are areas to play but the highlight is hand-feeding the gentle beasts. Reservations required for scheduled tours, mostly running weekends. $$–$$$.

Leavenworth Ski Hill. 10701 Ski Hill Rd., Leavenworth; (509) 548-5477; skileavenworth.com. When a vesture of snow settles on Leavenworth, residents and visitors alike head out to enjoy it. Snowshoeing, Nordic (cross-country) skiing, snow tubing, ski jumping, and rope tow are all popular snow sports at this in-town ski area run by the Leavenworth Winter Sports Club. Open daily when the snow falls. $$$.

Silvara Vineyards. 77 Stage Rd., Leavenworth; (509) 548-1000; silvarawine.com. A polished tasting room sits atop a hill overlooking Smallwood's (see next listing) and the valley. Silvara produces an easy-to-drink Cabernet Sauvignon amongst its varietals, and its grapes come from the Yakima Valley (see Southeast Day Trip 03). Open daily for tastings.

Smallwood's Harvest. 10461 Stemm Rd., Peshastin; (509) 548-4196. This spot may just appeal to the whole group: There is a petting farm, corn maze, fresh farm produce, a

becoming bavaria

Faced with a slumping logging industry in the 1960s, town leaders brainstormed ways to draw in tourists to the picturesque community of Leavenworth. After settling on the adoption of a Bavarian theme, hours of self-funded work transformed the town into an alpine village. Woodwork, murals, and Gothic-script signage add authenticity to the town. Other Bavarian-themed experiences include the morning alpenhorn serenade at the Enzian Inn and the schnitzel served at the in-town German restaurants.

While you wouldn't have seen a pair of lederhosen in the town a half century ago, you just might today. The community pride over the adopted heritage has grown so much so that census percentages of local residents claiming German ancestry increased from zero to more than 20 percent at one point.

wine-tasting room, and then the endless samples of the salsas, sauces, preserves, honeys, and other goodies produced under the Smallwood's label. Open daily. $.

where to eat

The Alley Cafe. 214 8th St., Leavenworth; (509) 548-6109; thealleycafe.com. Approaching on 8th Street, a sign directs diners, fittingly, to enter this intimate restaurant via the alley. Flower boxes in summer and a cozy warmth in winter greet diners. Expect hearty helpings and a full wine list. Open Fri to Sun for lunch; daily for dinner. $$–$$$.

Gustav's. 617 Hwy. 2, Leavenworth; (509) 548-4509; gustavsleavenworth.com. A simple grill and beer garden, Gustav's is a great destination for those seeking a sunny patio or retreating from the outdoors to warm up. Dozens of brews on tap make the pub a favorite with hikers or during Oktoberfest. Although the menu tends toward the heavy-eating side (think burgers and German sausages), there is also a refreshing variety of salads. Open daily for lunch and dinner. $–$$.

Pavz. 833 Front St., Leavenworth; (509) 548-2103; pavzcafebistro.com. Delicately crafted crepes served in a casual bistro make for a lighter dinner option. Tuck into a plate of seafood pasta followed by a chocolate gelato or fresh pear crepe. Or, make a crepe the main dish with filling options like roasted vegetables, spicy Italian sausage, or shrimp. The restaurant is open for lunch and dinner daily. $$–$$$.

Watershed Cafe. 221 8th St., Leavenworth; (509) 888-0214; watershedpnw.com. The menu features ingredients from all over the Pacific Northwest, from Hood Canal oysters to Washington apples. There's also a lovely patio to catch a casual cocktail. Open Thurs to Mon for dinner. $$$–$$$$.

where to stay

The Enzian Inn. 590 Hwy. 2, Leavenworth; (509) 548-5269 or (800) 223-8511; enzianinn.com. There's palpable family personality and hospitality for a 105-room hotel. The Enzian offers luxe comforts like down duvets, robes, indoor and outdoor pools, and an open-air hot tub. The buffet breakfast and alpenhorn serenade make a lovely start to the morning. Putt a round on the eighteen-hole putting green as mountain goats mow the grass and the Enzian's own waterfall adds a gentle white noise. $$–$$$$.

LOGE Leavenworth. 11798 US 2, Leavenworth; (509) 690-4106; logecamps.com. Riverside cabins and a hostel are tucked along the banks of the Wenatchee and offer more than meets the eye. Each is true to the wealth of outdoor activities in the area, and amenities include a communal campfire and deck, regular events, and cruiser bikes for local exploring. It's pet-friendly too. $–$$$.

leavenworth festivals

One would expect Leavenworth's Oktoberfest to be the biggest party in town, but in fact it's the annual Christmas Lighting Festival that draws the largest crowds and leads to fully booked rooms. Started in 1969, the Christmas lighting sees Leavenworth flick the switch on countless twinkling lights that harken from under the Bavarian eaves and crisp winter snows. The Christmas Lighting Festival generally runs the first three weekends of December, but the lights keep twinkling into February.

cashmere

On the south banks of the Wenatchee River, Cashmere features antiques shops, a twenty-building pioneer village, the Aplets & Cotlets candy factory, and a 9/11 Spirit of America Memorial. It's also the gateway to the Wenatchee Valley, beyond which apple orchards, dams, and forests stretch east.

getting there

Travel east from Leavenworth on US 2 for 11 miles (about 15 minutes). Turn to cross the Wenatchee River, and explore the tightly knit downtown of Cashmere on Division Street and Cottage Avenue.

where to go

Cashmere Chamber of Commerce. 103 Cottage Ave., Cashmere; (509) 782-7404; cashmerechamber.org. Located on the main street, it's open Mon to Fri. Additional info about local agriculture is available at cascadefarmlands.com.

Cashmere Cider Mill Tasting Room. 5420 Woodring Canyon Rd., Cashmere; gourmetcider@gmail.com. Cashmere Cider Mill offers tastings to visitors, its cider pressed from local Wenatchee Valley apples. There's also a hard cider tasting room on the property. Contact for hours. $.

Cashmere Museum and Pioneer Village. 600 Cotlets Way, Cashmere; (509) 782-3230; cashmeremuseum.org. An assembly of twenty or so relocated, original pioneer buildings stands outside the Cashmere Museum. From a schoolhouse and barbershop to hotel and doctor's office, the village could almost operate as its own community. The museum sheds light on life during the pioneer days with collections of Native American and pioneer artifacts and exhibits exploring the natural world. The village is open daily from Mar/Apr to Oct. Call ahead to confirm hours. $.

Liberty Orchards. 117 Mission Ave., Cashmere; (509) 782-2191 or (800) 231-3242; libertyorchards.com. Aplets & Cotlets, the sugar-coated fruit-and-walnut candies, have been produced by Liberty Orchards since the 1940s. From the preparation to cooking to packing, every factory tour has a sweet ending: a free sample of the candy. Free tours run daily approximately every 20 minutes. Closed weekends Jan to Mar.

Peshastin Pinnacles State Park. 7201 N. Dryden Rd., Hwy. 2; (509) 664-6373; parks.state.wa.us. Popular with rock climbers, sandstone slabs jut up to 200 feet into the air as mini craggy peaks at Peshastin Pinnacles State Park. This day-use park offers restrooms and picnic areas, plus excellent views when you explore zig-zagging trails. Open daily from mid-Mar to Oct. $.

where to eat

Brian's Bulldog Pizza. 107 Cottage Ave., Cashmere; (509) 782-1505; briansbulldogpizza.com. The local pride is infectious here, with orange and black (the colors of Cashmere High School) covering every surface. Pictures of recent sports teams fill the walls, while locals chow down on pizza or bowl at one of the neighboring four lanes. Open daily for lunch and dinner. $–$$.

Country Boys BBQ. 400 Aplets Way, Cashmere; (509) 782-7427; countryboysbbq.com. The bronze pig outside sits blissfully unaware that Country Boys BBQ is best known for its ribs. Outdoor picnic tables offer a relaxed summer feel, while the simple wood interior keeps the dining casual. Open Tues to Sat for lunch and dinner. $$–$$$.

apple country

Fruit stands are a staple in this area of the state, mostly stocking the valley's favorite varieties of apples, such as Fuji, Gala, Granny Smith, Braeburn, Golden or Red Delicious—and the state's new celebrity: Cosmic Crisp. For more on the local apple scene, head further east to the ***Washington Apple Commission Visitor Center*** *(2900 Euclid Ave., Wenatchee; 509-663-9600; bestapples.com).*

worth more time

Wenatchee Valley. Another 20 minutes further east on US 2 leads to Wenatchee and the banks of the Columbia River. The region is home to power-generating dams, such as **Rocky Reach Dam, Park and Discovery Center** (5000 Hwy. 97-A, Wenatchee; 509-663-7522; chelanpud.org).

There are also lots of good things growing thanks to the Columbia River, a source for agricultural irrigation. Plan a tour highlighting the local produce by stopping in at the **Washington Apple Commission Visitor Center** (2900 Euclid Ave., Wenatchee; 509-663-9600; bestapples.com). Or, enjoy the expert blend of lush and stark amid the trails, ponds, and evergreens of **Ohme Gardens** (3327 Ohme Rd., Wenatchee; 509-662-5785; ohmegardens.com). The gardens are open daily mid-Apr to mid-Oct.

southeast

day trip 01

southeast

hendrix and hydroplanes:
renton, kent, auburn

South of Seattle a horse-racing track, memorial to a guitar legend, and the area's only IKEA store blend in a curious mix of tourism. These communities along I-405 and SR 167 are quick to access and, because of their population density, are home to a unique complement of attractions that are often overlooked.

The diversity spans the Jimi Hendrix memorial and a library built over a river in Renton, fall pumpkin patches and a race-boat museum in Kent, and antiques and horse racing in Auburn.

renton

The city's growing downtown complements an interesting series of local attractions, including the polished granite of the Jimi Hendrix memorial. Riverside trails in Cedar River Park lead to the shores of Lake Washington, where a boathouse offers canoe and kayak rentals, or hop over to Gene Coulon Memorial Park for incredible views.

Excellent quality restaurants (think handsome steaks in historic eateries to interesting vegetarian) and a public library that spans the river create an eclectic mix of urban tourism.

getting there

Either follow I-5 south to the junction with I-405, which heads east to Renton, or take I-90 east to the junction with I-405 and then follow the interstate south. Travel time is 17 to 25

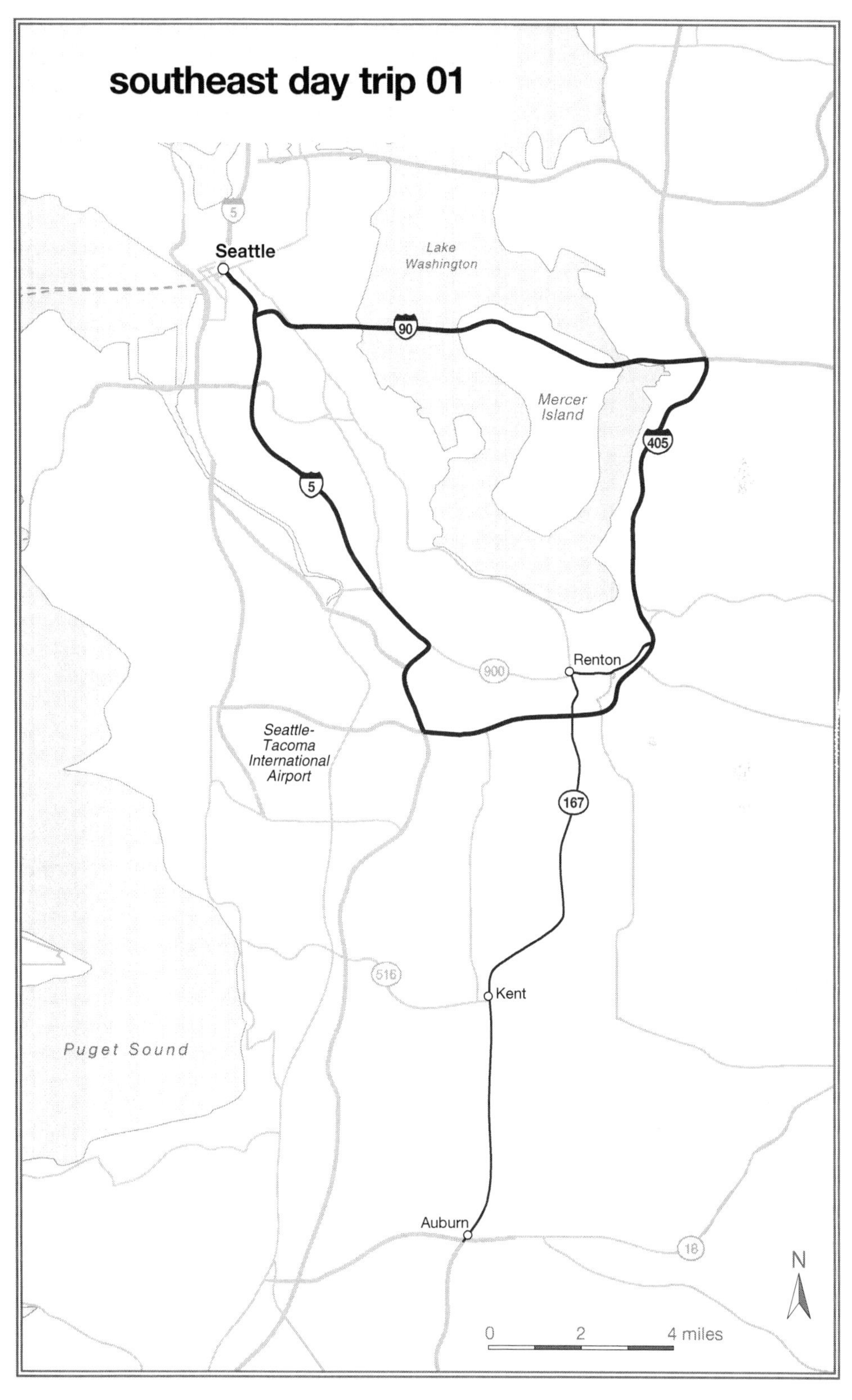
southeast day trip 01
5
Seattle
Lake Washington
90
Mercer Island
405
5
Renton
900
Seattle-Tacoma International Airport
167
516
Kent
Puget Sound
Auburn
18
N
0
2
4 miles

minutes, depending on traffic. Both Kent and Auburn are an easy distance from Renton along SR 167, also known as Valley Freeway.

where to go

Cedar River Trail. Cedar River Park Dr. off Maple Valley Hwy., Renton. This in-town trail is great for walking, running, and biking with about 12 paved miles. Attractions include river views, salmon spotting, and the river-spanning architectural gem of Renton Library near Liberty Park (100 Mill Ave. South; 425-226-6043; kcls.org). Paddleboard, canoe, or kayak rentals are available at the northern end, the Renton Rowing Center on Lake Washington (1060 Nishiwaki Ln.; 425-902-4848; canoe-kayak.com; $$$).

Gene Coulon Memorial Beach Park. 1201 Lake Washington Blvd. North, Renton; renton wa.gov. On the shores of Lake Washington, this expansive city park offers freshwater swimming plus games, boat launches, a fishing pier, and restaurants. The views from the beach and docks are spectacular.

Jimi Hendrix Memorial. Greenwood Memorial Park, 350 Monroe Ave. Northeast, Renton; jimihendrixmemorial.com. A large granite memorial is inscribed with lyrics and images familiar to Hendrix fans—including the musician's iconic electric guitar. In addition to being the resting place for Jimi Hendrix, the plot includes other Hendrix family members. Open daily during daylight hours.

Renton History Museum. 235 Mill Ave. South, Renton; (425) 255-2330; rentonwa.gov/rentonhistorymuseum. Housed in a 1942 Art Deco–style fire station, the museum preserves photos and artifacts from local history, including Renton's days of coal mining, logging, and pioneers. The museum is close to Veterans Memorial Park as well as a drinking fountain decorated with the portrait head of Chief Sealth. Open Tues to Sat. $.

where to shop

Fry's Electronic Store. 800 Garden Ave. North, Renton; (425) 525-0200; frys.com. A mecca for electronics, Fry's features specials on everything from laptops to housewares. Open daily.

IKEA. 601 SW 41st St., Renton; (425) 656-2980; ikea.com. As the only IKEA location in the Seattle area, this megastore is an undeniably popular destination. You'll find the same products from this iconic Swedish manufacturer online, but the store has the amazingly cheap Swedish eats you can only snag in person and the always cutely designed display rooms. Open daily.

where to eat

Berliner Pub. 221 Main Ave. South, Renton; (425) 277-1111; berlinerpub.com. Step into the lively beer hall vibe, where there are house-made sausages, fresh pretzels, and many beers on tap. The outdoor patio is family- and pet-friendly. Open afternoon to late night. $-$$.

Blossom Vegetarian Restaurant. 305 Burnett Ave. South, Renton; (425) 430-1610; blossomrenton.com. The spectrum of Vietnamese dishes are all meat-free, including the "beef" noodle soup and "chicken" fried rice. There's also a lovely patio garden. Open daily for lunch and dinner. $.

Melrose Grill. 819 Houser Way South, Renton; (425) 254-0759; melrosegrill.com. Since 1901 this clapboard building has welcomed travelers and locals for merriment. The Melrose Grill survived Prohibition (1918), a fire that burned the top two floors (1928), a stint housing a sparring ring (1972), as well as many owners over the last century. But the historic building has endured and nowadays operates as an intimate steakhouse. Although the menu includes some chicken and seafood, vegetarians may be happiest to head elsewhere. Open daily for dinner. $$$–$$$$.

kent

The city is an undemanding daytime destination with wonderful cafes, a polished shopping district, and tranquil downtown parks. In addition to a pleasant main street, Kent offers unique museums (think hydroplanes or a creative take on local history).

getting there

Travel south 6 miles on SR 167, also known as Valley Freeway, then take Central Avenue into downtown. Not accounting for traffic, the journey takes under 10 minutes.

where to go

Centennial Center Gallery. City of Kent Campus, 400 West Gowe St., Kent; (253) 856-5050; kentwa.gov. Although small and located in a municipal building, the breezeway-style gallery features stunningly good examples of Pacific Northwest art. Unfortunately, as the building is only open Mon to Fri, weekend day-trippers may be out of luck.

Hydroplane & Raceboat Museum. 5917 S. 196th St., Kent; (206) 764-9453; thunderboats.org. Dedicated to the speedy sport of powerboat racing, the museum hosts shows and lectures, as well as races in the summer Seafair Weekend Festival on Lake Washington. Exhibits include full-size hydroplanes (which look like floating UFOs), engines, race suits, and memorabilia. There's also a restoration shop. Open Tues to Sat. $$.

Kaibara Park. Railroad Ave., between Smith and Meeker Sts., Kent; kentwa.gov. A Japanese garden is on the doorstep of the library with stepping stones, a pond, and beautiful foliage. Burlington Green is another park, across the tracks. Both are easy to find near the shopping, railroad station, and dining district.

Kent Historical Museum. 855 E. Smith St., Kent; (253) 854-4330; gkhs.org. Exhibits at the museum strike a unique chord that goes beyond the pioneers: Perhaps learn about the Japanese-American internment experience during World War II; hear recordings of the high school band during its 1920s glory days; or see the collection of cream pitchers that number in the dozens. Open Wed to Sat. $.

Pacific Raceways. 31001 144th Ave. Southeast, Kent; (253) 639-5927; pacificraceways.com. With drag racing and a 2.25-mile road course, this motorsports venue has been in operation since 1960. Races generally run Apr to Oct. $$.

Pickleball Station. 22330 68th Ave. South, Kent; (253) 243-9858; pickleballstation.com. Besides a small museum dedicated to the Northwest origins of the sport, there's a host of courts just for pickleball and a drop-in schedule. Open daily. $.

where to eat

Café on Fourth. 124 4th Ave. South, Kent; (253) 859-5662; cafeonfourth.com. Breakfasts, quality sandwiches, pizzas, and espresso drinks are the core offerings—all with a bit of Hawaiian charm and occasional entertainment. Open Mon to Sat. $.

Wild Wheat Bakery Cafe and Restaurant. 202 First Ave. South, Kent; (253) 856-8919; wildwheatbakery.com. The menu items are creative and superb versions of familiar dishes. Ocean-inspired twists like a crab omelet complement the hearty soups, sandwiches, and bakery-fresh treats. Open daily for breakfast and lunch. $–$$.

auburn

Auburn is a family-oriented destination. Parks with disc-golf courses, festivals, and bocce ball courts add outdoor options that complement the museums and shops. A busy thoroughbred racing track—Emerald Downs—offers programming aimed at families, making it a fun, activity-filled, summer day-trip option.

The town originally went by the name Slaughter, but (no shocker) locals decided to rename the community given that the local hotel was called the Slaughter House. Some sources say the name *Auburn* comes from settlers who arrived from Auburn, NY. Others quote a line in an Oliver Goldsmith poem that begins "Sweet Auburn, loveliest village on the plain."

getting there

Auburn Way connects the downtowns of Kent and Auburn for a quick 6-mile trip. Or, take SR 167 from Kent and cut east on SR 18. Both routes take about 15 minutes without traffic.

where to go

Emerald Downs. 2300 Ron Crockett Dr., Auburn; (253) 288-7000 or (888) 931-8400; emeralddowns.com. From the "Call to Post" to the coming down the stretch, Emerald Downs provides a full day of race activities as well as dining options. Races run Fri to Sun from mid-Apr or May to mid-Sept. Admission charged for live racing events. $.

Game Farm Wilderness Park. 2401 Stuck River Rd., Auburn; (253) 931-3043 or (253) 931-3095 (info line); auburnwa.gov. Disc golf, camping sites, and festivals make the park a fabulous day-trip destination for families. Open year-round.

Les Gove Park. 910 9th St. Southeast, Auburn; auburnwa.gov. This downtown park is handy to the town museum and features bocce courts, plenty of play areas, and views of Mount Rainier. Plus there's a Sunday farmers' market. Open year-round.

Mary Olson Farm. 28728 Green River Rd. Southeast, Kent; (253) 288-7433; wrvmuseum .org. This 1880s farm is technically in Kent, but is run by the White River Valley Museum out of Auburn. A homestead, barn, and other farm buildings feature on the property, plus there's a salmon river, farm animals to greet, and orchard filled with apples and cherries. Open weekends late June to late Aug.

White River Valley Museum. 918 H St. Southeast, Auburn; (253) 288-7433; wrvmuseum .org. The museum connects the region's history through unique and insightful temporary exhibits and permanent displays telling Native American, pioneer, and railroad stories. Family programs are a large focus. Open Wed to Sun. $.

where to eat

Marvel Ukrainian Food & Deli. 615 C St. Southwest, Auburn; (253) 887-8181, marvel foodanddeli.com. There's a small dining area where diners can enjoy grocery purchases or items from the hot-food counter such as a variety of piroshky, borscht, and cabbage rolls. The family-run store stocks goods from Europe but also does much of the baking and cooking in-house. Open 8 a.m. to 9 p.m., Mon to Sat. $$.

worth more time

Flaming Geyser State Park. 23700 SE Flaming Geyser Rd., Auburn; (253) 735-8839; parks.state.wa.us. This park once featured a 20-foot flaming geyser and was privately run. Those days are no more. After stretched finances the park was transferred to the state and now small methane geysers—one known as the Bubbling Geyser—still warrant the park's name. It is no Old Faithful, but it does make a curious day-trip destination. Park facilities include access to the Green River, hiking and biking trails, and fire pits. Open year-round.

day trip 02

southeast

"the mountain"—mount rainier:
sunrise, paradise, longmire

One can truthfully say they've found Paradise in Mount Rainier National Park. This Paradise, however, is not so much a village as a gathering of buildings (a ranger station, visitor center, and a timber-framed inn) set below the snowy slopes of "The Mountain" where hikers, climbers, and day visitors converge.

Throughout the park the twisting roads, uncut timber, wind-blown vistas, creeping glaciers, and roaming wildlife all add immeasurable charm to a visit. Catching the park during the summer wildflower bloom (usually late July/early August) is spectacular. And if you're lucky, you'll spot some of the Packwood or Ashford herds of elk that roam wild.

Becoming the fifth national park in 1899, Rainier—or *Tahoma,* its Native American name—features the mountain at its center. The 14,410-foot peak is the highest in the state and towers above the other volcanoes in the Cascade Range. More than two million people make the trip here each year.

Mount Rainer's slopes are cloaked in twenty-six major glaciers, and its volcanic power has been quiet since the last reported eruption in 1894. But steam vents hiss near the summit, and volcanologists anticipate the mountain will erupt again. Although it's difficult to predict just when, the mountain appears to trigger lahars—giant mudflows and signs of a large eruption—every 500–1,000 years.

This day trip circles the mountain clockwise, starting at the freshly named Sunrise lookout. Visit the park in late summer for the wildflowers, when the lower slopes are dotted with asters, lupines, and red Indian paintbrush among countless varieties of blooms. In fall the chill of winter begins to hint. Watch for forecasts of snow in late September and October.

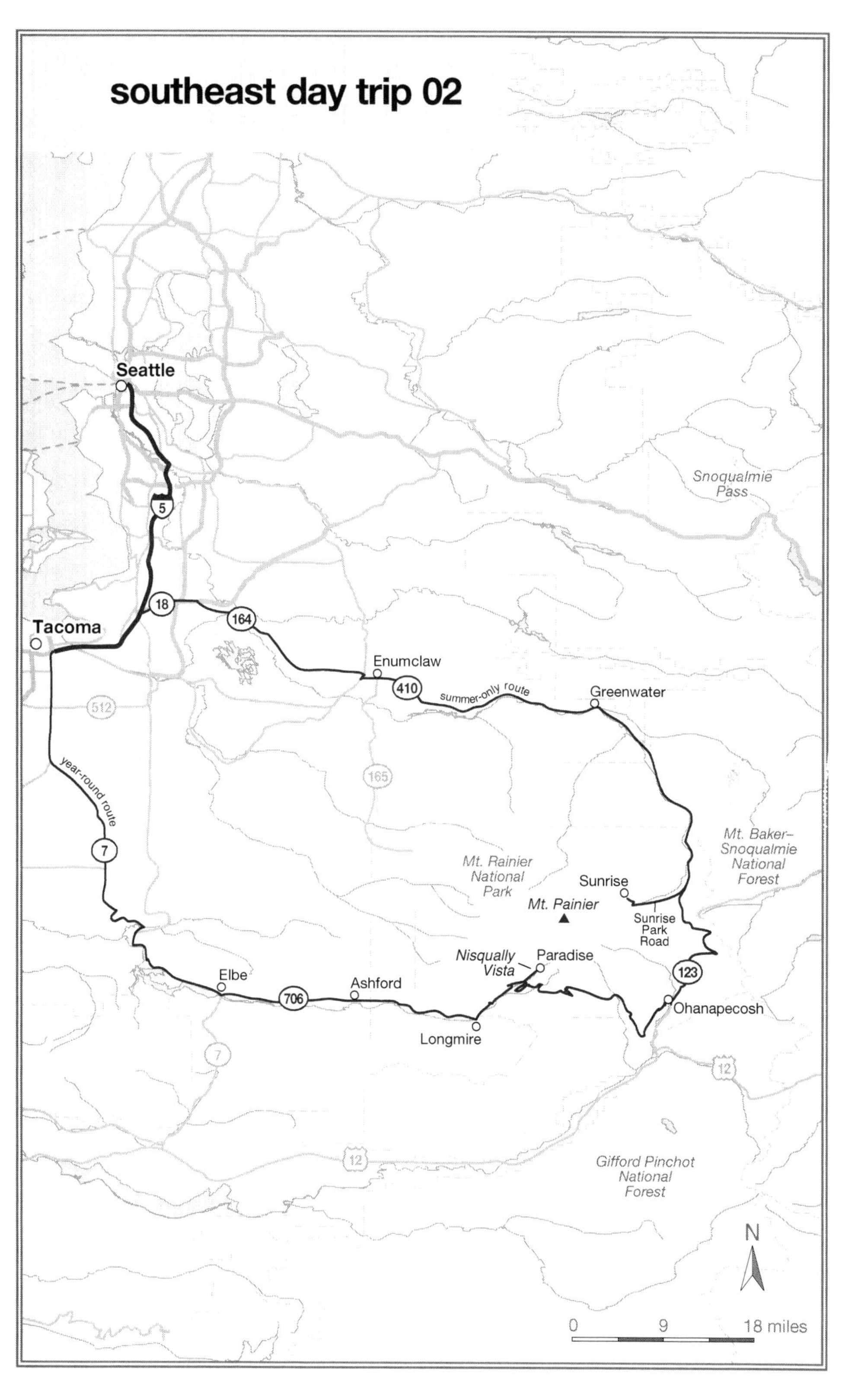
southeast day trip 02
Seattle
5
Snoqualmie Pass
18
164
Tacoma
Enumclaw
410
summer-only route
Greenwater
512
165
year-round route
7
Mt. Baker–Snoqualmie National Forest
Mt. Rainier National Park
Sunrise
Mt. Rainier
Sunrise Park Road
Nisqually Vista
Paradise
123
Elbe
706
Ashford
Ohanapecosh
Longmire
7
12
12
Gifford Pinchot National Forest
N
0
9
18 miles

If you can stay longer than a day, the park pass (priced by the vehicle; 360-569-2211; nps .gov/mora) is valid for up to seven days. And with endless lodging options, making a day trip into a weekend getaway is all too easy.

For excellent visitor information and events, see visitrainier.com.

getting there

The following route is a summer-only option since from November to May, SR 410 closes starting at the Crystal Mountain turnoff. Follow I-5 south of Federal Way to the junction with SR 18 at exit 142A. After heading east on SR 18, follow SR 164 southeast. From here the directions get a lot simpler and traffic lighter: Take SR 410 from Enumclaw through Greenwater to Sunrise, for a total of about 80 miles (1.5 hours) from Seattle.

Year-round, when SR 410 closes, begin the journey at the Nisqually entrance by taking I-5 south to exit 133 at Tacoma, then following SR 7 to Elbe and head east on SR 706.

sunrise

Sitting at 6,400 feet on Sunrise Ridge, this is the highest point in the park reachable by car. Of course the vantage affords stunning views looking at the northeast flank of Mount Rainier's 14,410-foot peak, a mountain climbers' camp, and the Emmons Glacier—the largest on the mountain. From here lookouts and hiking trails lead to fantastic views and ever-higher elevations.

Visitor services, including a visitor's center and restaurant, provide summer-only amenities and information.

getting there

Driving south on SR 410 through Mount Baker–Snoqualmie National Forest before entering the national park, make a right turn onto Sunrise Park Road. After 5 miles, keep straight (there's a left-hand turnoff heading to the White River Campground). For about 10 more miles, the route climbs the ridge through a series of switchbacks.

The road to Sunrise is generally open from July to early October. Total travel time is 2 to 2.5 hours from Seattle.

where to go

Crystal Mountain Ski Area. 33914 Crystal Mountain Blvd. (5 miles before the Sunrise turnoff); (360) 663-3050; skicrystal.com. Like many ski hills, Crystal Mountain finds a new life in summer, welcoming visitors to lush hiking trails and stunning displays of wildflowers. Ride the Mt. Rainier Gondola to gain more than 2,000 feet in elevation and get the best views while savoring a lovely scenic meal at the mountaintop Summit House Restaurant. In winter eleven lifts provide access to the more than fifty runs that make the hill the largest in Washington. Ski season generally runs mid-Nov to mid-Apr. $$$.

Sunrise Point. MP 13, Sunrise Park Rd., Mount Rainier National Park. Three-hundred feet lower than your eventual destination, Sunrise Point offers sensational views. The panorama includes five volcanoes: Rainier, Baker, Glacier Peak, Adams, and Hood are all within sight on a clear day. Accessible under the national park pass.

Sunrise Visitor Center. MP 16, Sunrise Park Rd., Mount Rainier National Park. Exhibits and information on hiking trails are available at the visitor center at the end of the road. A historic building, the visitor center and adjacent ranger accommodations were built in a blockhouse style yet are still dwarfed by the peak of Mount Rainier behind. Head to the left of the visitor center where there's a telescope that looks out to the glaciers of the volcano as well as climbers at Camp Schurman—which sits at 9,510 feet in elevation. For a short walk, take the trail to Emmons Vista. The stone balcony sits on the side of the hill and is ideal for group shots with Mount Rainier in the back row. Sunrise makes an easy departure point for day hikes with multiple trails fanning out from the visitor area. Open July to mid-Sept. Accessible under the national park pass.

where to eat

Summit House Restaurant. Crystal Mountain Ski Area; (360) 663-3085; crystalmountain resort.com. During summer this restaurant, sitting at a 6,872-foot elevation, serves sunset dinners on weekends and lunch daily. All winter long it's open to skiers and snowboarders. As with Sunrise Point, you get views of the region's ever-impressive volcanoes on clear days—especially from the lovely patio. Call ahead for hours. $$–$$$.

where to stay

Silver Skis Chalet. 33000 Crystal Mountain Blvd., Crystal Mountain Ski Area; (360) 663-2558 or (888) 668-4368; silverskischalet.com. Since there is limited dining on this side of Mount Rainier, bringing a few groceries and cooking in may be the best option. The kitchens at the condos are supremely stocked with everything you'd expect at home. Each has its own personality, depending on the owner, but generally the accommodations are cozy with clean linens and a friendly welcome. $$$–$$$$.

paradise

A one-way-in destination, Paradise is popular with all manner of visitors and has been for the past century: The iconic historic inn dates to 1917. Whether your style is sipping a glass of wine to the sounds of a live pianist or strapping on a helmet and crampons to climb a mountain, there's a version of Paradise just for you. Activities from this area include hiking, climbing, sledding, and snowshoeing.

Paradise sits on the southern flank on Mount Rainier at about 5,400 feet in elevation.

getting there

From Sunrise, take SR 410 then SR 123 south toward Ohanapecosh, before cutting west on Stevens Canyon Road. The final climb is on Paradise Valley Road, which is plowed year-round. Driving between Sunrise and Paradise takes about 1.5 hours.

Direct from Seattle, enter the park through the Nisqually entrance by taking I-5 south to exit 133 to Tacoma, then following SR 7 to Elbe and heading east on SR 706 through Longmire to Paradise.

where to go

Christine Falls. Located midway between Longmire and Paradise, this waterfall is an easy roadside stop to see two drops totaling about 69 feet. The stone bridge frames the lower falls. Further upstream is Comet Falls—more than four times larger! Accessible under the national park pass.

Grove of the Patriarchs. Stevens Canyon Rd., near the junction with SR 123, Mount Rainier National Park. About halfway between Sunrise and Paradise lies one of the shortest and most lovely hikes in the park. A well-worn trail leads to a suspension bridge spanning the Ohanapecosh River, taking visitors to a river island. The sandy paths skirt some of the largest trees in the park, including swollen trunks of western red cedar and Douglas fir. These trees seeded after a fire that roared through the area a millennium ago. Now river nutrients from seasonal flooding and the continual source of water keep these trees reaching upward. Accessible under the national park pass.

Henry M. Jackson Visitor Center. Paradise, Mount Rainier National Park; (360) 569-2211 (general park information line). Exhibits on ice climbing provide a new perspective on the park. Many hikes through the subalpine meadows have excellent mountain views, including the Nisqually Vista and Skyline trails. Open year-round; weekends only Oct to May. Accessible under the national park pass.

Narada Falls Viewpoint. Paradise Road/SR 706 (west of Paradise), Mount Rainier National Park. A short (but at times steep and slippery) trail leads to an excellent spot for admiring the 176-foot, two-tiered Narada Falls that is sourced from the Paradise River. Cascading below the road, the falls sometimes create a rainbow halo and remain a favorite photo stop. Accessible under the national park pass.

Reflection Lakes. Stevens Canyon Rd. From Paradise, travel 3 miles east to these lakes—most treasured when they perfectly reflect the graceful mountain on a clear day. A number of hikes weave through the area. Accessible under the national park pass.

names of mount rainier

The towering peak of Mount Rainier goes by many names. The Salish peoples call this volcano Tahoma, Takhoma, *and* Tacobeh*—names meaning "snowy peak" and "big mountain." But in 1792 Captain George Vancouver spied the mountain and named it after his superior, Rear Admiral Peter Rainier.*

Locally, however, you'll find Mount Rainier is most often simply referred to as "The Mountain."

where to eat & stay

Paradise Inn. 52807 Paradise Rd., Mount Rainier National Park; (360) 569-2275 or (855) 755-2275; mtrainierguestservices.com. The timber skeleton of the lodge tents a large social area with restaurants, gifts shops, and sitting areas. First opening in 1917, the inn now includes 121 guest rooms on the doorstep of the mountain. A large main-level area filled with couches and fireplaces creates a lively atmosphere for planning hikes, swapping wildlife encounter stories, and sharing photos with fellow visitors. Rooms available with shared or private bathrooms. In addition to a Sunday brunch, the restaurant serves breakfast, lunch, and dinner. Creative and hearty dishes include a bison Bolognese, a half-pound burger, and macaroni and cheese with crab. Open May to Sept only. Restaurant: $$–$$$. Rooms: $$–$$$$.

longmire

Less of a destination than Paradise, Longmire features the park's lone museum and a second historic lodge. This is also the location of the original park headquarters. It makes a convenient spot to gather information or stop for a meal, and at the Longmire General Store, there are cross-country ski and snowshoe rentals available in winter.

getting there

From Paradise, travel southwest on SR 706 for 11 miles (20 minutes) to Longmire.

Direct from Seattle, enter the park through the Nisqually entrance by taking I-5 south to exit 133 at Tacoma, then following SR 7 to Elbe and heading east on SR 706 to Longmire (about 2 hours).

where to go

Longmire Museum. Longmire, Mount Rainier National Park; (360) 569-6575. Telling the natural history as well as the history of the park from its 1899 establishment as the country's fifth national park, the Longmire Museum is part of a National Historic Landmark District. The building was originally the homestead of settler James Longmire and later housed the headquarters for the park. The log-and-stone building is now a museum. Next door, the Wilderness Information Center provides summertime information on trails and the backcountry. The museum is open daily year-round. Free with national park pass.

where to eat & stay

National Park Inn. 47009 Paradise Rd., Longmire, Mount Rainier National Park; (360) 569-2275 or (855) 755-2275; mtrainierguestservices.com. The smaller of the two national park inns, the Longmire lodge has the longest history in the park, stretching back to James Longmire finding hot springs in the area in 1883. About six miles from the Nisqually entrance, the year-round inn offers just twenty-five rooms, most with private bathrooms. An on-site restaurant serves breakfast, lunch, and dinner. Warming entrees include cedar-planked trout, elk burgers, and daily specials. Restaurant: $$–$$$. Rooms: $$–$$$$.

worth more time

Outside the Nisqually entrance, take a relaxing 14-mile trip through the scenery with **Mount Rainier Scenic Railroad** (54124 Mountain Hwy. East, Elbe; 360-492-6000 or 888-884-8338; mtrainierrailroad.com). Tracks leave Elbe, with its historic church, to cut a journey into the Mount Rainier foothills and visit the tiny village of Mineral, where there's a huge logging depot museum to explore. Tickets start at about $40 per adult. Trains run May to Oct with additional special events for holidays. $$$.

day trip 03

southeast

fruit bowl of the nation:
yakima

yakima

Arriving via I-82 on the outskirts of Yakima, you'll not mistake the glaciered slopes of Mount Rainier and the dark hulk of Mount Adams on the western horizon. But after the initial wows, it's the foreground that draws your attention: the stark desert, subtleties of millennia-old hills, and lush yet alien-looking agricultural lands.

Although the wide downtown streets are lined with century-old opulent buildings, there's also a new liveliness to the grandeur. Pause awhile and you'll find a Sunday farmers' market, stunning concert venue, and wine-tasting rooms. A large sector of life in the town surrounds the region's Mexican heritage. One-third of the population is of Mexican descent, and there are plenty of roadside taquerias and upscale Mexican restaurants to feed hungry travelers. Add in a blossoming wine industry with well over 100 wineries, burgeoning breweries that source hops from the local supply, and endless orchards, and the prospects for this middle-of-the-desert city look good.

Festivals throughout the year celebrate the bounty in many ways, from the spring barrel wine tasting to the fresh hops harvest and grape crush in the fall.

Receiving a mere 9 inches in annual rainfall, the city feels a world away from the dampness of the state's west coast. State Route 821, better known as Canyon Road, is north of town and leads to recreation sites, where fishing, hiking, and tubing are popular and relaxing come summer.

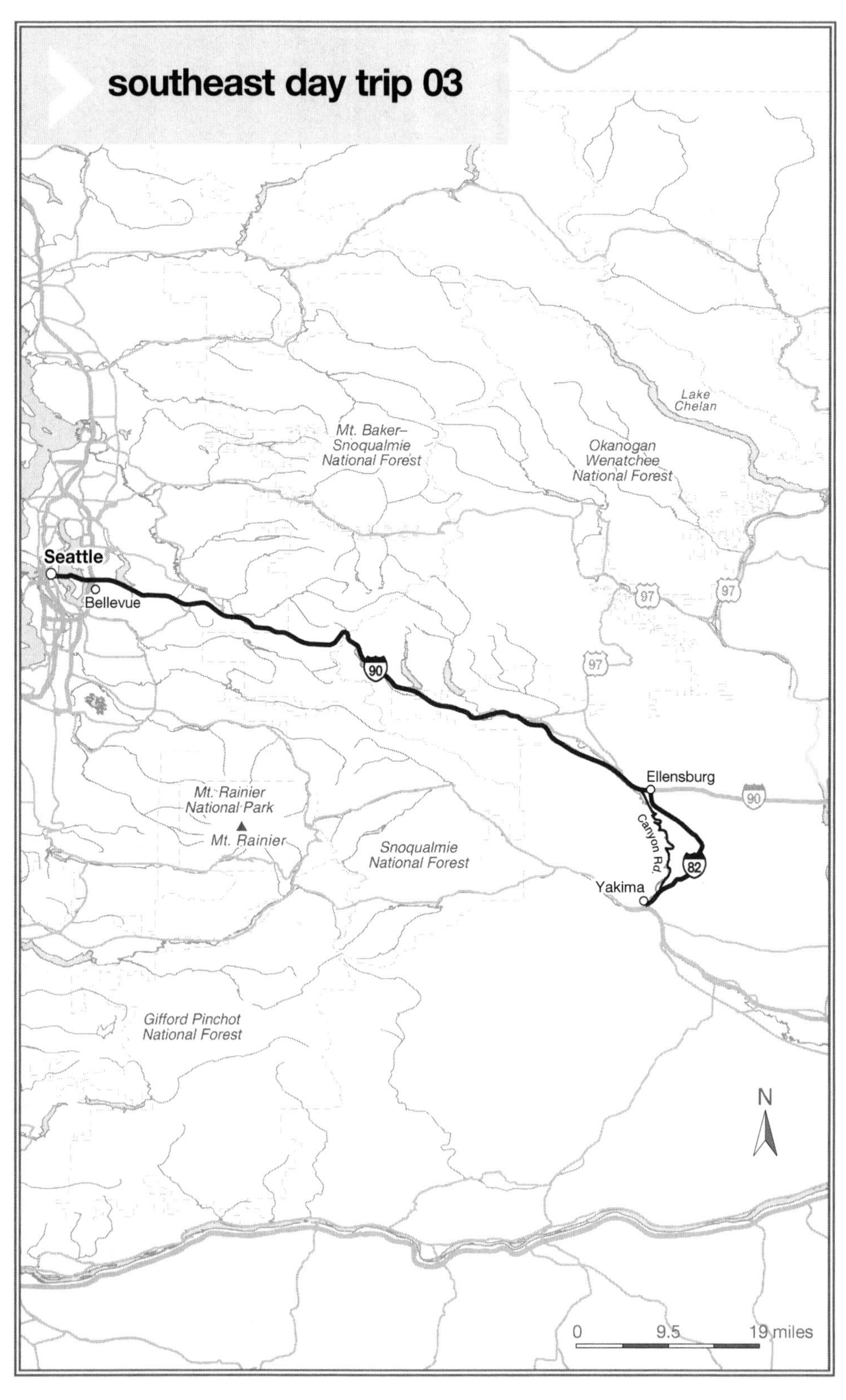

southeast day trip 03
Seattle
Bellevue
Mt. Baker–
Snoqualmie
National Forest
Okanogan
Wenatchee
National Forest
Lake
Chelan
97
97
97
90
90
Ellensburg
Canyon Rd.
82
Yakima
Mt. Rainier
National Park
Mt. Rainier
Snoqualmie
National Forest
Gifford Pinchot
National Forest
N
0
9.5
19 miles

canyon road along the yakima river

My preferred route to Yakima is along Canyon Road—a twisting, river-bottom route that follows the Yakima River between Ellensburg and its namesake city. In Ellensburg South Main Street becomes Canyon Road, officially known as SR 821. The route wends through desert hills and columned basalt formations to meet I-82 just north of Yakima. Hiking recreation areas, river rafting or float trips, and wildlife watching are all draws that keep visitors returning.

Between the local museums, quirky shopping experiences, winery tasting rooms, and a busy military base on the outskirts, Yakima and its wine region pour a unique taste of Washington.

getting there

Head east on I-90 for about 100 miles. Just past Ellensburg, exit onto I-82 and journey 32 miles south to Yakima. The route climbs and descends hill after hill, with a few scenic lookouts en route. The journey, without heavy traffic, takes a little over 2 hours.

where to go

Yakima Valley Visitor Information Center. 101 N. Fair Ave., Yakima; (509) 573-3388 or (800) 221-0751; visityakimavalley.org. With 100-plus wineries in the region around Yakima Valley, some planning is required to select the highlights (see Worth More Time at the end of this chapter for some suggestions). At the information center, get a head start by picking up winery and beer guides, hours, and trip itineraries—and even stocking up on a few bottles. The information center's hours change with the seasons, but it's generally open daily with longer hours on tasting weekends and in summer.

Cowiche Canyon Trails. End of Cowiche Canyon Rd., Yakima; (509) 248-5065; cowiche canyon.org. Following a creek and old railroad bed, this trail is an easy 3 miles from the east trailhead to the west end off Weikel Road. The conservancy group maintains 30 miles of trails, including a spur up to the farmhouse tasting room at Wilridge Winery.

The Seasons Performance Hall. 101 N. Naches Ave., Yakima; (509) 453-1888; the seasonsyakima.com. Built in 1917, the church with its stained glass, domed ceiling, and heavenly acoustics makes an excellent music venue and art gallery. Concerts and events here do the venue justice, bringing world-class jazz musicians, classical performers, and singer-songwriters to play the Seasons. Performances year-round. Tickets prices vary but are generally $10–25. $$$.

Yakima Area Arboretum. 1401 Arboretum Dr. (I-82 and Nob Hill Blvd.), Yakima; (509) 248-7337; ahtrees.org. Amidst the desert-like surroundings of Yakima, the 46-acre arboretum is a calm, cool, and green destination to explore. Japanese-style gardens, winding paths, and the Jewett Interpretive Center all call for a longer-than-planned stop. The interpretive center is open Mon to Sat; grounds open daily.

Yakima Valley Museum. 2105 Tieton Dr., Yakima; (509) 248-0747; yakimavalleymuseum .org. This modern museum edges beautiful Franklin Park. Exhibits inside trace the Native American and farming roots of the area and even provide a glimpse of the valley 25 million years in the past. Explore a pioneer home, see Yakima-iconic neon signs, trace the life of William O. Douglas, who served as Supreme Court Justice (1939–1975), or count the rings on 15-million-year-old trees. Open Tues to Sat. $.

Yakima Valley Trolleys. 306 W. Pine St. (at South Third Ave.), Yakima; (509) 249-5962; yakimavalleytrolleys.org. An old rail yard serves as home to the city's trolley routes. Trips either journey 5 miles through the Selah Gap to Selah, or make a straightaway along Yakima's Pine Street. Tours run on summer weekends but calling ahead is a must. $$.

where to eat

Cowiche Canyon Kitchen. 202 E. Yakima Ave., Yakima; (509) 457-2007; cowichecanyon .com. A large, modern eatery near the historic district, this restaurant serves American fare with style. Local produce and beverages as well as the bustling atmosphere all shine. Open daily for lunch and dinner. $$–$$$.

Essencia Artisan Bakery. 4 N. Third St., Yakima; (509) 575-5570. Off the main drag, Essencia serves light lunches and freshly baked goodies. The artisan bakery is open Mon to Sat for breakfast, coffee, and lunch; also open Sun when there's the downtown farmers' market. $–$$.

Santiago's. 111 E. Yakima Ave., Yakima; (509) 453-1644; santiagos.biz. Santiago's serves Mexican favorites, with specials often featuring what's in season in the Yakima Valley. Tacos, burritos, enchiladas, tamales, and chile rellenos are all on the menu, but so is a local-inspired Yakima-apple pork mole. Open Mon to Fri for lunch, Mon to Sat for dinner. $$–$$$.

where to stay

Birchfield Manor. 2018 Birchfield Rd., Yakima; (509) 452-1960; birchfieldmanor.com. Amidst hops fields and vineyards, this inn exhibits the true bounty of the wine and agricultural region. It's an ideal departure point for tasting tours, but also serves lavish meals in the reservation-only dining room. All the rooms have their own unique charm; some have jetted tubs while others have fireplaces and decks. The grounds include a pool and gardens. $$$.

Ledgestone Hotel. 107 N. Fair Ave., Yakima; (509) 453-3151; yakimawahotel.com. With 110 suites that are far larger than a typical hotel room, the Ledgestone was built primarily for those on an extended stay. Excellent amenities including fully equipped kitchens and comfy sitting areas. A downside is its highway-adjacent location, but that also makes it convenient for exploring. $$–$$$.

Orchard Inn Bed & Breakfast. 1207 Pecks Canyon Rd., Yakima; (509) 966-1283; orchardinnbb.com. Set amidst a hillside of cherry, pear, and apple orchards, this bed-and-breakfast offers a lovely getaway—especially when the trees fill with spring blossoms. You'll find each room offers a different feel, from the cooling Riesling room to the privacy of the Northwest room with its separate entrance. Private baths and expansive breakfasts enhance the comfort of the stay. The location is close to Cowiche Canyon, wine tasting, and downtown. $$.

worth more time

yakima area wineries and breweries

Bale Breaker Brewing Company. 1801 Birchfield Rd., Yakima; (509) 424-4000; balebreaker.com. Cascade hops fields (the region produces a third of the world's supply) surround the family-run taproom and lovely patio. Open daily.

Gilbert Cellars Tasting Room. 5 N. Front St., Yakima; (509) 249-9049; gilbert cellars.com. Sample a variety of fine wines in the sleek tasting room in the city's historic downtown. Visiting the winery (2620 Draper Rd.) requires booking ahead. Open daily.

Owen Roe. 309 Gangl Rd., Wapato; (509) 877-0454; owenroe.com. Savor views of the valley along with rich varietals like Pinot Noir, Cabernet Sauvignon, and Chardonnay. Open daily.

Treveri Cellars. 71 Gangl Rd., Wapato; (509) 877-0925; trevericellars.com. The sparkling wines complement the preciously lovely setting, with its backdrop of vineyards and desert hills. Open daily.

Wilridge Winery. 250 Ehler Rd., Yakima; (509) 966-0686; wilridgewinery.com. Atop a hill this tasting room and art gallery teases the senses. Stroll through the vineyards, part of the Naches Heights AVA (American Viticulture Area) or connect with Cowiche Canyon Trail—just watch out for rattlesnakes! Open daily Memorial Day to Labor Day; otherwise weekends only.

Rattlesnake Hills Wine Trail. rattlesnakehills.org. The next step in exploring beyond the Yakima area, this wine trail route connects the dots of wineries from Wapato to Sunnyside via Granger and Zillah.

Other area attractions include the Yakama Nation with its casino, restaurant, and **Yakama Nation Museum and Cultural Center** (100 Spiel-yi Loop, Toppenish; 509-865-2800; yakamamuseum.com) and the **American Hop Museum** (22 South B St., Toppenish; 509-865-4677; americanhopmuseum.org).

south

day trip 01

oregon trail and animal treks:
federal way, puyallup, eatonville

This day trip bridges city civilization and the wilderness that lies not far beyond. Walk through gardens of rhodies—the state's official flower—in Federal Way, then head south to hear about Ezra Meeker's days as hop king, mayor, and pioneer advocate in Puyallup. Finally venture into the forest to encounter wolves, cougars, and bears at Northwest Trek Wildlife Park.

Nature parks, animals, water slides, and pioneer villages prove family friendly, while the endless tales of Meeker's cross-nation treks, his bizarre construction projects, and the decor of Victorian hair sculptures will interest even the most reluctant historians.

federal way

Federal Way doesn't boast a historic or quaint downtown that may provoke the description of "strollable," but world-class gardens and fun family attractions make the city a worthwhile exit from I-5. Close to the interstate the absorbing theme park Wild Waves (a destination to remember for a summer heat wave) promises roller coasters, waterslides, and pools, while the state flower gets full billing at the Rhododendron Species Botanical Garden. Fun restaurants lighten the spirit in town.

Established when smaller lumber towns amalgamated under the same school district, Federal Way was first connected to Seattle and Tacoma by SR 99 (also called the Pacific

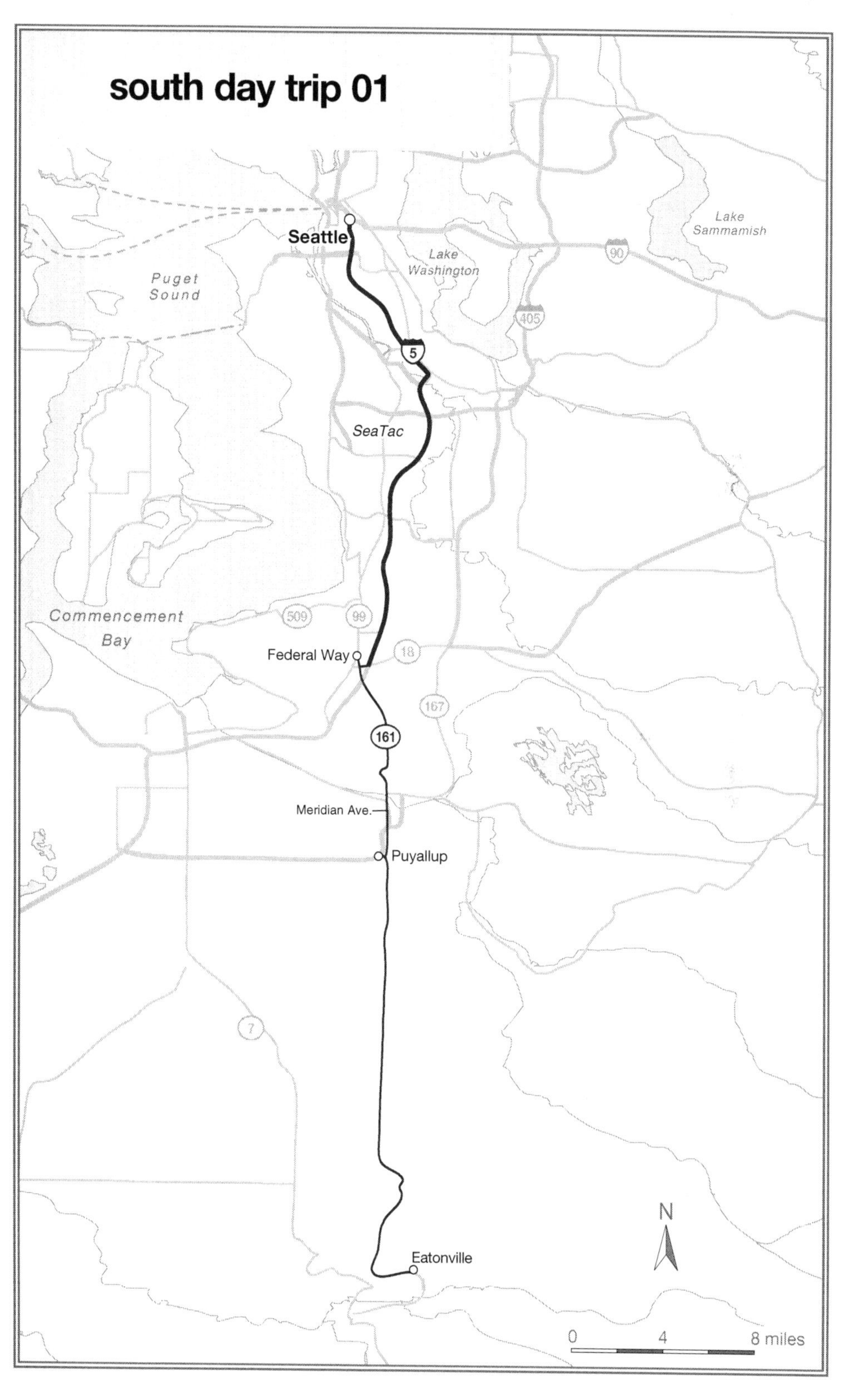
south day trip 01
Seattle
Lake Washington
Lake Sammamish
Puget Sound
90
405
5
SeaTac
Commencement Bay
509
99
18
Federal Way
167
161
Meridian Ave.
Puyallup
7
Eatonville
N
0
4
8 miles

Highway) in the late 1920s. Now you don't leave one city before entering another, and the boundaries of Federal Way abut Washington's largest urban districts.

getting there

With little traffic, travel at a mile a minute to Federal Way on I-5 south (22 miles, 22 minutes). Exit 143 leads to the commercial center while exits 142A and B lead to Wild Waves and the rhododendron garden. For a more leisurely drive, take SR 99 south. Remember, though, that leisurely also means stopping for miles of traffic lights.

where to go

Dash Point State Park. 5700 SW Dash Point Rd., Federal Way; (253) 661-4955; parks .state.wa.us. Perched on the western edge of Federal Way, this state park provides a secluded slice of Puget Sound recreation. Beachcombing and bird watching on the shore are favorite park activities along with camping, skimboarding at low tide, and hiking the 11 miles of forest trails. Open daily.

Pacific Bonsai Museum. 2515 S. 336th St., Federal Way; (253) 353-7345; pacificbonsai museum.org. This by-donation outdoor museum has about 60 carefully tended trees on display, from a collection of about 150. Some are estimated to be more than 500 years old. Open Tues to Sun.

Rhododendron Species Botanical Garden. 2525 S. 336th St., Federal Way; (253) 838-4646; rhodygarden.org. The rhododendrons number more than 10,000, and the soft shades of pink, yellow, and orange peak from Mar through May. Washington's state flower has a heritage that spans the globe, and the gardens include more than 700 species from dwarf rhodies to bushy blooms. The garden is located near the impressive Weyerhaeuser head offices. The rhododendron garden opens Tues to Sun. $$.

West Hylebos Wetlands Park. 411 S. 348th St., Federal Way; (253) 835-6901; hylebos .org. Close to the core of Federal Way, a 1.7-mile loop trail and boardwalk leads visitors on an interpretive route through the wetlands. Birds, including pileated woodpeckers and black-headed grosbeaks, feature as the bog's most active main residents, but look a little closer to see the frogs and perhaps even a weasel. Two historic cabins—the Denny and Barker Cabins, restored by the Historical Society of Federal Way—sit adjacent to the parking area. Open daily.

Wild Waves Theme Park. 36201 Enchanted Pkwy. South, Federal Way; (253) 661-8000; wildwaves.com. With water slides, amusement rides, rafting routes, and dining, this water-and-land theme park easily fills a hot summer day. Hours and open dates change with the weather and seasons, but the park is generally open daily from early June through Aug. $$$.

where to eat

Blue Island Sushi & Roll. 35002 Pacific Hwy. South, Ste. 101, Federal Way; (253) 838-5500. This is sushi for tire kickers. Diners face a conveyor belt loaded with small plates ranging from *gyoza* to edamame and California rolls. Color-coded plates denote the price, and diners are free to self-serve whatever catches their eye. Whether ultra hungry (and not looking to wait) or ultra cautious, Blue Island Sushi provides an engaging meal. Ordering directly from the menu is an option too. Open daily for lunch and dinner. $$.

Jimmy Mac's Roadhouse. 34902 Pacific Hwy. South, Federal Way; (253) 874-6000; jimmymacsroadhouse.com. Drop your peanut shells on the floor, eat your fill of fresh rolls, and order your steak just as you like it. The menu encompasses big portions of seafood, barbecue, and chicken delivered with cheeky humor by friendly staff. Steaks are a particular point of pride. Open daily for lunch and dinner. $$–$$$.

puyallup

Named for the long-resident Native Americans whose name means "generous people," Puyallup is the closest small community to the big city. In 1877 local-famous resident Ezra Meeker platted the city, and its prosperity grew based on hops and agriculture.

Even though Meeker's pioneer days are long gone, it is his influence that still draws visitors to Puyallup. A pioneer himself, the spry seventy-five-year-old Meeker journeyed the Oregon Trail again in 1906, wrote books, and lobbied politicians to raise awareness of its importance.

While the pioneer spirit lives on, Puyallup has also settled into a more modern mix of family festivals like the large Meeker Days Festival, a Saturday farmers' market, and the late-summer Washington State Fair.

getting there

From Federal Way, follow Enchanted Parkway south past Wild Waves. The route (also called SR 161) becomes Meridian Avenue and leads directly into downtown Puyallup (10 miles, 25 minutes).

where to go

Puyallup Sumner Chamber of Commerce. 323 N. Meridian, Puyallup; (253) 845-6755; puyallupsumnerchamber.com. Visitor info is available Mon to Fri.

Karshner Museum. 309 4th St. Northeast, Puyallup; (253) 841-8748; karctr.puyallup.k12.wa.us. This free museum is unusual in that it's owned by the school district and houses a diverse and educational collection of local history. Open 2 to 4 p.m. weekdays, from Sept to June.

Meeker Mansion. 312 Spring St., Puyallup; (253) 848-1770; meekermansion.org. Although best known as the home of Ezra Meeker, this ornate Victorian mansion was actually built at the direction and expense of his wife, Eliza Jane. Ezra, well off from growing hops, was happy living in a log cabin, but after a trip to England, Eliza Jane desired a more elaborate abode. Sure, said Ezra (or so I paraphrase)—if you pay for it. The house was built, and Eliza Jane retained the property title. But this is not the only quirky twist in the tale of the Meekers. From Ezra's cross-nation treks to revive the Oregon Trail to the city-block-long building he constructed to prevent access to a church (with whom he'd had a falling out), a visit to the Meeker home is illuminating and entertaining. Some original Meeker pieces furnish the house as well as the eerie but undeniably well-crafted Victorian-era sculptures made from locks of hair. The historical society has also lovingly restored ornate ceiling murals—the artist of which was long a mystery—and preserved the home of the city's founder. Open Wed to Sun. $.

Pioneer Park. 324 S. Meridian, Puyallup; cityofpuyallup.org/555/pioneer-park. On weekends this park becomes a convergence point for the city with an indoor/outdoor farmers' market (running Sat only mid-Apr to mid-Oct), a playground, and chess tables. The town library and cafes border the public space, which was once where the Meeker cabin stood. In addition to a statue of Ezra Meeker, view the now-ancient-looking ivy planted by Eliza Jane Meeker. Having grown thick like a tree with a heavy wood trunk in the 150 years or so since being planted, the Baltic ivy leans heavily on a concrete arbor. Open daily.

ezra meeker and the oregon trail

Prior to championing the history of the Oregon Trail, Meeker made a good living as a hop grower and also served as the first mayor of Puyallup. But an infestation of hop lice ruined crops and financially strained Meeker. After trips to the Klondike and various other business ventures, Ezra Meeker journeyed from his Puyallup home to Washington, D.C., in 1906 at the age of seventy-five with a singular purpose in mind.

His mission was to memorialize the Oregon Trail—a route blazed by pioneers that he too had traveled as a young man. With a wagon and two oxen named Dave and Dandy, Meeker made the journey, giving speeches and enlisting support en route.

He traveled the Oregon Trail again by cart starting in 1910, by automobile in 1916, and by airplane in 1924. He was planning a second journey by car, but died in 1928, aged ninety-seven, having secured the Oregon Trail history in the minds of many.

where to eat

Anthem Coffee & Tea. 210 W. Pioneer Ave., Puyallup; (253) 446-7941; myanthemcoffee.com. For a bite close to Pioneer Park, this welcoming coffeehouse offers varied options, from baked goods and espresso drinks to wine and pizzas. The vibe is lively. Open daily, from early morning until 7 p.m. $.

Powerhouse Restaurant & Brewery. 454 E. Main St., Puyallup; (253) 845-1370; powerhousebrewpub.com. The modern dining room, house-brewed beers, and historic red-brick architecture of the 1907 Puyallup substation create a lively destination for a meal. The menu spans pub fare (fish tacos, burgers, and fish-and-chips) as well as pastas, pizzas, and shareables. Open daily for lunch and dinner. $$–$$$.

eatonville

Although offering only a half-handful of things to do on the outskirts of town, the attractions near Eatonville are superb—whether it's silently watching wolves and listening to elks snort in the wilds of Northwest Trek Wildlife Park or dodging chickens amidst the aged timbers of a pioneer village.

Eatonville's proximity to Mount Rainier National Park (see Southeast Day Trip 02) also provides ever-stunning vantages of the mountain on a clear day.

getting there

To reach Eatonville, again head south on SR 161 passing Northwest Trek before reaching Washington Avenue and the town center (25 miles, 40 minutes from Puyallup).

where to go

Eatonville Visitor Information Center. 130 Mashell Ave. North, Eatonville; eatonvillechamber.com or eatonville-wa.gov. Located on the main route, the visitor center is open Fri to Sun from Memorial Day to Labor Day.

Northwest Trek. 11610 Trek Dr. East, Eatonville; (360) 832-6117; nwtrek.org. With cougar habitats, bear dens, eagle perches, and wolf lairs, the park offers so much to observe on self-guided walking tours. See animals from the Pacific Northwest in forest settings. A 40-minute tram tour travels into a restricted-access portion of the park where herds of animals are within sight of the roadway. Elk, deer, swans, and buffalo all amble past the naturalist-guided tram. Cafes, lots of parking, and interpretive signage make the park an easy trip to plan and fun experience for all. Open daily mid-Mar to Sept; Fri to Sun only from Oct to mid-Mar. $$$.

Pioneer Farm Museum & Ohop Indian Village. 7716 Ohop Valley Rd. East, Eatonville; (360) 832-6300; pioneerfarmmuseum.org. An 1880s homestead provides an enclave of pioneer life. Goats, cows, and horses all add to the farm feel. Or head to the Native American village to discover life in the Northwest before Europeans arrived. Open daily between Father's Day and Labor Day; weekends only mid-Mar to Father's Day and mid-Sept to Nov. Varied guided tours available. $$.

where to eat

Bruno's. 204 Center St. East, Eatonville; (360) 832-7866; eatbrunos.com. From burgers to clams to steaks, this downtown restaurant is a popular local choice. The large, easy feel to the dining room and ample parking complement a straightforward menu. Open daily for breakfast, lunch, and dinner. $$–$$$.

Cottage Bakery. 212 Washington Ave., Eatonville; (360) 832-1959; cottage-bakerycafe .com. The cute little yellow house is just as lovely inside, with warm wood and tasty home-style sandwiches, soups, and salads—all with views of Mount Rainier on the horizon. $.

day trip 02

museum city:
tacoma

tacoma

Let's not even touch on Tacoma's past. Instead, explore the city's revitalized downtown—a combination of timeless museums, polished dining, gorgeous city parks, palpable history, and elevated architecture that create a striking vibe.

At the center of downtown lies the museum district. The worthy feature presentations include the Museum of Glass with its working hot shop, the Northwest-focused Tacoma Art Museum, and the in-depth Washington History Museum. The luminescent Chihuly Bridge of Glass connects these core attractions. And there's also a multi-museum attraction pass if you're set on visiting a few.

But around the city you'll find more excellent museums: A museum of treasured manuscripts lies near a lush park, the fur trading–era re-creation at Fort Nisqually, and the aerodynamic-looking LeMay Car Museum near the Tacoma Dome. The Tacoma Link Light Rail makes it easy to get around, connecting the theater district to the Tacoma Dome. There's also the lively presence of the University of Washington Tacoma campus.

Whether it's catching a show in the tightly knit theater district or venturing west to take Ruston Way and Wilson Way Bridge to the 760-acre woodland Point Defiance Park (with its zoo, aquarium, and scenic Five-mile Drive), the raft of attractions in Tacoma eclipses any old reputation with one that's fresh, fun, and forward.

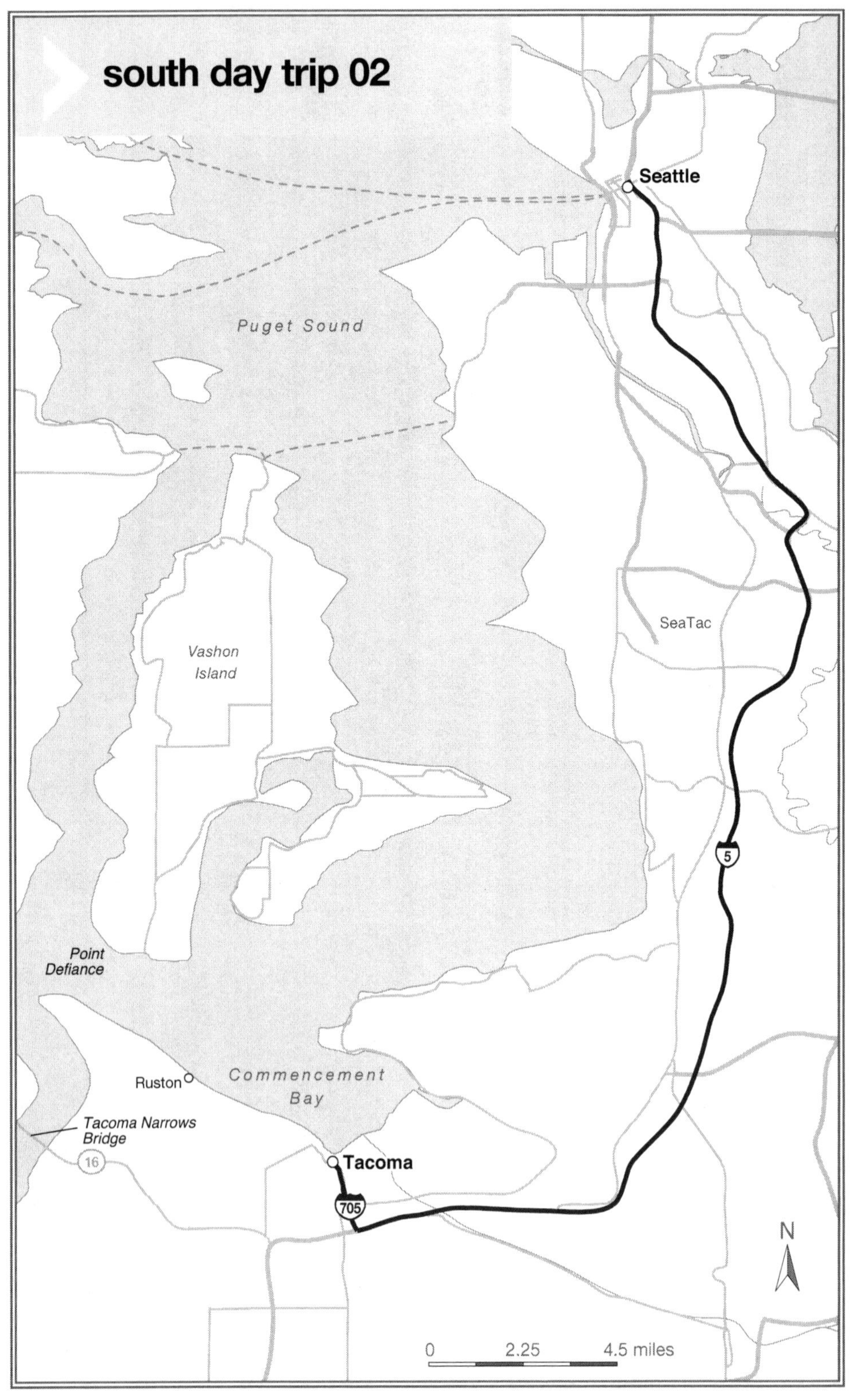
south day trip 02
Seattle
Puget Sound
SeaTac
Vashon
Island
5
Point
Defiance
Ruston
Commencement
Bay
Tacoma Narrows
Bridge
16
Tacoma
705
N
0
2.25
4.5 miles

getting there

From Seattle, head south on I-5 to exit 133. The short stretch of I-705 leads into town (35 miles, 35 minutes without traffic).

where to go

Tacoma Visitor Information Center. 1516 Commerce St., Tacoma; (253) 284-3254 or (800) 272-2662; traveltacoma.com. Located in the Greater Tacoma Convention Center and within a short distance of the downtown museums and dining, the information center offers brochures (but is not staffed) weekdays and when there's an event.

Children's Museum of Tacoma. 1501 Pacific Ave., Tacoma; (253) 627-6031; play tacoma.org. Focusing on hands-on exhibits, the Children's Museum sparks imagination with adventurous exhibits. Open Wed to Sun (with additional special hours). Admission is pay-what-you-can.

Fort Nisqually Living History Museum. 5519 Five-mile Dr., Tacoma; (253) 404-3970; fort nisqually.org. This Hudson's Bay Company outpost has defensive blockhouse-style towers, a granary, blacksmith shop, and actors who reenact history and bring the year 1855 to life. Although not originally at this location, Fort Nisqually recalls Puget Sound's first European settlement, which sat beside Nisqually River in present-day DuPont. The visitor center is generally open daily in summer and Wed to Sun from October to May. The Living History Museum is open the same hours, although the number of costumed interpreters can range from one (on weekdays) to dozens (for special events). Call ahead to confirm hours to ensure you catch the very worthwhile living-history interpreters. $.

Foss Waterway Seaport. 705 Dock St., Tacoma; (253) 272-2750; fosswaterwayseaport .org. Featuring historic boats, a working boat shop, as well as ocean sea-life exhibits such as the skull of a fin whale, the large and beautiful museum sits right on the waterfront. It was once a wheat warehouse and is another example of just how much this port city is transforming. Open Wed to Sun. $$.

Job Carr Cabin Museum. 2350 N. 30th St., Tacoma; (253) 627-5405; jobcarrmuseum .org. This pioneer cabin is known as the birthplace of Tacoma. Hands-on kids' activities comprise the majority of the exhibits inside the cabin, and there are occasional guided history walks through Old Town to see historic homes or Tacoma "firsts." Located just one block from the cabin's original site, the building is an authentic reconstruction and sits affront the grassy Old Town Park. It is worth pulling over for the views of Commencement Bay alone! Open Wed to Sat; closed during Jan. $.

Karpeles Manuscript Museum. 407 S. G St., Tacoma; (253) 383-2575. Sure, you've heard of Einstein's Theory of Relativity, the Bill of Rights, or the Wedding March. Seen them? Likely not. Karpeles Manuscript Museums around the country hold such paper treasures.

The handsome brick Tacoma location near Wright Park is no exception: It houses ancient Egyptian tablets, treaties that abolished the slave trade, letters by novelist Gaston Leroux (author of *The Phantom of the Opera*), and Florence Nightingale's documents. Exhibits rotate so call ahead to confirm the current showings. Open Tues to Fri.

LeMay America's Car Museum. 2702 E. D St., Tacoma; (253) 779-8490; lemaymuseum.org. This speedy museum near the Tacoma Dome impresses with hundreds of automobiles on display from custom to classic, and car history to racing. Open daily. $$.

Museum of Glass. 1801 Dock St., Tacoma; (253) 284-4719; museumofglass.org. Indoors and out, the Museum of Glass twinkles with lightness and transparency. The outside exhibits make an excellent first impression, whether it's crossing Dale Chihuly's Bridge of Glass with its Venetian Wall and undersea-like flowers of the Seaform Pavilion, or pausing at the reflecting pool around Martin Blank's *Fluent Steps*. Inside the museum visitors feel the heat in the hot shop and can admire rotating exhibits. Open daily from Memorial Day to Labor Day; Wed to Sun year-round. $$.

Point Defiance Park. 5400 N. Pearl St., Tacoma; (253) 305-1088; metroparkstacoma.org. Hiking trails, a waterfront promenade, landscaped gardens, historical museums, and Owen Beach—as well as the separately introduced Point Defiance Zoo & Aquarium and Fort Nisqually Living History Museum—all make Point Defiance a true local favorite. Five-mile Drive guides visitors through a full loop of the park. Wildlife sightings are practically guaranteed—particularly raccoons that clamor toward vehicles because (against warnings not to by park officials) many visitors stop to feed the critters. With road-crossing wildlife and distracted drivers, it is best to drive slowly. Wilson Way Bridge connects the park to Ruston Way with waterfront views along the way. Open daily.

glass artist dale chihuly

Looking at the Venetian Wall on the Chihuly Bridge of Glass in Tacoma, the word "prolific" immediately springs to mind: The 80-foot span wows with 109 glass sculptures—all intricate, elaborate, and unique pieces.

Chihuly's process of creation involves numerous glass artists working together to create multi-elemental sculptures. The Tacoma native is credited with pushing glass art toward this collaborative work method. In Tacoma you can see works produced at his Lake Union studio at the Museum of Glass, Tacoma Art Museum, Union Station, Hotel Murano, and even at a bar: the Swiss Restaurant & Pub.

Point Defiance Zoo & Aquarium. 5400 N. Pearl St., Tacoma; (253) 404-3800; pdza.org. These animal houses explore above and below the ocean. Tigers, red wolves, and Asian elephants highlight the world's diminishing on-ground species, while shark, octopi, and eels rule the underwater aquariums. Family programs and a friendly approach to engaging visitors (dive with the sharks, anyone?) make the zoo and aquarium a top destination. Open daily, except closed Tues and Wed from Nov to Feb. $$.

Tacoma Art Museum. 1701 Pacific Ave., Tacoma; (253) 272-4258; tacomaartmuseum.org. Since its 1935 establishment the Tacoma Art Museum has compiled a world-class collection. A large exhibit of Dale Chihuly glass art makes a fitting complement to a Tacoma day trip, while Northwest art exhibits explore Native American culture and nature. Open Tues to Sun. $$.

Tacoma Arts Live. 901 Broadway Ave., Tacoma; (253) 591-5894 or (800) 291-7593; tacomaartslive.org. The theater district pops to life in the evening. It centers on the three performance venues: Pantages, Rialto, and Theatre on the Square. From opera and comedy to ballet and symphonies, the venues stage works from Tacoma and the nation's foremost performers. $$$.

Tacoma Nature Center. 1919 S. Tyler St., Tacoma; (253) 404-3930; metroparkstacoma.org. Seventy-one acres of parkland lie around Snake Lake. The Nature Center focuses on families and introducing kids to the plants and animals that make a home in the park—and offers extra fun in the play area Discovery Pond. While the grounds and trails are open daily, the visitor center provides information Mon to Sat.

Tacoma Historical Society Museum. 919 Pacific Ave., Tacoma; (253) 472-3738; tacomahistory.org. This addition to the city's fine museum collection presents rotating local history exhibits in a 1903 building. Open Wed to Sat.

Union Station. 1717 Pacific Ave., Tacoma; unionstationrotunda.org. In the heart of Tacoma's museum district, Union Station stands out as a beautiful and historic destination. Although now operating as a courthouse and rental facility for functions, its first and former life was as the Pacific-coast terminus of the Northern Pacific Railroad. Look for glass works by Dale Chihuly. Open weekdays 8 a.m. to 5 p.m.

W. W. Seymour Botanical Conservatory. 316 S. G St., Tacoma; (253) 404-3975; metroparkstacoma.org. The glass dome insulates a tropical paradise of plants. Each month brings a vibrant new bloom from spring tulips through summer orchids, fall chili peppers, and holiday displays of poinsettias. Located on the east side of Wright Park, the conservatory is surrounded by old-growth trees and grassy hills. Open Tues to Sun. $.

Washington State History Museum. 1911 Pacific Ave., Tacoma; (253) 272-3500 or (888) 238-4373; wshs.org. This state history museum delves deep into the state's past, including the Great Hall of Washington History that retraces the peoples and places, sounds and sights of Washington history. Open Tues to Sun. $$.

where to eat

Indochine. 1924 Pacific Ave., Tacoma; (253) 272-8200; indochinedowntown.com. With curtained partitions, warm-toned wood, and a candle-lit atmosphere, this museum-district restaurant creates a subdued feel while still drawing vibrancy from the nearby University of Washington. The Dungeness crab wontons use the best of the Northwest, while Thai favorites like drunken beef noodles and panang curry are more hearty options. There's also an inventive cocktail menu and a large patio. Open for lunch and dinner Tues to Sun. $$–$$$.

TAM Café. 1701 Pacific Ave., Tacoma; (253) 272-4258 ext. 3023; tacomaartmuseum.org/visit/tam-cafe. This slice of an eatery fits into the museum with all the neatness of a Rothko painting. Hearty soups, inventive sandwiches, and Pacific Northwest eats provide healthy options on a small but thoughtful menu. Open Tues to Sun for lunch. $–$$.

Tatanka. 4915 N. Pearl St., Ruston; (253) 752-8778; tatankatakeout.com. Buffalo is the main ingredient of a quick, healthy menu at this restaurant that is located close to Point Defiance Park. Chili, tacos, burritos, melts, and burgers are available with bison meat, plus a handful of veggie dishes with beans or tofu. While you wait, admire the buffalo-themed kitsch in the dining room. Open Wed to Sun for lunch and early dinner. $–$$.

THEKOI. 1552 Commerce St., Tacoma; (253) 272-0996; thekoitacoma.com. A spacious dining room and full bar give this sushi restaurant a more formal feel. The bento boxes and sushi combos are expected, but a few unique items are hidden in the large Japanese-fusion menu. Order the carpaccio tuna or salmon served with onion and citrus, or from the long list of specialty rolls—ranging from the Cowboy Crunch to the Volcano Lobster. Open daily for lunch and dinner. $$.

where to stay

Courtyard by Marriott. 1515 Commerce St., Tacoma; (253) 591-9100; marriott.com. Most Marriott guest rooms follow a predictable standard, but the wing that incorporates a historic building rates as truly special. Three floors of unique and historic suites merge modern comfort with classic architecture. The location is fantastic—it's the closest to the museum district. $$$–$$$$.

Hampton Inn. 8203 S. Hosmer, Tacoma; (253) 539-2288; hamptoninntacoma.com. Despite its proximity to I-5, the rooms are quiet. Add the out-of-downtown discounts, beds of heavenly comfort, friendly greetings, and extras (that include a pool, fitness center, and free breakfast) and this location provides a convenient base location, especially if exploring further south. $$–$$$.

Hotel Murano. 1320 Broadway Ave., Tacoma; (253) 238-8000; hotelmuranotacoma.com. A modern design befitting a newly modern city, Hotel Murano features more than 300 guest rooms as well as fine art of the caliber that you'll also see in the local museums. Tours of the international collection, which features art from more than forty artists, can also be arranged in advance. The hotel seizes on Tacoma's glass-art pride and plays with glass forms in the decor like the bedside lamps and lobby chandelier. Amenities include a fitness room, spa, dining, and a lobby bar. Top-level suites have unbeatable views. $$–$$$$.

worth more time

south of tacoma

Lakewood. Appealing attractions in this small city include the English **Thornewood Castle** (253-584-4393; thornewoodcastle.com; guests only), which was shipped across the world piece by piece, the European-inspired grounds of **Lakewold Gardens** (12317 Gravelly Lake Dr. Southwest, Lakewood; 253-584-4106; lakewoldgardens.org), and the historic **Fort Steilacoom** (9601 Steilacoom Blvd. Southwest, Lakewood; historicfortsteilacoom.org), established in 1849. The community is located about 20 minutes from the Tacoma museum district.

LeMay Collections at Marymount. 325 152nd St. East, Tacoma; (253) 272-2336; lemaymarymount.org. Cars are most associated with the LeMay name—and there are more than 1,500 in this immense fleet—but the collections here go far beyond, including a Rodin sculpture garden and other surprises. As a former military academy, Marymount is an attraction in itself, and a variety of guided tours and experiences are available. Open Tues to Sun. $$.

day trip 03

mount st. helens:
mount st. helens, longview and kelso

On May 18, 1980, Mount St. Helens erupted, sending a massive landslide and ripping explosion into the surrounding valley and a globe-circling cloud of ash into the sky. Now four decades later, the destruction is still evident with blast-felled trees, replanted forests, and a gaping mouth in the side of the mountain—which was once a smooth snowy peak like Mount Baker or Mount Rainier.

This day trip climbs along Spirit Lake Highway, which is metered by visitor centers. Be sure to check the weather before heading up the highway to Johnston Ridge—low clouds can obscure the crater and lava dome, making the trip a disappointment without the awesome views. Either call the visitor center (360-274-2140) or view the mountain via the observatory's web cams at fs.fed.us/gpnf/volcanocams/msh.

After admiring the mountain, great food and accommodation options are just 15 minutes south on I-5 in Longview and Kelso, on the Columbia River.

mount st. helens

Since Mount St. Helens erupted on May 18, 1980, this area has transformed. The mud-swamped buildings have been shoveled out, showing the extent of the landslide, trees have re-rooted, polished visitor centers sit as sentries watching the volcano, and a smoothly paved highway makes the area easily accessible. But amidst this transformation, signs of the

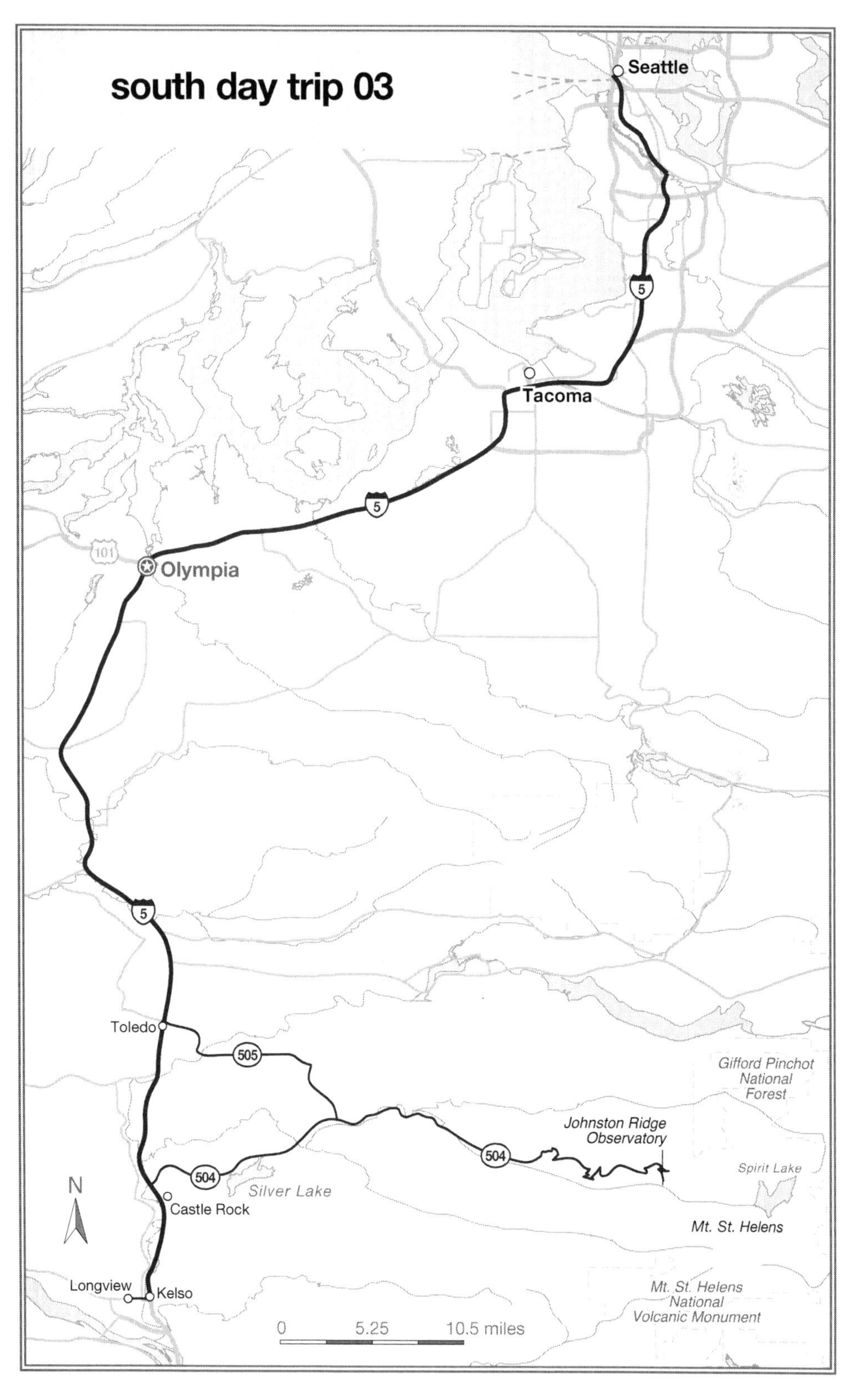
south day trip 03
Seattle
5
Tacoma
5
101
Olympia
5
Toledo
505
Gifford Pinchot
National
Forest
Johnston Ridge
Observatory
504
Spirit Lake
504
Silver Lake
N
Castle Rock
Mt. St. Helens
Longview
Kelso
Mt. St. Helens
National
Volcanic Monument
0
5.25
10.5 miles

destruction still remain: toppled trees in the blast zone, the moonscape of the Toutle River, and a still-active lava dome in the mountain's immense crater.

While there are a small number of communities within easy reach of the monument, including Toledo, Kid Valley, Silver Lake, and Castle Rock, overall the area's services remain rather scarce. But there are a variety of visitor centers and viewpoints along Spirit Lake Highway, so budget your trip to allow for plenty of time at your destination: Johnston Ridge Observatory, where the main attraction is viewing the blasted crater of Mount St. Helens. The national monument is a place of education and remembrance, and an unparalleled opportunity to see the immense potential force of Mother Nature.

getting there

Follow I-5 south for about 100 miles. Take exit 63 and pick up SR 505 that leads through Toledo before coming to a T-junction with SR 504—Spirit Lake Highway. Climb this memorial highway to Johnston Ridge Observatory. The one-way trip to the ridge summit is less than a 3-hour straight drive from Seattle, but visitor centers and viewpoints make the journey a leisurely trip with lots to see en route.

where to go

Along Spirit Lake Memorial Highway, there are a number of lookout opportunities—such as Castle Lake Viewpoint at MP 40—as well as the following stops:

Forest Learning Center. MP 33, 17000 Spirit Lake Memorial Hwy.; (360) 414-3439; weyerhaeuser.com. On a good day you'll be rewarded with views of elk herds in the Toutle River Valley. If not, head inside to explore the hands-on forest and volcano exhibits. Along the highway blast-felled trees and replanted forests show the effects of the eruption on the forest and surrounding industry—the learning center puts this into perspective. Open daily mid-May to mid-Sept.

Science and Learning Center at Coldwater. MP 43, 19000 Spirit Lake Memorial Hwy.; (360) 274-2131; mshslc.org. Though primarily focused on school groups, this educational facility is open weekends in the off-season. It overlooks Coldwater Lake and the mountain. Watch for elk or venture into the blast zone on the Winds of Change Trail. Open weekends from Nov to Apr.

Johnston Ridge Observatory. MP 52, 24000 Spirit Lake Memorial Hwy.; (360) 274-2140; fs.usda.gov. The jewel of the visitor centers, Johnston Ridge Observatory connects the events of May 1980 to what you see today. Track seismic activity on the mountain's new lava dome, measure your own seismic force, and watch the short film that dramatically reveals what happened beneath Mount St. Helens to create such an intense explosion. Open daily from mid-May to Oct. $.

surrounding towns

Castle Rock is a small city that's held onto its heritage along the quaint main street. Bookshops and cafes encourage a slower pace, and it's also home to additional information centers:

Mount St. Helens Visitor Center. 3029 Spirit Lake Memorial Hwy., MP 5, Castle Rock; (360) 274-0962; parks.wa.gov. Run by Washington State Parks, the interpretive center has exhibits on wildlife and geology. A trail leads to Silver Lake and a wetlands boardwalk. Traveling from Seattle and venturing the extra distance along I-5 to visit this center first adds about 10 minutes in travel time, or it can be

"vancouver! vancouver! this is it!"

Two months before the explosive day, Mount St. Helens started to show serious signs of unrest. In mid-March 1980 scientists measured increasing numbers of earthquakes that in turn triggered worrisome avalanches, ash, smoke, and cracks in the crater.

The world watched intently with extensive television coverage, tracking the mountain as it rumbled. Information centers and roads closed, and throughout the month of April 1980, more steam and ash emerged from the depths of the mountain. As the crater grew steadily wider, the north flank also began to bulge. Though the mountain quieted for a period, the bulge continued to grow—some began wondering if it was a false alarm.

Then, on Sunday, May 18, 1980, at 8:32 a.m., an earthquake rumbled one mile below the volcano. The earthquake caused the mountain's swollen north flank to collapse, falling away from the mountain in a massive landslide. The mountain—its tightly bottled pressure now uncorked—erupted with a force that flattened the valley up to 15 miles away.

It was amid this devastation that USGS volcanologist David Johnston radioed his last message: "Vancouver! Vancouver! This is it!"

Hot ash and the blast killed fifty-seven people. Mudflows (or lahars) measuring dozens of feet deep coursed through the Toutle River Valley like a tsunami of mud, overtaking homes. As you'll see, the valley is still recovering.

Even though the blast reduced the height of the mountain by more than 1,300 feet, smaller eruptions have formed a new lava dome in the crater. On a visit to the Johnston Ridge Observatory, in roughly the same spot where David Johnston radioed his last message, look for the seismographs tracking the on-going rumblings at the lava dome.

visited in conjunction with dinner in Longview and Kelso. Open daily from Mar to Oct; closed Tues and Wed from Nov to Feb. $.

Mount St. Helens Creation Center. 147 Front Ave. NW, Castle Rock; (360) 274-5737; mshcreationcenter.org. Seizing on the sequence of events during the eruption at Mount St. Helens, the center questions if the same forces could have sculpted other ancient natural monuments, such as the Grand Canyon. The theories do require a bit of explaining, but dedicated volunteers staff the site and are keen to present the creationist take. Open Mon to Sat.

where to eat

Fire Mountain Grill. 9440 Spirit Lake Memorial Hwy., Toutle; (360) 274-5217. The last stop for eats when heading along the highway, this friendly restaurant has lovely river views from the back patio. Elk burgers, fish-and-chips, and sandwiches don't stray too far from the norm. Open daily for lunch and dinner. $$.

longview and kelso

Longview offers the best services close to Mount St. Helens. If you are extending your trip to an overnight, the town will provide the most comfortable choices for dining and accommodation as well as some fun nightlife options, such as a theater-pub in Kelso where you can sip a local brew while taking in a first-run movie. Add to that a historic mansion and a bridge built just for squirrels in the town center, and this corner of the state beside the Columbia River serves up a few surprises. Unusual annual events include the cultural **Kelso Highlander Festival** and a summer **Squirrel Fest.**

getting there

Reach Longview-Kelso by returning along Spirit Lake Highway to I-5. Exit 39 leads to the dining and accommodation options in Kelso and Longview. One way, it's about 2 hours from Seattle.

where to go

Kelso Visitor and Volcano Information Center. 105 Minor Rd., Kelso (near I-5); (360) 423-8400. Open daily, this spot has information on both the local area and the main attraction: Mount St. Helens. Check out the view of the volcano from the "volcano cam"—some days Mount St. Helens is vestured in clouds and not visible. Open daily; closed Sun Nov to Mar.

Civic Center. Washington Way and Olympia Way, Longview. Public buildings like the library and city hall border a grassy square in the middle of town where benches, shady trees, and monuments create a pleasant spot to relax. Look for the "Nutty Narrows Bridge"—a span built in 1963 for the resident squirrels. There's even a summer **Squirrel Fest** (lvsquirrelfest .com). Open daily.

Cowlitz County Historical Museum. 405 Allen St., Kelso; (360) 577-3119; cowlitz.wa.us/ museum. Just before the Allen Street Bridge, the Cowlitz County Historical Museum draws on the logging history that flourished alongside the Columbia River. From the Cowlitz Native American tribes to the eruption that shook the Northwest, the museum presents photographs and artifacts retelling the stories. Open Tues to Sat.

Kelso Theater Pub. 214 S. Pacific Ave., Kelso; (360) 414-9451; ktpub.com. Pizza (from small to large made-to-order pies), sandwiches, salads, and beer are available to theatergoers who want to combine dinner and a movie. A friendly staff provides a welcoming spot to escape for an evening. If dining in front of the big screen isn't your style, arrive early and take a table at the Backstage Café next door, where the candlelit setting makes for a cozy evening. The theater is open 30 minutes before movies start. $.

Lake Sacajawea Park. 3223 NE Nichols Blvd., Longview; (360) 442-5421; mylongview .com. Rhododendron gardens, an arboretum, fishing areas, and a playground within this city park complement the pretty Japanese garden set on an island. It's a 3.5-mile easy walk around the lake with many spots to pause. Park open daily.

where to eat

Backstage Café. 216 S. Pacific Ave., Kelso; (360) 414-9451; ktpub.com/backstage. Located next to the Kelso Theater Pub (and serving from the same kitchen), the cafe offers a more dinner-like atmosphere to enjoy freshly made pizzas, pastas, and sandwiches. Service is excellent and the historical feel of the building adds to the charm. Open for dinner daily; Mon to Fri for lunch. $–$$.

Grounds for Opportunity. 413 Pacific Ave., Kelso; (360) 703-3020. In this learning cafe, students gain job skills while serving up hot breakfasts, varied sandwiches, and heaping salads. Open Wed to Sun for breakfast and lunch. $.

Monticello Wood Fired Pizzeria. 405 17th Ave., Longview; (360) 747-6031; monticellopiz zeria.com. Step into the expansive Monticello Hotel, which has many stories and lives to its years, and bask in the opulence of this Longview landmark. There's a large pizza oven at this casual eatery that turns out simple, thin-crust pies. Open daily for lunch and dinner. $–$$.

where to stay

Red Lion. 510 Kelso Dr., Kelso; (360) 636-4400; redlion.com. The rooms are large and relaxing—perfect when returning from a day of exploring Mount St. Helens. Rooms at the back of the hotel front the Coweeman River. A pool, coffee shop, and restaurant all complement the clean, bright, and comfortable suites. $–$$.

southwest

day trip 01

southwest

the independent state:
vashon island, maury island

The locals are friendly and the ideas are liberal on Vashon Island, where most attractions and restaurants harbor an independent spirit. Request an island map when at the ferry ticket window, and then take the 20-minute ferry from Fauntleroy to the north end of the island.

From end to end Vashon Island is a mere half-hour drive. Instead work your way slowly south through local wineries, community museums, lovely parks and gardens, boutique shops, and welcoming restaurants. Add to the relaxed exploration with a trip across the portage to Maury Island—an even smaller and quieter spot than Vashon.

While driving on the island, you'll likely encounter lots of cyclists and dogs. Vashon is a friendly spot with plenty of terrain to explore on two wheels or with four-legged friends. And it's especially welcoming for events like the community-minded Vashon Island Strawberry Festival.

vashon island

Vashon is the bigger island of the two. As such, it has the majority of attractions, restaurants, and accommodations. That's not to say the attractions are numerous, but the lavender farms, gardens, and roadside llamas add life and color to this agricultural island. It's just big enough to get lost in the mazes of roads yet quiet enough to stand on a beach alone. Easy explorations here don't require traveling long distances.

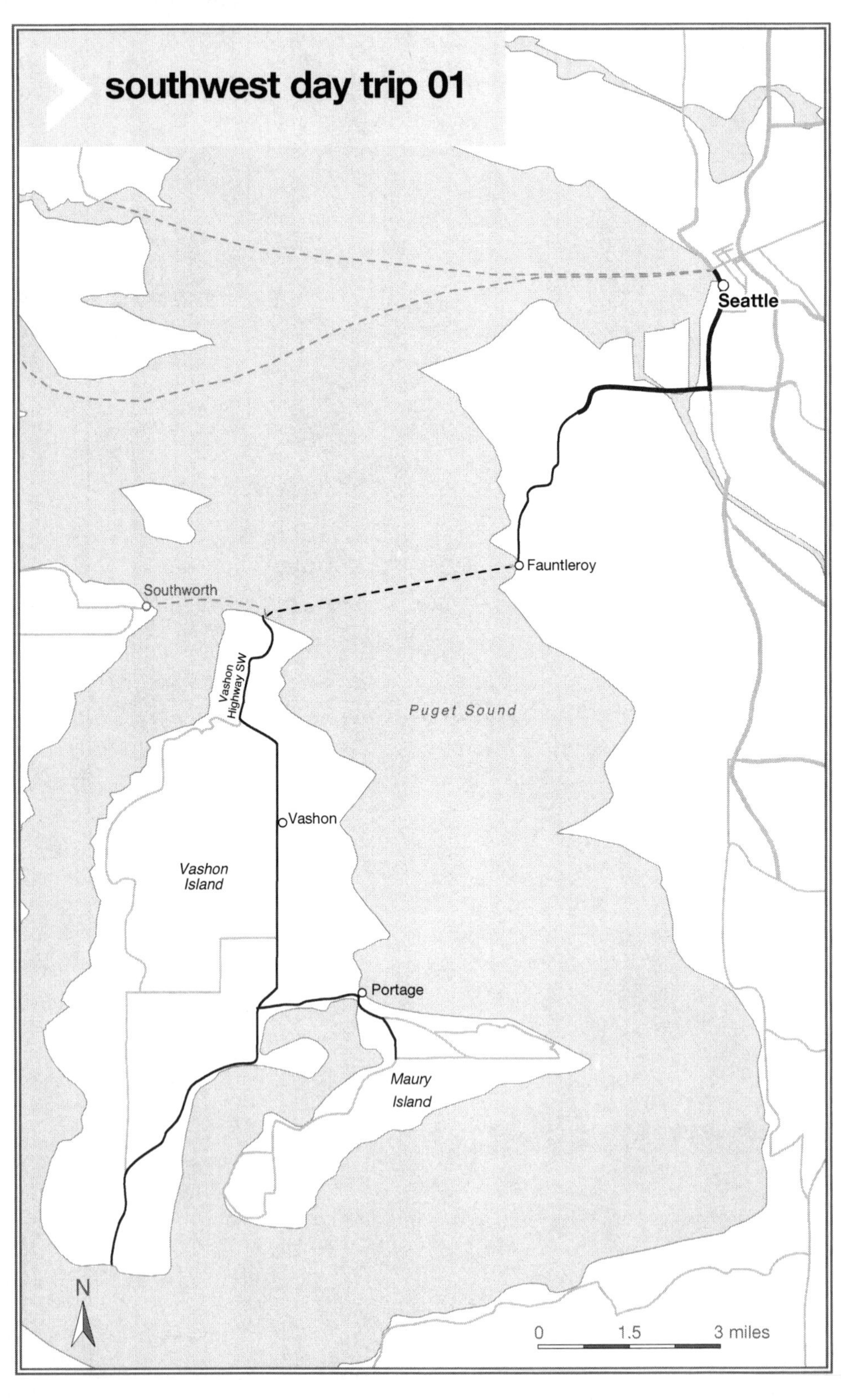

southwest day trip 01
Seattle
Fauntleroy
Southworth
Vashon Highway SW
Puget Sound
Vashon
Vashon Island
Portage
Maury Island
N
0
1.5
3 miles

First a home for Coast Salish people, settlers came to Vashon Island starting in the 1860s to homestead, log, and establish farms. The island culture has developed as a curious independence despite its proximity to the dense urban areas of Tacoma and Seattle. Artists are in particularly strong force here, and one of the best ways to get a feel for the island is through the self-guided spring and holiday art studio tours from **Vashon Island Visual Artists** (vivartists.com).

getting there

Ferries make more than twenty journeys daily from Fauntleroy to Vashon. The south end of Vashon Island is also accessible from Tacoma, where a ferry runs with similar frequency from Point Defiance to Tahlequah. A commuter passenger-only ferry runs from Pier 50 in Seattle to Vashon on weekdays only.

where to go

Vashon Maury Island Chamber of Commerce. 17141 Vashon Hwy. Southwest, Vashon; (206) 463-6217; vashonchamber.com. The local info center is open Mon to Fri and occasional weekends.

Burton Acres Park and Jensen Point. Southwest Burton Dr., Vashon Island; vashon parks.org. The park looks out to Maury Island. The beach is an easy spot for renting kayaks or stand-up paddleboards (206-259-3978; vashonadventures.com) and is also dog friendly. Open daily.

Mukai Farm & Garden. 18017 107th Ave. Southwest, Vashon; mukaifarmandgarden.org. This is a rarity, a woman-designed Japanese garden from the mid-century. The Mukai family ran a large strawberry farm from the 1920s until WWII, when they left Vashon due to the Japanese Exclusion Act. Post-war, they returned to continue running the farm. Grounds are open daily for self-guided tours with occasional open houses.

Palouse Winery. 12431 Vashon Hwy., Vashon Island; (206) 567-4994; palousewinery.com. This small island winery draws its name from the rolling hills in eastern Washington. Producing a delicate Riesling, an unusual Viognier, and a powerful Cabernet Franc amongst other varietals, the winery is easy to find—just up the hill after arriving on the Fauntleroy-Vashon ferry. Open weekends.

Vashon Center for the Arts. 19600 Vashon Hwy. Southwest, Vashon; (206) 463-5131; vashoncenterforthearts.org. With exhibitions, performances, and classes, this arts center attracts a strong local crowd. Gallery open Tues to Sat.

Vashon Maury Island Heritage Museum. 10105 SW Bank Rd., Vashon; (206) 463-7808; vashonheritage.org. An old Lutheran church houses informative displays on the various epochs of Vashon history. From the Native American communities to the logging and agriculture industries, the bright museum lovingly presents the island's tales. The stories of water transportation to the island are also pivotal—even now ferries and boats are Vashon's only link to the rest of Puget Sound. Open Wed to Sun. $.

where to shop

The island's agricultural heritage is always growing, with commercial nurseries and gardening shops to visit. Plus, there's an in-season farmers' market on Saturdays at the Village Green (17505 Vashon Hwy. Southwest).

The Country Store & Farm. 20211 Vashon Hwy. Southwest, Vashon Island; (206) 463-3655; countrystoreandfarm.com. For more than five decades, this store has stocked varieties of local jams, clothing (especially gardening gear), and gifts—not to mention lots of community feel. Ten acres feature summer blooms and fall foliage as well as a berry u-pick. Open daily.

Lavender Hill Farm. 10425 SW 238th St., Vashon Island; (206) 463-2322 (summer); lavenderhillvashon.com. Mid-summer there is a distinct shade of pale purple and an ever-relaxing aroma around the farm—it's the many varieties of fragrant lavender rooting here. Summer farm tours highlight the many uses of this aromatic herb. Or stop in for a glass of lavender lemonade and a bundle of blooms from the u-pick. Open Wed to Sun from late June to July.

Nashi Orchards. 16906 SW 107th Ave., Vashon; (206) 734-5551; nashiorchards.com. Pouring cider and perry crafted from the orchard's own apples and pears, this tasting room offers a delicious way to experience the 27-acre property. Open weekends only.

where to eat

Cafe Luna. 9924 SW Bank Rd., Vashon; (206) 463-0777; cafelunavashon.com. Vashon is a friendly community and Cafe Luna offers excellent coffee, homemade soups, and hot grilled sandwiches for a great lunch stop. Open daily from breakfast through afternoon. $.

The Hardware Store. 17601 Vashon Hwy., Vashon; (206) 463-1800; thsrestaurant.com. The ever-social booth seating and a warming menu create a welcoming feel at the Hardware Store. This restaurant, on the main Vashon road, was indeed once a hardware store and is the island's oldest commercial building. Now instead of nails and appliances, Vashoners come here for plates of buttermilk fried chicken, Pacific cod fish-and-chips, and daily specials. Next door is a sister business, the cooking school Relish (relishvashon.com). Open daily for breakfast, lunch, and dinner. $$.

Vashon Island Coffee Roasterie. 19529 Vashon Hwy., Vashon; (206) 463-9800; tvicr.com. The fresh allure of coffee acts as the ultimate temptress. With a small selection of eats and lots of seating on the outdoor veranda, it's tough not to take a few minutes to sit here and relax as you adjust to island time. Open daily with breakfast and lunch hours. $.

home of betty macdonald

From living and writing on Vashon Island, Betty MacDonald went on to become a best-selling author known for her humorous autobiographical tales. Her most-read title is the 1945 book The Egg & I, *recounting her first marriage and days of chicken farming in the Chimacum Valley near Port Townsend. Another book published in 1954,* Onions in the Stew, *captures her time on Vashon Island. She also wrote the children's Mrs. Piggle-Wiggle series while living on the island. To gain a little insight into her life, you can stay at her former farm and steep in the writer's former surroundings (11835 99th Ave. Southwest, Vashon; 206-567-4227; bettymacdonald farm.com).*

where to stay

AYH Ranch. 12119 SW Cove Rd., Vashon; (206) 463-2592; ayhranch.com. Get a feel for the old West with options to sleep in a tepee and gather around a campfire. For the non-pioneers, however, there is also plenty of comfort with cute cabins and log-house rooms. The grounds offer lots to explore. Reservations recommended. $–$$.

Belle Baldwin House. 11408 SW Cedarhurst Rd., Fern Cove Nature Preserve, Vashon; (206) 463-9602; vashonparks.org. This secluded house offers three bedrooms and a waterside setting. Rubber boots, a full kitchen, and a fireplace create a fully equipped retreat. Admire the views of Puget Sound from an Adirondack chair on the porch. A prominent physician lived here in the late 1800s, and his daughter, Belle Baldwin, became the first female physician in the state in 1912. Three bedrooms can sleep up to seven. Minimums range from two to seven nights. $$$–$$$$.

maury island

Vashon Island's little brother makes a complementary side trip. Cross between the islands at the military-constructed community of Portage and head off the traveled path to Point Robinson Lighthouse. From the rocky beaches of the island, appreciate the views of Tacoma and Mount Rainier on a clear day.

where to go

Maury Island Marine Park. SW 244th St. and SW 248th St., Maury Island; kingcounty .gov. Although covering more than 300 acres and with a mile of shoreline, this large park has few trails. The route down the shoreline is steep, but the views of Mount Rainier are worth the trip.

Point Robinson Park. 3705 SW Point Robinson Rd., Maury Island; (206) 463-9602; vashonparks.org. Since 1885 this lighthouse has stood as a beacon for vessels navigating fog and rough conditions. On summer Sundays there are tours of the light, which was automated in 1978. The former lighthouse-keepers' quarters also now serve as vacation rental properties through the Vashon Park District (vashonparks.org).

where to stay

Maury Cottage. 5313 SW Point Robinson Rd., Maury Island; (206) 463-4558; maurycottage.com. As the cottage is the only guest accommodation on the property, it provides an independent, restful lodging option complete with star-studded skies, quiet nights, and coffee or tea on the garden patio. The deep-soaking tub provides an insulated escape. Welcoming hosts help keep the secret of this tranquil corner of the island. No credit cards. $$.

day trip 02

state capital:
olympia, tumwater, chehalis

Olympia offers the grandeur of a state capital—including palatial buildings and palpable history—but with an independent undercurrent. Beneath its marble surface the Washington state capital does things a little differently with a lively waterfront district, large farmers' market, and the alternative influence of Evergreen State College. Tour the grand state capitol campus, step up to an espresso bar at Batdorf & Bronson for a coffee tasting, let the kids explore at a science center, or tour the waterfront during **Olympia Harbor Days.**

Just south of Olympia, and barely distinguishable as city borders go, lies Tumwater and its historical attractions. Preserved historic buildings include a home built by Bing Crosby's pioneer grandfather. Nearby, visitors can enjoy a meal overlooking the tumult of Tumwater Falls on the Deschutes River.

This day trip ends in Chehalis where museums, railroads, and quaint cafes provide a picturesque small town to explore.

olympia

Just as Washington is no ordinary state, Olympia is no ordinary state capital. Beyond the ornate domes and facades of the capitol buildings, visitors will uncover a diverse community, university-fueled nightlife, and urban market district. In fact, the local farmers' market, coffee-tasting room, and waterfront parks embody the Washingtonian spirit (think good food, coffee, and the outdoors) far better than any grandiose architecture.

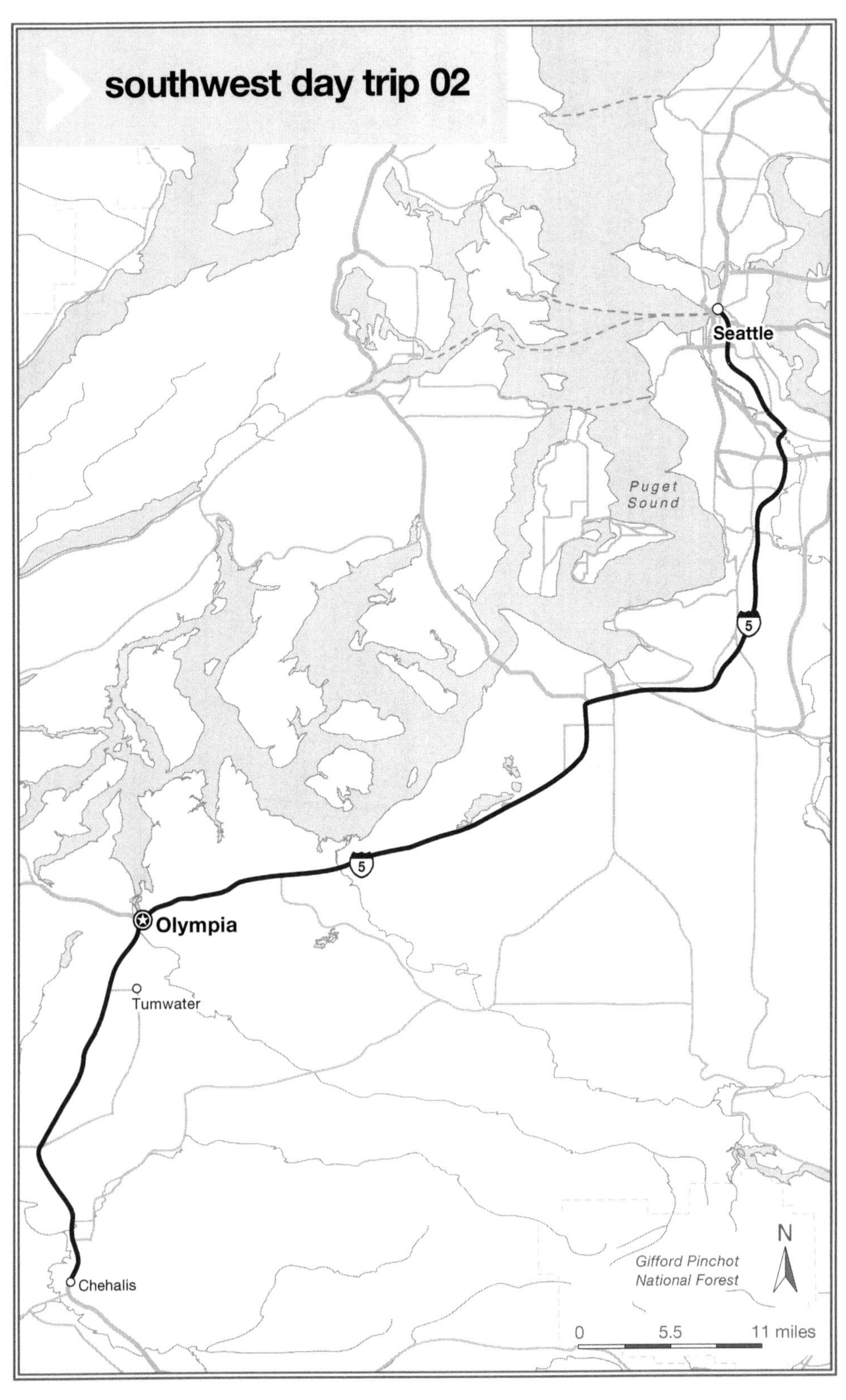
southwest day trip 02
Seattle
Puget Sound
5
5
Olympia
Tumwater
Chehalis
Gifford Pinchot National Forest
N
0
5.5
11 miles

getting there

Head south on I-5 from Seattle (60 miles, 1 hour). Exit 105 leads to downtown Olympia and the state capitol campus.

where to go

Experience Olympia and Beyond Visitor Information. 103 Sid Snyder Ave. Southwest, Olympia; (360) 763-5656; experienceolympia.com. This source for visitor information is open daily.

Batdorf & Bronson Tasting Room. 200 Market St. Northeast, Olympia; (360) 753-4057; batdorfcoffee.com. Yes, Washingtonians do take their coffee this seriously: This tasting room is certainly not to be mistaken for a cafe. You won't find cozy seating or sugary syrups here. Instead the "brewmasters" illuminate the subtle flavors and roasts of the beans. For a more coffee-cozy atmosphere, visit the cafe location of **Batdorf & Bronson Coffeehouse** (516 S. Capitol Way) or the **Dancing Goats Espresso Bar** (111 Market St. Northeast), which is across the street from the tasting room. The cafes are open daily, while you'll find coffee brewing in the tasting room Wed to Sun.

Billy Frank Jr. Nisqually National Wildlife Refuge. 100 Brown Farm Rd., Olympia; (360) 753-9467; fws.gov/nisqually. Migratory birds find sanctuary in this protected section of the Nisqually River Delta. The 3,000-acre refuge includes boardwalks, trails, and a visitor center plus bird-friendly natural habitat (planning a trip within two hours of high tide provides the best viewing). The visitor center is open Wed to Sun while the refuge is open daily during daylight hours.

Capitol Lake. 5th Ave. Southwest and Water St. Southwest, Olympia. The artificial lake has particularly lovely views of the state capitol building. A 1.5-mile sidewalk trail rings the lake perimeter, with a spur leading uphill to the capitol campus. Paths and sidewalks also connect to Interpretive Park at the south end, which is close to Tumwater Falls. Open daily.

Hands On Children's Museum. 414 Jefferson St. Northeast, Olympia; (360) 956-0818; hocm.org. For kids ten and under, this museum has varied indoor exhibits to touch and experience, as well as an outdoor playground with a lighthouse looking out to Budd Inlet. Open daily. $$.

Old State Capitol and Sylvester Park. 600 Washington St. Southeast, Olympia; (360) 725-6000; k12.wa.us. Originally built from Chuckanut-area stone as a courthouse, this 1892 building across from Sylvester Park became the seat of the legislature in the early 1900s. Fires, renovations, and earthquakes have changed its appearance over the years, but a major 1980s restoration saw the building revitalize its public function: It is now the Office of Superintendent of Public Instruction. Visitors can admire the storied building from Sylvester Park.

Olympia Farmers' Market. 700 Capitol Way North, Olympia; (360) 352-9096; olympiafarmersmarket.com. Live entertainment and local producers create a vibrant market atmosphere that is one of the largest open-air markets in the state. Seafood, produce, flowers, desserts, and cheeses are all available at the covered but breezy market. Goods are on sale Thurs to Sun from Apr to Oct; weekends only Nov and Dec; Sat only Jan to Mar.

Percival Landing Park. 217 Thurston Ave. Northwest, Olympia; olympiawa.gov/city-services/parks. A small slice of park connects with a waterfront boardwalk stroll past great dinner restaurants and marinas. Moored at the docks is the tugboat *Sand Man*—a historic vessel that has been restored as a floating museum (tugsandman.org). The park is open daily while the tugboat is often open weekends.

Washington State Capitol Campus. 14th Ave. Southeast and Capitol Way, Olympia; (360) 902-8880 (tours); des.wa.gov. Arriving in Olympia via I-5, the legislative building—the largest on the state capitol campus—forms a majestic opening frame. The largest brick-and-concrete dome in North America rises well above Olympia's tree-lined streets. Climb the forty-two steps to the entrance and explore the campus buildings on a variety of tours. The most popular tour (running daily with departures between 10 a.m. and 3 p.m.) showcases the marble halls, pioneer statutes, and a Tiffany chandelier. On Wed only, by-reservation tours visit the governor's mansion.

WET Science Centre. 500 Adams St. Northeast, Olympia; (360) 664-2333; wetsciencecenter.org. From water conservation to the Puget Sound environment, this center looks at the wet stuff in many ways. On hot days East Bay Public Plaza is a draw for its wading stream and simulated wetland. It's next door to the Hands On Children's Museum and has free admission. Open Mon to Sat.

where to eat

Cascadia Grill. 200 4th Ave. West, Olympia; (360) 628-8731; cascadiagrill.com. A cozy corner restaurant, Cascadia Grill borrows a little from many cuisines to build a menu that feels like it has all your favorite dishes. Expansive vegetarian and vegan offerings range from pasta to schnitzel. Open daily for lunch and dinner, and there's often live music too. $$–$$$.

The Budd Bay Cafe. 525 Columbia St. Northwest, Olympia; (360) 357-6963; buddbaycafe.com. Cedar-planked or blackened salmon, tiger prawns, and Dungeness crab cakes complement the waterfront views. Arrive early for dinner Sun to Thurs and snag the well-priced sunset dinner specials that include a starter, entree, and dessert. Open daily for breakfast, lunch, and dinner. $$–$$$$.

The Lemon Grass Restaurant. 212 4th Ave. West, Olympia; (360) 705-1832; thelemongrassrestaurants.com. This modern dining room is divided into an upscale dining spot and bar in one half and a more casual spot to grab a quick meal in the other. Fresh and flavorful

Thai and Vietnamese dishes span noodles, curries, and rice dishes. Open Mon to Sat for lunch and dinner; closed Sun. $$–$$$.

where to stay

Swantown Inn Bed-and-Breakfast. 1431 11th Ave. Southeast, Olympia; (360) 753-9123; swantowninn.com. This historic, family-run inn provides excellent service and lovely rooms with regal textiles, deluxe king-size beds, and private baths. A Victorian garden enhances the spacious house (which once included a ballroom that is now an event space). Spa massages are particularly leisurely with plenty of time to relax before and after. It's a 1-mile walk to downtown and the historic district, allowing visitors to easily indulge in the excellent local restaurants and breweries. $$–$$$.

tumwater

Once the end of the pioneer Oregon Trail, Tumwater now sits at the south end of Capitol Lake. The community—then known as New Market—was one of the first non-Native settlements in the state and was positioned to harness the power of Tumwater Falls on the Deschutes River. Now historical attractions and views of the power-generating falls highlight a quick tour of the city.

getting there

From Olympia, follow Capitol Way south as it crosses I-5 and become Capitol Boulevard. Turn onto E Street Southwest to access the historical attractions along Deschutes Way.

where to go

Crosby House Museum. 703 Deschutes Way Southwest, Tumwater; (360) 943-9884; ci.tumwater.wa.us. Built by Nathaniel Crosby III for his new bride, Cordelia Jane Smith, the Crosby House dates to the 1860s. Beyond the pioneer-period furnishing, the house draws interest because the Crosbys were the grandparents of famous actor and singer Bing Crosby. The neighboring Henderson House is not open regularly but was the original home of an Olympia Brewery brewmaster. Open Sun only from Apr to Oct.

Olympic Flight Museum. 7637 Old Hwy. 99 Southeast, Tumwater; (360) 705-3925; olympicflightmuseum.com. A collection of about twenty vintage planes spans World War II to Vietnam. The Father's Day weekend Olympic Air Show is the best chance to see them in the skies. Open Tues to Sun. $.

Tumwater Falls Park. 110 Deschutes Way Southwest, Tumwater; (360) 943-2550; olytumfoundation.org. The drop of the falls presented a powerful opportunity to the pioneers who first settled nearby—and then later to Olympia Power and Light Company and the Olympic

Brewing Company. There are three sections to the falls, with the lower falls being the largest and most impressive. Footbridges and a riverside trail connect them. Open daily.

where to eat

Falls Terrace Restaurant. 106 Deschutes Way Southwest, Tumwater; (360) 943-7830; fallsterrace.com. A large dining area with lots of windows provides views of Tumwater Falls on the Deschutes River. Enjoy signature dishes such as halibut with crab and shrimp, steak, or salmon. Lunch is more casual, with sandwiches, burgers, and fish-and-chips. After a meal, stroll over the bridges and along the river to the lower falls and the historic park. Open daily for lunch and dinner. $$–$$$$.

chehalis

Railroads and Ezra Meeker's historic travel along the Oregon Trail feature most prominently in the town, along with its lovely old-timey main street of cafes and shops on North Market Boulevard. The town preserves its heritage with a passion, including rides on a 1916 steam train. But it wasn't always so: Chehalis was one of just three towns that broke its promise to Meeker by not erecting an Oregon Trail marker. In 2006 the town finally fulfilled that promise.

getting there

Follow I-5 south, taking exit 79 or 77 for Chehalis. Or take the slower route: Old 99 Highway Southeast to Tenino, then drive SR 507 to Centralia. Gold Street and National Avenue lead south to Chehalis.

where to go

Centralia-Chehalis Chamber of Commerce. 500 NW Chamber of Commerce Way, Chehalis; (360) 748-8885; chamberway.com. It's open Mon to Sat. The site experiencechehalis .com is another great local resource.

Chehalis-Centralia Railroad. 1101 Sylvenus St., Chehalis; (360) 748-9593; steamtrainride .com. Another example of Washington's great love of railroads, this train steams out of a station on the outskirts of Chehalis alongside the Chehalis River. The 1916 Baldwin generally offers two route options on summer weekends: a 13-mile round-trip to Milburn and an 18-mile round-trip ticket to Ruth. Full-price tickets start at about $17, with additional options for seasonal train rides and dinner on the rails. $$–$$$.

Lewis County Historical Museum. 599 NW Front Way, Chehalis; (360) 748-0831; lewiscountymuseum.org. A finely restored train station now houses the Lewis County Historical Museum. Exhibits of course include train history but also the histories of Native Americans and pioneer life. Open Tues to Sat. $.

Veterans Memorial Museum. 100 SW Veterans Way, Chehalis; (360) 740-8875; veterans museum.org. The 9,000-square-foot museum has a September 11 display that includes fragments of the fallen World Trade Center, and a Korean War exhibit recalling America's "forgotten war." Open Tues to Sun from Memorial Day to Labor Day; then closed Sun and Mon. $.

Willapa Hills State Park Trail. 900 Block, Hillburger Rd.; (360) 753-1519 (Millersylvania State Park); parks.state.wa.us. From Chehalis this trail heads 56 miles west out to Willapa Bay on the Pacific coast. It was once a logging railroad, though not all sections are now paved or surfaced with gravel. $.

Wolf Haven. 3111 Offut Lake Rd. Southeast, Tenino; (360) 264-4695; wolfhaven.org. By-reservation tours venture into this quiet sanctuary where wolves are treated as the wild animals they are. It neighbors an area similar to the strange, bumpy topography of the Mima Mounds. Open Fri to Mon from Apr to Sept; weekends only Oct to Mar. $$.

where to eat

Sweet Inspirations. 531 N. Market Blvd., Chehalis; (360) 748-7102. Be treated as a local at this cafe, where the historic main street of brick buildings adds charm to the menu offerings of fresh, hot comfort food. The dishes are diner style with full breakfasts plus well-done classics such as grilled sandwiches, steaks, and homemade soup. Open Mon to Sat for breakfast, lunch, and early dinner. $–$$.

day trip 03

southwest

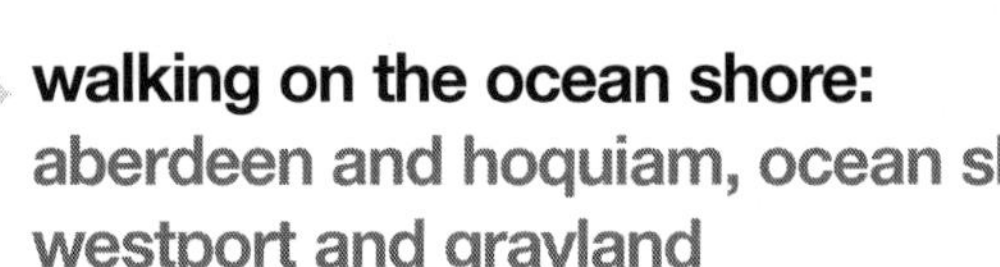

walking on the ocean shore:
aberdeen and hoquiam, ocean shores, westport and grayland

Grays Harbor is a Seattle seaside getaway and a whole lot more. Drive directly on the sandy beaches at Ocean Shores, recall the grunge scene at Kurt Cobain's home in Aberdeen, or admire burgundy fields of cranberry harvests near Westport.

Grays Harbor features unique birdlife and distinct geography. Aberdeen and Hoquiam (both industry towns) sit at the head of the harbor, while Westport and Ocean Shores face each other across the harbor mouth. Life beside the ocean is rich, filled with razor-clam dinners, trips to the casino, strolling the boardwalk, buying fresh fish direct from the marina, surfing waves, and embarking on whale-watching excursions.

This day trip also offers perhaps the largest concentration of state parks. Most front the ocean and make serene destinations for clamming, camping, or watching the surf roll in, and gray whales visit the coastal waters in May.

Add historical museums, interpretive centers, and opportunities to boat, fish, hike, and build sand castles and this day trip so easily becomes either a longer getaway or the first of many.

aberdeen and hoquiam

There's a hidden glamour amid the industrial faces of Aberdeen and Hoquiam—separate cities although I include them together because their downtowns sit a mere 5 minutes apart. Visit the former homes of lumber barons at Hoquiam Castle and the Polson Museum, ornate

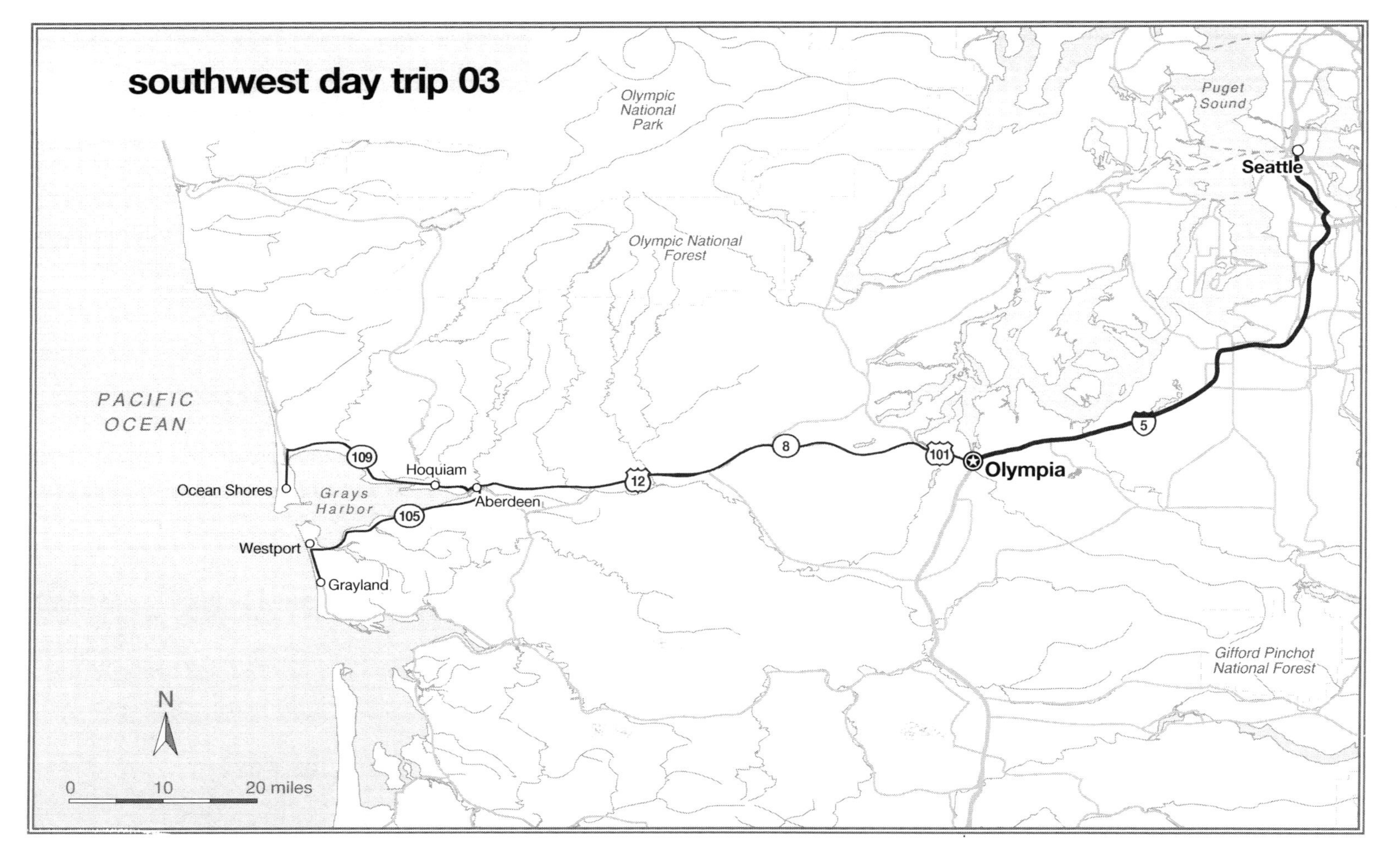
southwest day trip 03
Olympic National Park
Puget Sound
Seattle
Olympic National Forest
PACIFIC OCEAN
109
Hoquiam
Ocean Shores
Grays Harbor
Aberdeen
105
Westport
Grayland
12
8
101
Olympia
5
Gifford Pinchot National Forest
N
0
10
20 miles

properties that recall the prosperity of the lumber age. At the head of Grays Harbor where the Chehalis River meets the ocean, the communities also provide access to protected wildlife areas and mark seasons with events such as the Grays Harbor Shorebird and Nature Festival.

Add into the mix famous former residents—who include Nirvana singer and guitarist Kurt Cobain and the founder of Boeing, William Boeing—and the towns prove surprisingly worth exploring.

getting there

From Seattle, take I-5 south to exit 104, just south of Olympia. Head west first on US 101, then continue on SR 8. SR 8 becomes US 12 at Elma and takes the final stretch to Aberdeen (2 hours, 110 miles).

From Aberdeen, SR 109 heads to Ocean Shores (25 miles, 40 minutes) while SR 105 cuts a route along the opposite shore of Grays Harbor to Westport (20 miles, 30 minutes).

kurt cobain and seattle grunge

Born in Aberdeen in 1967, Kurt Cobain lived in Hoquiam briefly before his family moved to Aberdeen—a lumber town. When his parents divorced, the 9-year-old Cobain experienced a huge life change. He moved between parents, towns, and family friends throughout his teenage years before moving out on his own and dropping out of school.

Cobain started playing music early. He began as a drummer in the school band and then picked up guitar at age fourteen. The Aberdeen punk band the Melvins held a strong influence over the young musician and artist.

Nirvana took form when Cobain convinced fellow Aberdeen resident Krist Novoselic to start a band—the beginnings of Nirvana. They recorded their first album with Chad Channing on drums and later changed drummers to Dave Grohl. With their 1991 album Nevermind, *Nirvana brought attention to the Seattle grunge scene and became the biggest band of the early 1990s.*

Despite this success, Cobain was found dead with a shotgun pointed at his chin on April 8, 1994. Much speculation has emerged over his death, and many books have since been published rehashing his heavy drug use, marriage to Courtney Love, and Aberdeen childhood.

where to go

Grays Harbor Visitor Information Center. 506 Duffy St., Aberdeen; (360) 532-1924; discovergraysharbor.com. Pick up a guide to the coast at the chamber and visitor center. Open Mon to Fri.

Aberdeen Museum of History. aberdeenmuseumofhistory.com. Unfortunately, a massive fire in 2018 destroyed the museum and many exhibits at 111 East Third St.

Grays Harbor Historical Seaport. 500 N. Custer St., Aberdeen; (360) 532-8611; historical seaport.org. This is home port for two tall ships, *Lady Washington* and *Hawaiian Chieftain*. The vessels travel around, so call or check the website to make sure they are there for your visit.

Grays Harbor National Wildlife Refuge. 1131 Airport Way (off Paulson Road), Hoquiam; fws.gov/graysharbor. Tidal flats are a haven for shorebirds. Each spring on their return migration, shorebirds flock to the marshes and grasses that comprise this 1,500-acre refuge. And these birds certainly need the rest stop—some are stopping en route between South America and the Arctic, a 7,000-mile journey. Open daily.

Hoquiam's Castle. 515 Chenault Ave., Hoquiam; hoquiamcastle.com. Now a private residence, this former bed-and-breakfast is beautiful to admire from the street. The elegant three-story wooden structure with towers and an arched veranda is a twenty-room mansion built by lumber baron Robert Lytle in 1897.

Kurt Cobain Memorial Park. Under Young Street Bridge. A series of monuments and memorials remember Nirvana frontman Kurt Cobain. Visitors can embark on a self-guided tour to the places in Aberdeen where Cobain lived, slept, and went to school—including from his first house in Aberdeen at 1210 E. First St. and the "Come As You Are" sign on Highway 12 that welcomes people to the city.

The Polson Museum. 1611 Riverside Ave., Hoquiam; (360) 533-5862; polsonmuseum .org. Spacious grounds include railroad displays, artifacts from the lumber industry, a blacksmith shop, and the large Polson mansion. The twenty-six-room mansion, built by another lumber-rich family, was a wedding gift to Arnold Polson from his uncle Robert Polson. The museum includes two acres of grounds on the banks of the Hoquiam River. Historical maps, photos of the Polson family's time in the house, and preserved furnishings make the museum an excellent stop year-round. Open Wed to Sun. $.

where to eat

Breakwater Seafood & Chowder House. 306 S. F St., Aberdeen; (360) 532-5693; break waterseafood.com. With a lovely patio overlooking the Wishkah River, this cheery eatery serves Pacific bounty—ranging from halibut-and-chips to a crowd-pleasing clam chowder. There's also a fish market on-site. Open daily for lunch and early dinner. $–$$.

satsop nuclear power plant

South of US 12, you may spot the two massive, eerie-looking cooling towers of the Satsop Nuclear Power Plant—or what was intended to be a plant at least. In the 1970s plans were forged to build two nuclear power plants here, but by the mid-1980s costs and safety concerns had mushroomed.

With more than $2 billion invested in the Washington Public Power Supply System (WPPSS) project but funds gone, the site was transferred to the county and the WPPSS project earned the unfortunate moniker of "Whoops." Now the project has been revitalized as a business park (satsop.com).

ocean shores

Most windows in Ocean Shores homes are saved for the second level—maximizing the views of the Pacific Ocean and sandy beaches reaching as far as the horizon.

Drive on the sand, visit a hands-on wildlife interpretive center, fly a kite in the intense ocean winds, dig for razor clams, or test chance at the local casino. Accommodations, most offering easy access to the beach, line the roads and make this a summertime city for those seeking a beach getaway from Seattle.

The community sprung up as a vacation destination in the 1960s, benefitting from celebrity promotion by singer and actor Pat Boone—who also hosted tournaments at the Ocean Shores Golf Course. It still has a touch of that promo feel, but nothing trumps the simple joys of beachcombing.

getting there

From Aberdeen, SR 109 heads to Ocean Shores (25 miles, 40 minutes).

where to go

Ocean Shores Visitor Information Center. 120 W. Chance a la Mer, Ocean Shores; (360) 289-9586 or toll-free (800) 762-3224; tourismoceanshores.com. Accommodation, business, and tide info is available in the convention center. Open daily.

Coastal Interpretive Center. 1033 Catala Ave. Southeast, Ocean Shores; (360) 289-4617; interpretivecenter.org. Hands-on natural history exhibits have plenty of appeal—everything from sea critters to the inner ear of a whale. The center illuminates the environment of Grays Harbor, and helpful docents are available to answer questions. Open daily Apr through Sept; weekends only from Oct through Mar.

Damon Point Trail. Off Discovery Ave. Southeast, Ocean Shores. At low tide a two-mile strip of dune grass and sand leads to Damon Point. Go for a short hike that contrasts views of the protected harbor and the wild ocean. This former state park is next to the 683-acre Oyhut Wildlife Recreation Area, which provides one of the rare nesting grounds in the state for the snowy plover.

Ocean City State Park. 148 SR 115; (360) 289-3553; parks.state.wa.us. The area's rich sea life meant that Native Americans long visited this spot for its abundant food sources. Many cooking and hunting artifacts have been found in the area. Nowadays clamming, fishing, driving on the sands, and camping are popular state park activities. Open daily.

where to eat

Emily's. 78 SR 115, Ocean Shores; (360) 289-6038; quinaultbeachresort.com. With made-to-order items such as razor-clam steaks, Pacific halibut, and prime rib, Emily's offers the most diverse local menu. A handsome dining room has snapshots of the ocean and beach views. The restaurant is named for a respected elder in the Quinault Nation, and around Quinault Beach Resort and Casino, you'll see beautiful photography revealing the Native history and heritage. There are also buffet options at the casino. Hours are variable, but on-site restaurants at the complex are open daily for breakfast, lunch, and dinner. $$$–$$$$.

where to stay

The Judith Ann Inn. 855 Ocean Shores Blvd. Northwest, Ocean Shores; (360) 289-0222; judithanninn.com. With the appearance of a Cape Cod mansion but the hardy vinyl siding required to withstand the Pacific storms, these vacation rentals offer a true seaside getaway. Jetted tubs stand out as the perfect spot from which to watch the sunset, while the gas fireplaces make the inn a cozy spot for the winter-storm-watching season. All the suites have separate bedrooms with king-size beds and full kitchens. While the decor in most suites is a tad dated, the spacious 900-square-foot layouts are ideal for longer stays. Two-night minimum. $$$.

westport and grayland

Westport retains its old-fashioned seaside charm while still offering varied accommodations, dining, and tour options. It's not just the harbor winds and seafood restaurants you'll savor, but also the local surf culture, oceanside parks, viewing towers, scenic lighthouses, and beaches prepped for sand-castle building.

A boardwalk helps protect the fishing fleets that find a safe harbor at Westport. There are many spots to view the ocean juxtaposed against the boats hunkered down in port, and on a day with swells, surfers catch waves at a break called the Groynes.

Add in the pastoral charm of nearby Grayland, where cranberry farmers harvest the tart berries each fall, and this destination rates as a personal favorite.

getting there

From Aberdeen, SR 105 cuts a route along the southern shore of Grays Harbor to Westport (20 miles, 30 minutes). Grayland is just south of Westport.

where to go

Westport-Grayland Chamber of Commerce. 2985 S. Montesano St., Westport; (360) 268-9422 or toll-free (800) 345-6223; cometowestport.com. Helpful local advice is available throughout the week at the Y intersection. Open daily.

Grayland Beach State Park. 925 Cranberry Beach Rd., Grayland; (360) 267-4301; parks.state.wa.us. A beach day: that's what the nearly 1.5 miles of this state park beachfront warrants. Camping, clamming, crabbing, and watching the ocean are all top activities for parkgoers. Open daily.

Twin Harbors State Park. 3120 SR 105, Westport; (360) 268-9717; parks.state.wa.us. Once a military training ground, Twin Harbors now welcomes the area's beachgoers. As with other local state parks along this stretch, camping, clamming, and bird watching are popular thanks to the dunes, sands, and park facilities. Open daily.

Westport Aquarium. 321 East Harbor St., Westport; (360) 268-7070. The aquarium is a tiny spot with display tanks and a touch tank. The facilities are basic, but there's lots to fascinate kids about the underwater world at the town's doorstep. Open daily during summer; call ahead for winter hours. $.

Westport Light State Park. 1595 Ocean Ave., Westport; (360) 268-9717; parks.state.wa.us. Walk the Westport Light Trail from the marina and viewing tower to Westport Light. Surfable breaks, car-free beaches, and bird watching are additional attractions at the park. Built in 1898, the lighthouse is also called Grays Harbor Lighthouse (open Thurs to Mon from Feb through Oct) and is run by the Westport Maritime Museum. The park is open daily.

Westport Maritime Museum. 2201 Westhaven Dr., Westport; (360) 268-0078; wsbhs.org. You'll find a unique set of local-focused exhibits here, ranging from cranberries to the impressive Destruction Island Lens that dates to 1888. Skeletons of minke and gray whales along with other sea mammals draw curiosity in the outdoor display buildings. The museum building once housed the coast guard station. Open Thurs to Mon year-round; closed Tues and Wed. $.

westport surfing

Westport thrives on a small, local community of surfers. Surf shops offer advice, sales, and rentals. ***Surf Shop*** *(207 N. Montesano St.; 360-268-0992; westportsurfshop.com) and* ***Steepwater Surf Shop*** *(316 N. Montesano St.; 360-268-5527; steepwatersurf.com) both provide rentals starting at about $40. For beginners, enquire about summer surf lessons.*

As the Pacific stays cold year-round, be sure to grab booties and gloves with your board and wet suit.

where to eat

Bennett's Fish Shack. 2581 Westhaven Dr., Westport: (360) 268-7380. There's fish-and-chips of course, but other excellent eats include the Cranberry Coast chicken salad with local berries, crab cakes, halibut sandwiches, tacos, and burgers. There's also a location in Ocean Shores. Open daily for lunch and dinner. $$–$$$.

Westport Winery. 1 S. Arbor Rd., Aberdeen; (360) 648-2224; westportwinery.com. Driving from Aberdeen, you can't miss Westport Winery's lighthouse that is constructed miles from the heaving Pacific. This winery has lovely grounds and an excellent on-site restaurant—Sea Glass Grill—serving such local and ocean bounty as Dungeness crab dip, fish-and-chips, and oysters. Sample many varietals as well as fruit wines in the cheery tasting room. Open daily for breakfast, lunch, and dinner. $$–$$$.

where to stay

Chateau Westport. 710 W. Hancock Ave., Westport; (360) 268-9101; chateauwestport.com. Just minutes from the beach, Chateau Westport is the local resort with an indoor pool, disc golf, and other activities, plus a secluded location. Guest rooms offer simple, clean accommodations from which to explore the area. Things are more upscale in the suites that include fireplaces, kitchens, and saunas. There's free breakfast plus an on-site espresso bar in summer. $$–$$$.

LOGE Westport. 1416 S. Montesano St., Westport; (360) 268-0091; logecamps.com. This combination property infuses local surf culture into the guest rooms, hostel, camping sites, and communal areas. A cafe, board rental service, bicycles, and welcoming staff add to the getaway vibe. $–$$$.

grayland cranberries

You'll only need two hints as to what you'll find down Cranberry Road—it's red and tart. In Grayland boggy acres of the berries line the miles of road. Farmers harvest in mid-fall, coinciding with the mid-October Cranberry Harvest Festival. The wet harvest method is the most fun to watch as farmers flood the fields and the ripe cranberries float to the surface.

Ocean Spray Beach Resort. 1757 SR 105, Grayland; (360) 986-6500; oceanspraybeachresort.net. Each self-contained cottage is painted and decorated with an individual style. Some cottages were built as army barracks during World War II. Spacious interiors, full kitchens, and large sitting areas nicely complement the fresh linens and friendly hosts. There's a cleaning area, if you're fishing, clamming, or crabbing, plus a fire pit and children's play area to keep families entertained. $$.

west

day trip 01

in the navy:
bremerton, port orchard, gig harbor

The Kitsap Peninsula reveals cities tied to the ocean—whether through the naval base, boat building, or fishing heritage. In Bremerton revitalization projects are creating an ever-changing city to explore. Parks dotted with synchronized fountains, museums, and restaurant patios cluster around the ferry dock and overlook the transportation hub that's a 1-hour ferry ride from Seattle.

On the opposite side of Sinclair Inlet, Port Orchard preserves the history of the lumber industry and mixes it with the community's present-day artists.

Further south, in ever-quaint Gig Harbor, parks and marinas line the waterfront and recall a strong sailing heritage. The small city bustles with tours, markets, and events.

Wherever you venture on the Kitsap Peninsula, you are never far from Puget Sound—and that saltwater beauty is the thread of this day trip.

bremerton

A strong naval presence and dubious reputation persist a bit in Bremerton, Kitsap's largest city. But arrive by ferry, stroll the waterfront boardwalk, and watch the dance of water in Harborside Fountain Park and those ideas quickly fade. Naval and puppet museums as well as public art and a marina create a vibrant and varied city so close to Seattle via ferry.

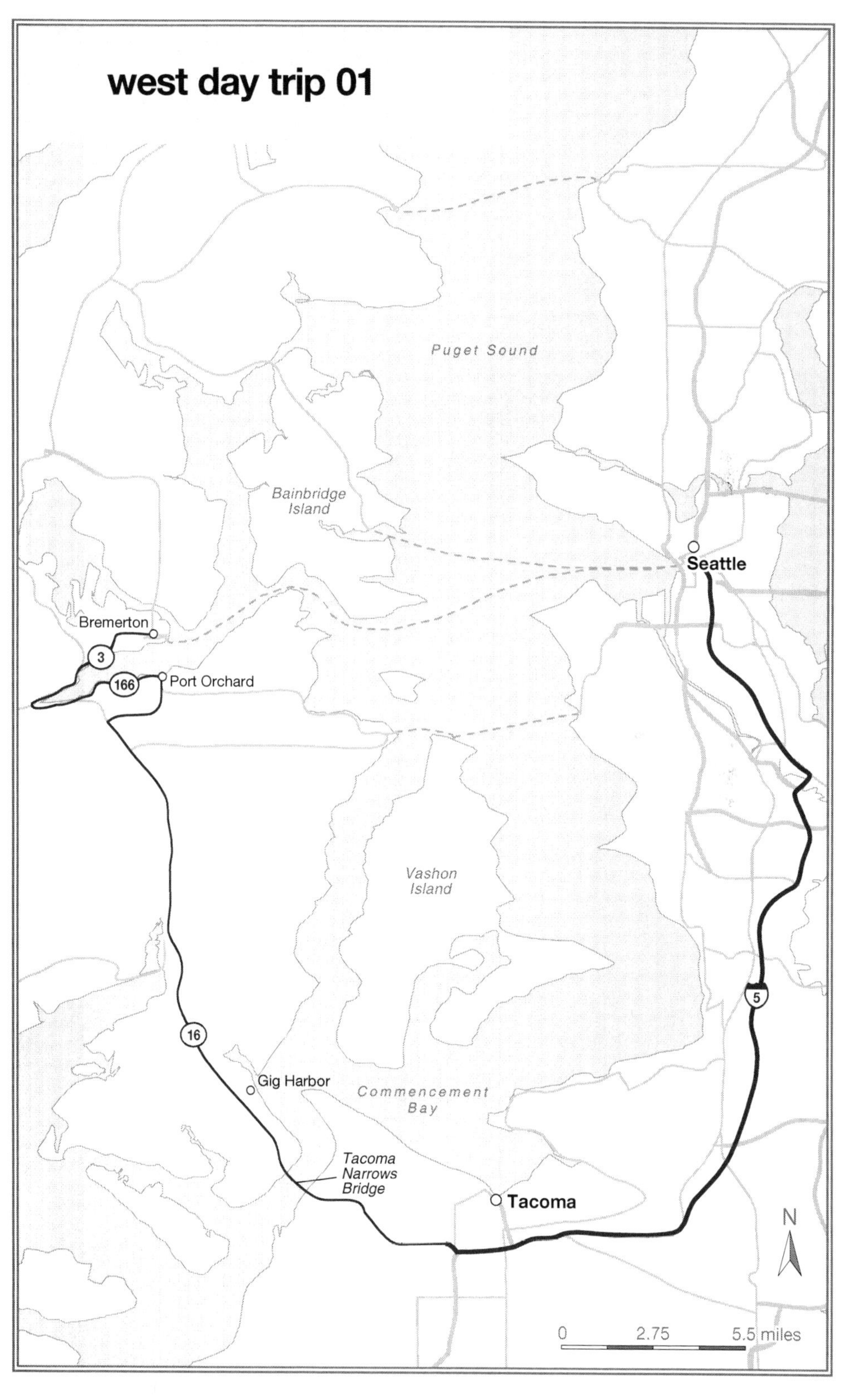
west day trip 01
Puget Sound
Bainbridge Island
Seattle
Bremerton
3
166
Port Orchard
Vashon Island
16
5
Gig Harbor
Commencement Bay
Tacoma Narrows Bridge
Tacoma
N
0
2.75
5.5 miles

getting there

Take the Seattle-Bremerton ferry, which runs more than a dozen times daily and takes about 60 minutes. From Bremerton, Port Orchard sits on the other side of Sinclair Inlet—9 miles away via a string of state highways: SR 3, SR 16, and SR 166.

When Southwest Bay Street splits off to Port Orchard, SR 16 continues to Gig Harbor, which can also be reached via Tacoma and the Tacoma Narrows Bridge (45 miles, 45 minutes from Seattle).

where to go

Bremerton Chamber of Commerce and Visitor Center. 409 Pacific Ave., Bremerton; (360) 479-3579; bremertonchamber.org. The visitor center is open Mon to Fri, with additional days when possible.

Bug & Reptile Museum. 1118 Charleston Beach Rd. West, Bremerton; bugmuseum.com. Visit live slithering reptiles and creepy crawlies like tarantulas, scorpions, and beetles at this free attraction and shop, located near the naval shipyard. Open daily.

Elandan Gardens. 3050 W. SR 16, Bremerton; (360) 373-8260; elandangardens.com. Elandan Gardens offers a rare and lovely glimpse of the special art of bonsai. The trees have a distinctly Pacific Northwest appeal: ponderosa pine, Douglas fir, and Rocky Mountain juniper. Acres of gardens snake between paths, ponds, and stone boulders and are interesting throughout the varied seasons. Open Tues to Sun from Apr to Oct; Fri to Sun Nov to Mar. $.

Kitsap Historical Society & Museum. 280 Fourth St., Bremerton; (360) 479-6226; kitsapmuseum.org. From farm, cottage, and pioneer life to the shipbuilding and forestry industries, this museum covers the region's past with a passion—and it's free! It shares a location with the Valentinetti Puppet Museum. Open Wed to Sat.

Ilahee State Park. 3540 NE Sylvan Way, Bremerton; (360) 478-6460; parks.state.wa.us. From harvesting oysters to throwing horseshoes, this state park provides an escape on Port Orchard Bay. Water activities take advantage of the moorage, dock, and boat ramp. Open daily.

Puget Sound Navy Museum. 251 First St., Bremerton; (360) 479-7447; pugetsoundnavymuseum.org. In a historic building near the ferry terminal and Puget Sound Naval Shipyard, exhibits display collections of naval artifacts and documents. Open daily June to Sept; closed Tues from Oct to May.

USS *Turner Joy*. 300 Washington Beach Ave., Bremerton; (360) 792-2457; ussturnerjoy.org. The ship, which was launched in 1958, is restored to recall its days of Vietnam action. A ship tour explores the destroyer, heading below decks to the crew cabins, engine room, and galley. Open daily Mar through Oct; closed Mon and Tues Nov to Feb. $$.

bremers of bremerton

In 1891 William Bremer platted the community on the shores on Sinclair Inlet and later secured the building of Puget Sound Naval Shipyard in Bremerton. By the 1970s the Bremer family still owned a large portion of the commercial buildings in the downtown core, and ownership had fallen to sole heir Edward, one of William and Sophia Bremer's three children.

A condition of the inheritance was that the heir could never marry. Sounds a bit like a bad fairytale, but in reality it had a devastating effect on the downtown. Under Edward's ownership and changing economic times, buildings deteriorated and the downtown district crumbled. Reports say the ferry terminal closed when a floor caved in under someone's foot. Edward fought legal battles to keep malls out of the downtown, and by the mid-1980s many brand-name tenants had left the waterfront, opting for lower taxes in Silverdale.

Revitalization projects like the boardwalk, waterfront fountains, and public museums have brought new life to the city.

Source: Seattle Post-Intelligencer *article "Remaking downtown Bremerton City now has chance to get ball rolling" by Gil Bailey. Published October 28, 1987.*

Valentinetti Puppet Museum. 280 Fourth St., Bremerton; (360) 479-6226; ectandpuppets.org. Enter the world of puppetry at this unique museum where ventriloquist dummies, Thai puppets, and miniature theater sets show the diversity of the art. It shares a location with the local history museum. Open Wed to Sat.

where to eat

Anthony's. 20 Washington Ave., Bremerton; (360) 377-5004; anthonys.com. Few reliable restaurant choices feature in downtown Bremerton, but from Anthony's you can watch ferries dock and admire waterfront fountains. Local seafood and Washington beef steaks offer an upscale menu that matches the panorama. Open daily for lunch and dinner. $$–$$$.

port orchard

This small community on Puget Sound looks out on the bright lights and naval shipyards of Bremerton on the opposite side of Sinclair Inlet. Yet Port Orchard shines in its own right with museums, waterfront dining, a Saturday farmers' market, and a busy main street. In addition to a waterfront boardwalk and marina, historical museums and an art gallery attract visitors to the small but entertaining downtown district.

The city, once called Sidney, thrived with the lumber industry and is the seat of Kitsap County.

getting there

From Bremerton, follow SR 3 south and merge shortly thereafter onto SR 16. Southwest Bay Street (SR 166) follows the shore, leading to downtown Port Orchard. A Kitsap Transit foot ferry runs every half hour on weekdays and Saturdays from Bremerton to Port Orchard (kitsaptransit.org).

where to go

Hobbit House. The Brothers Greenhouses, 3200 Victory Dr. Southwest, Port Orchard; (360) 674-2558; brothersgreenhouses.com. There's delightful imagination at play in this nursery, with a life-size hobbit house to visit. The structure is complete with a round door, chimney, and mossy roof. Wander the gardens, displays, and house for free. Open daily.

Log Cabin Museum. 416 Sidney Ave., Port Orchard; sidneymuseumandarts.com. Look for the lone log house on busy Sidney Avenue. Constructed by a Civil War veteran in 1914, the cabin recreates the daily life of yesteryear. Open weekends in summer.

Manchester State Park. 7767 E. Hilldale Rd., Port Orchard; (360) 871-4065; parks.state .wa.us. A 5-mile drive northeast of town, this park was once part of the Puget Sound defense system—and you can step inside this history with the old torpedo warehouse. Hiking trails, waterfront access, and camping all feature. Open daily. $.

Sidney Art Gallery and Museum. 202 Sidney Ave., Port Orchard; (360) 876-3693; sidney museumandarts.com. The first-floor gallery and second-floor museum fascinate visitors with a diverse look at the community in the past and present. Shops, a school, and a doctor's office envision snippets of Kitsap history, while the gallery livens the ground level with local art and monthly exhibitions. Open daily.

where to eat

Port Orchard Public Market. 715 Bay St., Port Orchard. The public market building hosts seasonal events and is also home to a couple of casual eateries like **The Dock Bar & Eatery** (360-602-0276), which serves bar staples like battered seafood, burgers, and sandwiches and is open daily for lunch and dinner. $–$$.

gig harbor

Once a mecca for boatbuilding, the small city of Gig Harbor has evolved into an upscale community with a vibrant waterfront life that remembers its early days. The Harbor History Museum, historic net sheds, and interpretive signs preserve the boatbuilding and fishing heritage, while shops and restaurants create a modern small-town feel. Dine on the waterfront then stroll past luxury marinas, waterfront parks with boat access, and the public pier—it's all part of exploring this safe harbor.

Summer is the time to visit, with trolley service to get around town and guided waterfront walking tours (253-514-0071; gigharborwaterfront.org).

getting there

SR 16 is the fastest route connecting Port Orchard to Gig Harbor (18 miles, 25 minutes). But the Kitsap Peninsula offers many by-ways to explore. You can also arrive in Gig Harbor via Tacoma and the Tacoma Narrows Bridge (45 miles, 45 minutes from Seattle).

where to go

Visitor Information & Interpretive Center at the Skansie House. 3207 Harborview Dr., Gig Harbor; (253) 853-3554; gigharborguide.com. This visitor center shares the historic **Skansie Netshed** (skansiebrothersnetshed.com) with the organization **Harbor WildWatch** (harborwildwatch.org). Open Wed to Sun from Apr to Sept; reduced hours or closures in the off-season. There's also a year-round visitor center open Mon to Fri at 3125 Judson St. (253-851-6865; gigharborchamber.net).

Gig Harbor Parks. Much of the city's greenspace also takes advantage of the waterfront. Along the shoreline, pocket parks provide great amenities such as the viewing platform and plaza at Ancich Waterfont Park. Nearby, Eddon Boat Park is a mid-century boatyard now preserved as a park, with the **Gig Harbor Boat Shop** (253-857-9344; gigharborboatshop .org) retaining the connection to maritime skills. Open daily.

Harbor History Museum. 4121 Harborview Dr., Gig Harbor; (253) 858-6722; harborhis torymuseum.org. This museum exhibits the area's boatbuilding culture and more. There's

galloping gertie

It's best to read about the history of Tacoma Narrows Bridge after a safe crossing. In 1940 the first Tacoma Narrows Bridge opened and soon earned the nickname Galloping Gertie—called such because of the way the bridge swayed and shook in the wind. Just months after opening, the bridge completely collapsed into the waters below, killing a dog that was trapped in an abandoned car. Amazingly the bridge's buckling twists are caught on camera; they are worth searching for online.

The replacement bridge, which was completed in 1950 and an expansion added in 2007, has earned a far more reassuring moniker: Sturdy Gertie.

a restored fishing vessel in the adjoining boatshed, and also an 1893 schoolhouse on the grounds. Open Tues to Sun during summer; Wed to Sat during winter.

Tacoma Narrows Park. 1502 Lucille Pkwy. Northwest, Gig Harbor; (253) 858-3400; penmetparks.org. This small park gives big views of the bridges and Narrows Passage. Open daily.

where to eat

Brix 25°. 3315 Harborview Dr., Gig Harbor; (253) 858-6626; harborbrix.com. Hailed for its polish, Brix 25° boasts both an impressive menu and scenery. Upscale dishes like halibut, crab, and filet mignon put the focus on quality and allow presentation to shine along with harbor views. Neighboring **Net Shed No. 9** (3313 Harborview Dr.; 253-858-7175; netshed9.com) serves inventive breakfast and lunch options, and is even closer to the water's edge. Open Thurs to Mon for dinner. $$$–$$$$.

Tides Tavern. 2925 Harborview Dr., Gig Harbor; (253) 858-3982; tidestavern.com. You don't become the longest-serving restaurant in town on nothing; Tides serves up excellent happy hours, fish-and-chips, clam chowder, plus towering burgers on a stellar waterfront patio. 21+. Open daily for lunch and dinner. $$–$$$.

where to stay

The Maritime Inn. 3212 Harborview Dr., Gig Harbor; (253) 858-1818 or toll free (888) 506-3580; maritimeinn.com. Without sacrificing any of their intimate quality, the guest rooms at the Maritime Inn are fresh and clean with queen- or king-size beds, waterfront views, fridges, and fireplaces. The location is superb for exploring the neighborhood feel of Gig Harbor. $$$.

day trip 02

west

chief sealth, swans, and vikings:
bainbridge island, suquamish, poulsbo

From within sight of Seattle to the grave of the city's namesake, the Suquamish leader Chief Seattle, this day trip explores the heart of the Kitsap Peninsula. Just close enough to be a relaxing journey, just far enough to be a getaway, you can walk through Norwegian-influenced Poulsbo, the regal gardens on Bainbridge Island, or the age-old Native American home of the Suquamish at Old Man House Park.

Museums explore the marine world, cultural stories, and local history, while gardens and parks invite you for a day outdoors.

bainbridge island

Within such a short distance of Seattle, the hidden back streets of Bainbridge Island still offer some seclusion despite being a heavily gentrified region of large homes on the water. But the locals are friendly, and the polish of the island yields lovely waterfront dining, lavish gardens, scrumptious baked treats, and wineries.

getting there

About two dozen times daily, ferries sail for Bainbridge Island from Seattle (terminal at 801 Alaskan Way, Pier 52). The 35-minute crossing is clogged with afternoon rush-hour traffic, so try to avoid peak travel times (usually about 3 p.m. to 7 p.m.).

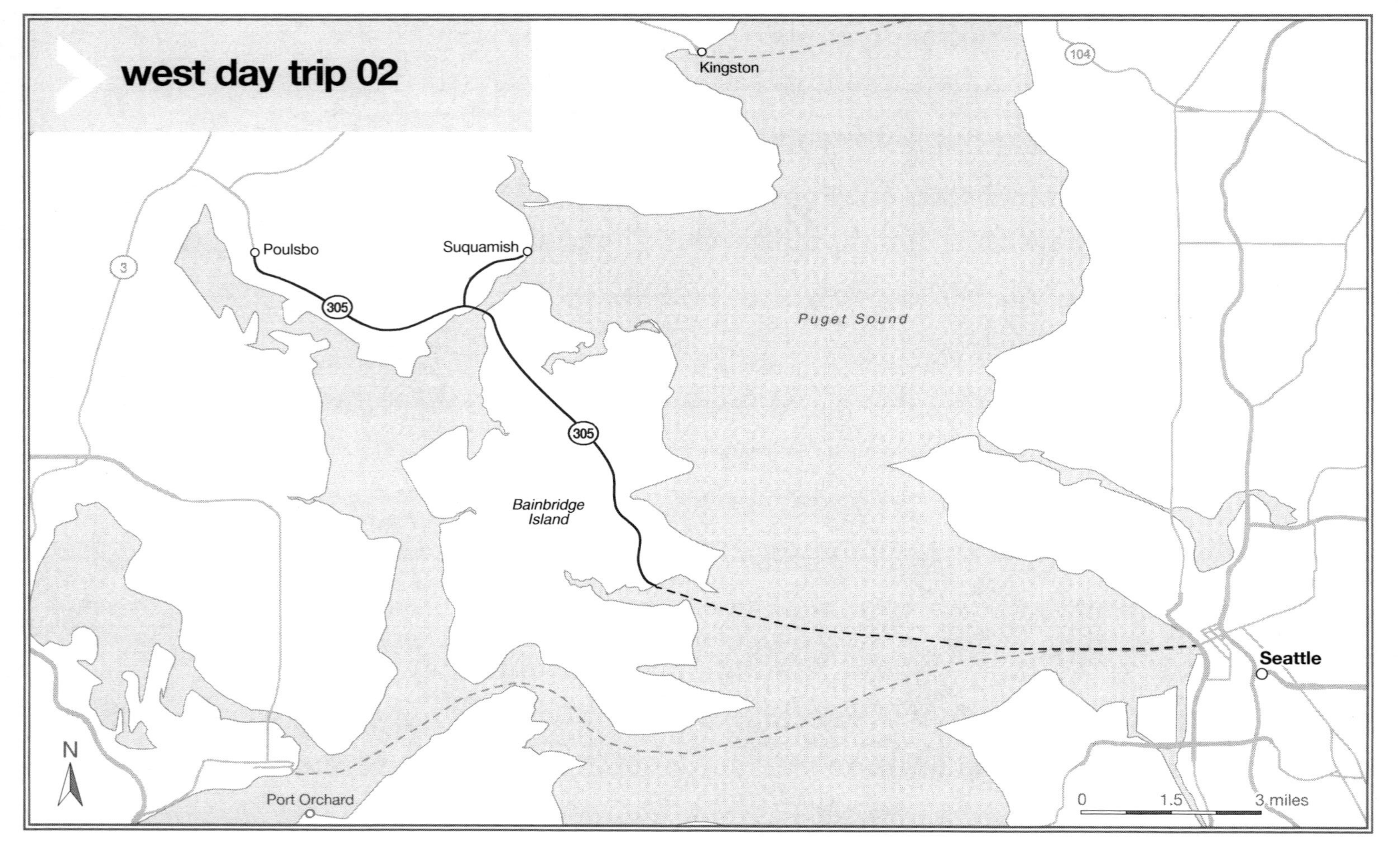
west day trip 02
Kingston
104
Poulsbo
Suquamish
3
305
Puget Sound
305
Bainbridge Island
Seattle
N
Port Orchard
0
1.5
3 miles

Alternately, catch a ferry from Edmonds to Kingston and begin in the Poulsbo area. Driving up from Bremerton is a third option, and avoiding the ferries altogether and arriving by land via Tacoma and Gig Harbor is a fourth. Keep in mind that these alternate routes all add about an hour to the travel time to reach Bainbridge.

where to go

Bainbridge Island Historical Museum. 215 Ericksen Ave. Northeast, Bainbridge Island; (206) 842-2773; bainbridgehistory.org. Located in a 1908 schoolhouse, the museum draws on local history from early to modern days of Bainbridge Island. The history of Puget Sound links to shipping, fishing, ferries, and a World War II fort. Open daily. $.

Bainbridge Island Japanese American Exclusion Memorial. Pritchard Park, 4192 Eagle Harbor Dr., Bainbridge Island; bijac.org. More than 200 Japanese Americans—most of them citizens—were exiled from the island in 1942 and became the first incarcerated during World War II. The memorial keeps that injustice alive.

Bainbridge Island Museum of Art. 550 Winslow Way East, Bainbridge Island; (206) 842-4451; biartmuseum.org. This free museum exhibits contemporary works from local artists. BIMA Bistro offers patio lunches daily from a simple but inventive menu. Open daily.

Bloedel Reserve. 7571 NE Dolphin Dr., Bainbridge Island; (206) 842-7631; bloedelreserve.org. The house is purely palatial and the grounds even more so: A human-made waterfall, serene swans, and stooping willows all add a regal note to the Northwest gardens of rhodies and conifers. The reflection, moss, and Japanese gardens all have a sacred air of preservation and veneration. About half of the 150 or so acres remain forested while the rest contains the manicured beds, sweeping garden scenes, and a visitor center. Open Tues to Sun year-round. $$.

Kids Discovery Museum. 301 Ravine Ln. Northeast, Bainbridge Island; (206) 855-4650. There's a busy schedule of special events at this children's museum, plus a variety of exhibits to inspire exploration. Open daily. $.

Fort Ward Park. 2241 Pleasant Beach, Bainbridge Island; biparks.org. Checkered with concrete relics of World War II, this island park provides a mix of activities from beachcombing to boating and biking. In the early 1900s the navy established Fort Ward to help protect Puget Sound Naval Shipyard in Bremerton. After serving as a training base and radio station during the war, the navy decommissioned the fort in 1958. Open daily.

Waterfront Park. 301 Shannon Dr. Southeast, Bainbridge Island; (206) 842-2306; bainbridgewa.gov. At five-and-a-half acres, Waterfront Park is just a small slice of shoreline by the city dock. But playgrounds, boat rentals, and benches—not to mention events and festivals—make it a lovely spot from which to enjoy the water. For kayak rental information, check with **Exotic Aquatics** (206-842-1980; exoticaquaticsscuba.com).

biking bainbrige

You won't drive far on Bainbridge Island without encountering a cyclist. With its wide road shoulders and off-main routes, the island endears itself to bikers. To join the pedal parade, check in with ***Bainbridge Classic Cycle*** *(740 Winslow Way East; 206-842-9191; classiccycleus.com) with year-round rentals and a museum showing bikes dating back more than a century, or Bike Barn Rentals (206-842-3434; bikebarnrentals.com), which offers summer rentals near the ferry dock.*

where to eat

Blackbird Bakery. 210 Winslow Way East, Bainbridge Island; (206) 780-1322; blackbirdbakery.com. Vegan chocolate loaf cake doesn't get better than this; it will even have nonvegans calling it yummy. From quiches to cookies all the baked goods here earn top honors—the only downside is choosing just one. Okay, maybe two. Open daily from about 6 or 7 a.m. to 6 p.m. $.

Harbour Public House. 231 Parfitt Way Southwest, Bainbridge Island; (206) 842-0969; harbourpub.com. This fun-loving pub offers marina views and well-priced, tasty eats. Organic greens, local meats, and west coast seafood show care in the menu. Most of the dishes can be customized with extras. Open daily for lunch, dinner, and late night. $$–$$$.

where to stay

The Eagle Harbor Inn. 291 Madison Ave. South, Bainbridge Island; (206) 842-1446; theeagleharborinn.com. Fresh with a European feel, the inn features classic comforts, lots of natural light, and works by Pacific Northwest artists. Large patios and well-tended gardens add space and privacy to the guest suites that range from hotel rooms to townhouses. $$$–$$$$.

suquamish

The community of Suquamish captures the spirit of the Pacific Northwest before European settlement encroached. A red-cedar festival hall that was once the largest on Puget Sound—stretching about 600 feet along the beach during the 1800s—is now commemorated at Old Man House Park. The park also treats visitors with great views of boat traffic and marine life heading through Agate Pass.

In Suquamish, part of a larger area known as Port Madison Indian Reservation, many come to visit the grave of Chief Seattle—the respected leader of the Duwamish and Suquamish tribes.

The community also hosts **Chief Seattle Days,** with canoe races and more, in mid-August.

getting there

From Bainbridge, head north on SR 305 and cross the Agate Pass Bridge (about 7 miles). Turn right onto Suquamish Way Northeast. From this main route, Division Avenue leads to Chief Seattle's grave to the north and Old Man House Park to the south.

where to go

Chief Seattle's Grave, St. Peter's Mission Cemetery, 7076 NE South St., Suquamish. The grave of the revered and respected Suquamish leader draws visitors who come to pay their respects. The headstone reads "Seattle, Chief of Suquamish, and Allied tribes. Died June 7, 1866. The firm friend of the whites, and for him the City of Seattle, was named by its founders." Religious offerings of flowers, trinkets, coins, and tobacco surround the grave site, which is adjacent to the church of St. Peter's Mission. Open daily.

Old Man House Park. NE McKinstry St. and S. Angeline Ave. Northeast, Suquamish. This small waterfront park marks the former location of a roughly 600-foot longhouse and festival hall that had a history of lodging dozens of Suquamish families. The house, made of red cedar, stood parallel to the tide lines and featured a sloping roof rather than the more common gabled roof. The park is open daily.

chief sealth

Also called Si'ahl as well as Chief Sealth, Chief Seattle—the name which ties him most closely to the city named for him—remains a revered leader for his strong and peaceful leadership. His famed 1854 speech urged respect for Native American land rights and ecological care. But dispute remains, however, over the exact content of Chief Sealth's Lushootseed-language speech as there is no original written version.

For a century the Suquamish community has celebrated ***Chief Seattle Days*** *with memorials, songs, dances, fireworks, canoe races, and salmon dinners. The festival occurs in mid-August (360-598-3311; suquamish.nsn.us).*

Suquamish Museum. 6861 NE South St., Suquamish; (360) 394-8499; suquamish museum.org. The large museum houses exhibits as well as arts and crafts that illustrate the history, culture, and storytelling of the Suquamish. Timelines share the deep cultural history of the Salish people. Open daily. $.

poulsbo

The one-time hamlet of Poulsbo attained its Norwegian heritage authentically—from Scandinavian settlers who immigrated here in the 1880s. The town's location on a fjord affront the peaks of the Olympic Mountains is a picturesque spot, especially from the lovely vantage of Waterfront Park. Stop in at Scandinavian bakeries and restaurants, admire the pretty white-and-blue First Lutheran Church, walk through the heritage downtown district, or explore the depths of the ocean at the marine science center.

But perhaps the town festivals are best reason to visit. Viking Fest celebrates Constitution Day in Norway on May 17 and includes parades, races, and a vendor market, while the Midsommarfest hosts folk dancers for the summer solstice.

getting there

Head 10 minutes (5 miles) west of the Agate Pass Bridge on SR 305 to reach Poulsbo.

where to go

Poulsbo Fish Park. 288 NW Lindvig Way, Poulsbo; (360) 779-9898. In this large and well-loved city park, there's a boardwalk, bridges, and wildlife-viewing platforms on Liberty Bay Estuary. Across the road in Nelson Park is the late-1800s Martinson Cabin, preserved to recall the pioneer days by the local historical society. Park open daily.

Poulsbo Heritage Museum. 200 Moe St. Northeast, Poulsbo; (360) 440-7354; poulsbo history.com. Exhibits introduce this unique city and how it has been shaped by land and salt water. It's located within the city hall complex. Open Wed to Sat. Admission is free.

Maritime Museum. 19010 Front St. NE, Poulsbo; (360) 994-4943; poulsbohistory.com. With a visitor center also, this water-focused museum illuminates the life along the twisting coastline of Kitsap Peninsula. Admission is free.

SEA Discovery Center. 18743 Front St. Northeast, Poulsbo; (360) 598-4460; wp.wwu .edu/seacenter. A tidepool touch tank and aquariums with Puget Sound critters fill the facility. Overlooking the town marina, the center prioritizes education, and kids especially will enjoy the ocean-life exhibits. Open Tues to Sun in summer; open Thurs to Sun from Oct to June. Closed Sept.

where to eat

Central Market. 20148 10th Ave. Northeast, Poulsbo; (360) 779-1881; central-market.com/poulsbo. It's a grocery store, yes, but it's also a community gathering spot with fantastic grab-and-go dishes, sushi eatery, and cafe with seating. Open daily. $–$$.

Sluys' Poulsbo Bakery. 18924 Front St. Northeast, Poulsbo; (360) 779-2798; sluyspoulsbobakery.com. Find baked treats of every kind, including the Norwegian *lefse* flat bread. Open daily. $.

Sogno di Vino. 18830 Front St. Northeast, Poulsbo; (360) 697-8466; sogno-di-vino.com. Wine and pizza make a simple and tasty combination. The pizza is baked in a wood-fired oven, and toppings such as fennel sausage, smoked salmon, Gruyere, prosciutto, and rosemary tease the senses. The small but spot-on menu also offers fresh pastas and smaller starters. A warm, friendly vibe permeates throughout. Open daily for lunch and dinner. $$–$$$.

worth more time

U.S. Naval Undersea Museum. 1 Garnett Way, Keyport; (360) 396-4148; navalunderseamuseum.org. From ocean science to combat, this free museum unveils the hidden world of undersea operations. The torpedo displays are particularly impressive. Open daily; closed Tues Oct to Apr.

day trip 03

west

hood canal:
shelton, allyn, union and hoodsport, quilcene

Fishermen awake before dawn to launch their boats where the Olympic Mountains meet a saltwater fjord—the only one in the Lower 48. Although homes overlook a large portion of Hood Canal, state parks with beaches also provide access to stretches of waterfront where visitors can harvest oysters and clams in season (and with a license). Every turn delivers understated views of forest, water, and wildlife.

This day trip takes a roundabout route following the C-curve of Hood Canal from its terminus at the Theler Wetlands near Belfair out to the Hood Canal Floating Bridge that marks its connection with Puget Sound. Through Olympic forests, past waterside oyster bars, and beside fishing docks, it's a route of discovery that traces the length of this interesting waterway.

The timeless scenic drive of the Hood Canal area also offers plenty of rewarding activities, whether it's touring a garden nursery, fish hatchery, wine-tasting room, or chainsaw-carving gallery.

shelton

Shelton was established as, and still is, a logging town: The piles of timber at the waterfront mill, tree slices serving as town greeting signs, and working railroad lines attest to that. But often with a strong industry comes wealth, and Shelton hints at a measure of prosperity with some lovely early-twentieth-century historical architecture in the downtown. And, firmly

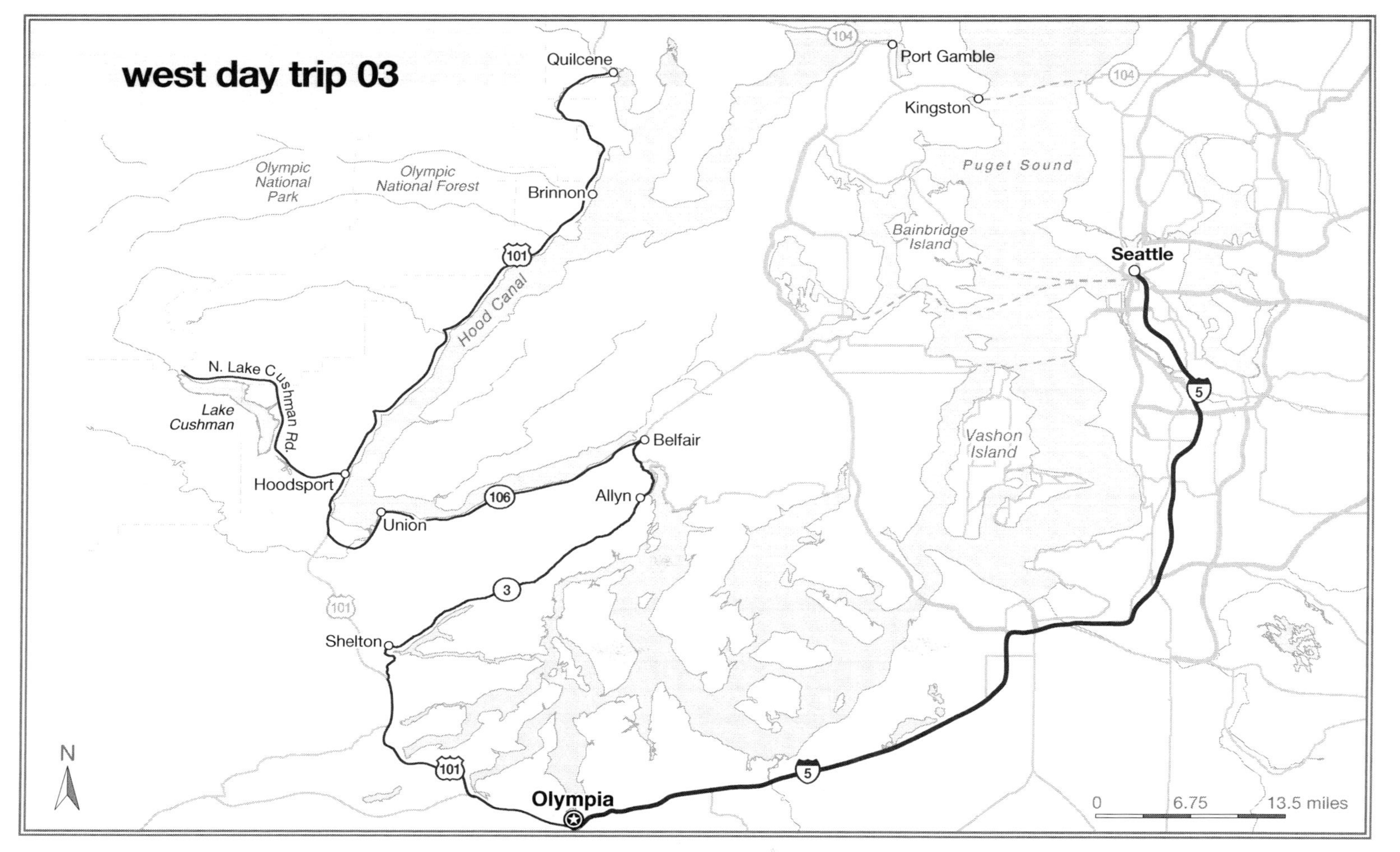

west day trip 03
Quilcene
Port Gamble
Kingston
104
Puget Sound
Olympic National Park
Olympic National Forest
Brinnon
Bainbridge Island
Seattle
101
Hood Canal
N. Lake Cushman Rd.
Lake Cushman
Hoodsport
Belfair
Vashon Island
5
Allyn
106
Union
3
Shelton
N
Olympia
0
6.75
13.5 miles

planted in the present, there's also a farmers' market on Saturdays and OysterFest shucking competitions in October.

getting there

From Seattle, head south on I-5 to exit 104, which meets US 101 at Olympia. Just before Shelton, SR 3 spurs off US 101. Take SR 3 to downtown Shelton (80 miles, 1.5 hours). This road trip cuts a leisurely route along SR 3 to the head of the canal then along SR 106 to the lower shore, meeting again with US 101 as it heads north into the Olympic Peninsula. The total tour takes about 2 hours from Shelton to Quilcene.

Another option is to begin the drive at Allyn—taking the Fauntleroy-Southworth ferry and hopping west on State Routes 160, 16, and 3.

Alternately, flip the drive on its head to begin at the mouth end of Hood Canal by taking the Edmonds-Kingston ferry and traveling along SR 104 as it crosses the Hood Canal Bridge and meets with US 101.

where to go

Shelton Visitor Center. 230 W. Railroad Ave., Shelton; (360) 426-2021; sheltonchamber .org. Look for the red caboose on Railroad Avenue for local guidance. There's also a county chamber of commerce across the street at 215 W. Railroad Ave. Open weekdays only.

Mason County Historical Museum. 427 W. Railroad Ave., Shelton; (360) 426-1020; masoncountyhistoricalsociety.org. From pioneers to oysters and the logging industry, the museum explores the history of Shelton and Mason County in a 1914 building that was once the town hall and library. Open Tues to Sat.

Squaxin Island Tribe Museum. 150 SE K'wuh-deegs-altxw, Shelton; (360) 432-3839; squaxinislandmuseum.org. The Squaxin are known as the People of the Water—it's no surprise considering the water that surrounds and laces the Kitsap Peninsula. Murals dominate this beautiful museum telling the stories of an ancient people, while the woven baskets reveal a more subtle tale. Outside the museum, there are serene gardens for a stroll. Open Tues to Sat. $.

Vance Creek Railriders. 421 W. Hanks Lake Rd., Shelton; (541) 519-4200; vcrailriders .com. Hop into a unique bicycle-of-sorts: designed specifically to pedal along train tracks. The tour follows Simpson Logging Company Railway lines. Tours run Thurs to Mon from May to early Oct at set times. $$$.

Wild Felid Advocacy Center of Washington. 3111 E. Harstine Island Rd. North, Shelton; (360) 427-4466; wildfelids.org. Book ahead for tours to see the incredible wildcats housed at this sanctuary, with species that include leopard, tiger, lynx, and more. $$$.

where to eat

Ritz Drive-In. 325 S. 1st St., Shelton; (360) 427-9294. A simple burger shack where the classics headline the menu doesn't disappoint—including the excellent milk shakes. Open Mon to Sat for lunch and dinner. $.

The Strip Steakhouse. 405 W. Railroad Ave., Shelton; (360) 432-5844. A small, well-planned menu includes classic cuts of steak as well as burgers and the odd chicken or seafood dish. Cozy but with lots of seating, the intimate dining room is one of the few options downtown. Open Mon to Sat for lunch and dinner. $$–$$$.

allyn

To drive the full shore of Hood Canal, first venture out of the way on SR 3 to the small town of Allyn. Right on the waterfront, it offers a sheltered vantage and sandy beach on the North Bay of Case Inlet plus a dose of local quirkiness. Visit a chainsaw-carving school, kayak the calm waters, or hike through preserved wetlands and see a whale skeleton. Or just relax on a waterfront patio—the choice is yours.

getting there

SR 3 leads from Shelton to Allyn and Belfair, near the head of the canal (18 miles, 25 minutes).

where to go

George Kenny's School of Chainsaw Carving. 18351 E. SR 3, Allyn; (360) 275-9570; chainsaw-carving-school.com. It's nearly impossible to miss this: Just look for the Vikings, eagles, bears, and beavers placed alongside the highway. The school holds classes for chainsaw carvers and exhibits the cedar-carved work for all to enjoy. Each July during Allyn Days, it's the center of the competition circuit. Open daily.

North Bay Kayak. 18350 SR 3, Allyn; (360) 535-2198; allynhouseinn.com. Recreational kayaking or paddleboarding can be easy and a fun way to explore the calm waters of Hood Canal. Hourly or daily rentals are available with rates starting at about $20 for one hour to about $60 for a full day. $$$.

Theler Wetlands. 22871 NE SR 3, Belfair. About 3 miles of trails with diverse wildlife are located behind a childcare center. There's also a shuttered exhibit center with a gray whale skeleton. The wetland spans marsh, farmland, and forest and sits where the Union River meets Hood Canal. No dogs are allowed on the trails. The wetlands are open daily.

The Salmon Center. 600 NE Roessel Rd., Belfair; (360) 275-3575; pnwsalmoncenter.org. The focus of this educational center is protecting salmon—but llamas, gardens, and exhibits give an interesting and engaging perspective. Open Mon to Fri.

Twanoh State Park. 12190 E. SR 106, Union; (360) 275-2222; parks.state.wa.us. Halfway between Belfair and Union, this longtime favorite park is known for its warm swimming waters. Other draws include shellfish harvesting, hiking trails, and a variety of activities from volleyball to horseshoes. Open daily.

where to eat

Lennard K's Boathouse Restaurant. 18340 E. SR 3, Allyn; (360) 275-6060; lennardks.com. This casual bayside dining room and patio offers a taste of the west coast with cedar plank salmon, halibut, and fried oysters. There's lots more on the standard pub-style menu, including bar staples like burgers, salads, pizzas, and sandwiches. Open Tues to Sun for lunch and dinner. $$–$$$.

union and hoodsport

At the "Great Bend" of Hood Canal sit the two towns of Union and Hoodsport, about 15 minutes apart and both with incredible mountain and water views. This area remains a hotbed for commercial fishing, where waking at dawn yields serene shots of boats out early, nets already in the water. With local wineries, access to Olympic National Park, and the area's best accommodations, Union and Hoodsport sparkle.

There are plenty of stopping places, including roadside attractions such as the historic Dalby Waterwheel, which first provided electricity in 1923.

getting there

Follow SR 106 west along the canal to Union. At the junction with US 101, head north to Hoodsport.

where to go

Hood Canal Visitor Information Center. 150 N. Lake Cushman Rd., Hoodsport; (360) 877-2021; explorehoodcanal.com. This visitor center opens daily and provides information about Olympic National Park and Forest, with rangers on-site Fri to Mon in summer.

Hoodsport Winery. 23501 US 101, Hoodsport; (360) 877-9894; hoodsport.com. One of the first wineries in Washington, Hoodsport Winery produces fruit wines that sparkle with color. Whether it's the apple, blackberry, pear, or rhubarb wine, or perhaps one of the more traditional varietals such as Chardonnay or Cabernet Sauvignon, there exists no shortage of bottles to uncork. There's also the Stottle Winery tasting room in the cute waterfront strip of businesses. Open daily.

Hunter Farms. 1921 E. SR 106, Union; (360) 426-2222; hunter-farms.com. More than a century old, this farm offers a bit of everything—from nursery plants to Christmas trees (with fresh summer berries and a pumpkin patch in between). Open daily.

Lake Cushman. SR 119, west of Hoodsport. With remote-feeling resorts, national park access, and boat rentals, this large reservoir lake encourages visitors to linger. There's not much around, except a few basic vacation services for cabins and then the wilderness beyond. The Staircase Ranger Station for Olympic National Park (open in summer) lies at the end of the road.

Potlatch State Park. 21020 US 101, Shelton; (360) 877-5361; parks.state.wa.us. The shady waterfront park is a destination for shellfish harvesting including famed Hood Canal oysters. Watch for the local wildlife, including elk and birds. There's also year-round camping. Open daily. $.

where to eat

Hama Hama Oyster Saloon. 35846 US 101, Lilliwaup; (360) 877-5811 or (888) 877-5844; hamahamaoysters.com. Fresh oysters and smoked salmon reel in visitors to the Hama Hama Seafood Store. The shop sits waterside on the main route, about 15 minutes north of Hoodsport. The outdoor oyster bar, which serves mainly seafood, is open daily in summer; winter hours can vary, but usually Fri to Sun. Afternoons only. $–$$$.

where to stay

Alderbrook Resort & Spa. 10 E. Alderbrook Dr., Union; (360) 898-2200; alderbrookresort.com. This posh luxury resort and spa on Hood Canal features thoughtfully designed guest rooms as well as private cottages. The warm stone hearth and Northwest feel of the lobby gives way to bright guest rooms—like traversing forest to meadow. King-size beds, scenic views, frequent live music, and an on-site spa and restaurant all let you tuck in to the experience. $$$–$$$$.

Glen Ayr Resort. 25381 US 101, Hoodsport; (360) 877-9522; garesort.com. Pull up in your RV, moor your boat, or drive in and grab a guestroom—this waterfront resort accommodates many travelers. Balconies allow for excellent morning views with a coffee and panorama of Hood Canal. Facilities include an indoor hot tub, a rec room with pool table, and outdoor area to spark up a barbecue. $–$$.

quilcene

The wilds begin in Quilcene, which sits on the edge of Olympic National Forest. Tucked in the nook of Quilcene Bay, the area (which, at first glance, doesn't present itself as much of a destination) offers attractions such as a fish hatchery, historical museum, and access to national forest camping. This is also a destination for classical music, with an impressive lineup of artists performing in Olympic Music Festival concerts.

where to go

Olympic National Forest Quilcene Ranger Station. 295142 US 101, Quilcene; (360) 765-2200; fs.usda.gov/olympic. For details on exploring the national forest—the lands that ring the national park—stop in to gather guides and guidance. Easy excursions include following the Hamma Hamma Living Legacy Trail to a historic guardhouse dating to the 1930s, or driving the well-maintained gravel road to Mt. Walker Viewpoint to look out over Puget Sound. Open daily Memorial Day to Labor Day; otherwise closed weekends.

Dosewallips State Park. 306996 US 101, Brinnon; (360) 796-4415; parks.state.wa.us. Elk herds are known to wander through the campground here. There's an unusual combo of both fresh- and saltwater access, plus cabin rentals. Open daily. $.

Quilcene Historical Museum. 151 E. Columbia St., Quilcene; (360) 765-4848; quilcene museum.org. This small community museum provides Native American and pioneer perspectives on this lumber town. Open Fri to Mon, from mid-Apr through mid-Sept. $.

Quilcene National Fish Hatchery. 281 Fish Hatchery Rd., Quilcene; (360) 765-3334; fws .gov/quilcenenfh. Adult salmon return in fall, making the autumn the most active time to see

eastern side of olympic national park

Hood Canal trims the southeastern corner of the national forest, which buffers Olympic National Park. A few roads spur into the wilderness, providing access. For all areas of the park, the central visitor center lies in Port Angeles but is reachable for questions on the area adjacent to Hood Canal as well (3002 Mount Angeles Rd.; 360-565-3130; nps.gov/olym).

From Brinnon, FSR 2610 strikes up to Dosewallips alongside Dosewallips River, although a road washout necessitates a 5-mile hike to the campground.

SR 119 provides a more traveled route from Hoodsport to Staircase, where there are hiking, picnic, and camping facilities near Lake Cushman.

fish spawning in Quilcene River. As with many Washington hatcheries, staff members or volunteers provide tours to groups, but they are also eager to answer questions as they go about their tasks. Open weekdays year-round.

Whitney Gardens and Nursery. 306264 US 101, Brinnon; (360) 796-4411 or (800) 952-2404; whitneygardens.com. Wander the gardens to see rhododendrons, magnolias, and blooming bulbs in a Northwest floral paradise spanning seven acres. Open daily year-round, although Mar through June is the best time for blooms and Oct wows with fall colors. $.

where to eat

101 Brewery at Twana Road House. 294793 US 101, Quilcene; (360) 765-6485; 101 brewery.com. Standard fare includes pizza, burgers, and large breakfasts. But the small restaurant is also a friendly and welcoming spot to start or end a road trip over a house microbrew beer. Open daily for breakfast, lunch, and dinner. $–$$.

northwest

day trip 01

northwest

whidbey island:
langley, greenbank, coupeville, oak harbor

This long island on the Pacific coast is only about 10 miles across at its widest. And yet throughout the island, decommissioned army outposts, historic farms, welcoming gardens, and diverse eateries punctuate the miles of coastline. There's also a growing crop of wineries, breweries, and distilleries. Events and festivals mark all the seasons, from murder mystery weekends to whale festivals and seafood celebrations.

On the western front, batten down the hatches for storm watching, oceanside hiking, and views of the snow-capped Olympic Mountains. Historical buildings and mussel farms find a safe harbor in the shelter of the east side of the island. Throughout your visit, you'll hear that you're now "on island"—it means slow down and enjoy the scenery.

Whidbey boasts perhaps the highest density of accommodations in the state. Sifting through the inns, B&Bs, cabins, cottages, and vacation rentals takes some work. To ease the effort, visit the lodging section of whidbeycamanoislands.com.

getting there

Travel north on I-5 to exit 182. The Mukilteo Speedway (or SR 525) cuts northwest to the ferry at Mukilteo and I-405 heads south. Running on the hour and half hour throughout the day, the ferry takes just 20 minutes to transport you to Clinton—and island time!

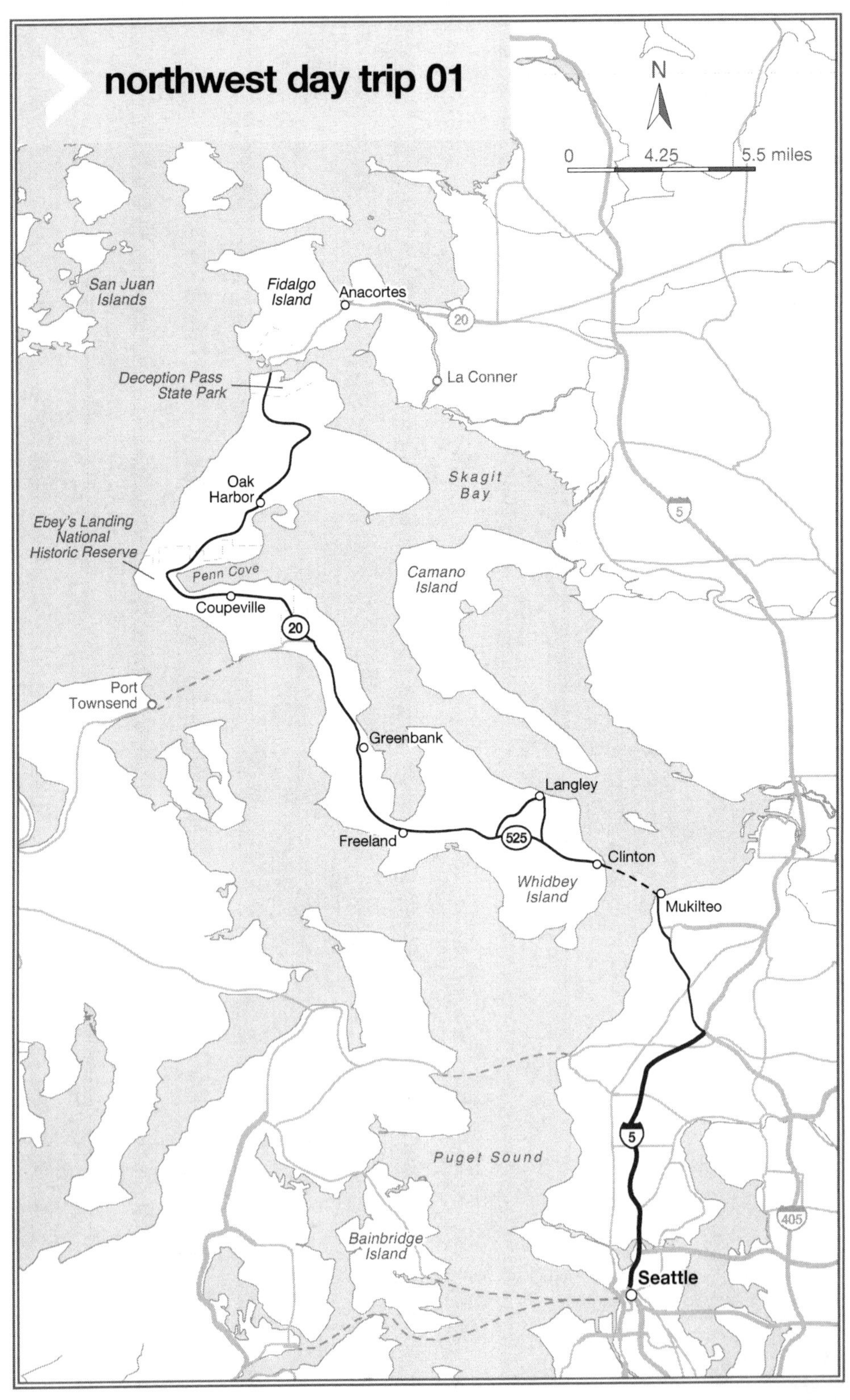

northwest day trip 01
N
0
4.25
5.5 miles
San Juan Islands
Fidalgo Island
Anacortes
20
La Conner
Deception Pass State Park
Oak Harbor
Skagit Bay
5
Ebey's Landing National Historic Reserve
Penn Cove
Coupeville
20
Camano Island
Port Townsend
Greenbank
Langley
Freeland
525
Clinton
Whidbey Island
Mukilteo
5
Puget Sound
405
Bainbridge Island
Seattle

langley

After a ferry ride across Possession Sound from Mukilteo, Langley makes a pretty first destination with its seaside shopping, varied restaurants, and unusual events like Langley Mystery Weekend. There's a whale bell to ring when orcas or gray whales are feeding offshore, and a Welcome the Whales Parade harkens their return each spring.

getting there

Follow SR 525 from the Clinton ferry dock and turn north onto Langley Road to reach Langley—about 10 minutes from the ferry.

where to go

Langley Visitor Information. 208 Anthes Ave., Langley; (360) 221-6765; visitlangley.com. Open daily, the visitor center provides the local scoop on events and accommodations. Closed Sun Oct to Mar.

Langley Whale Center. 105 Anthes Ave., Langley; (360) 221-7505; orcanetwork.org. Learn more about some of the original visitors to Whidbey: orca whales, gray whales, and humpbacks. Exhibits and information also provide insight into more Puget Sound marine life. Open Thurs to Mon, and generally extra days in summer.

Seawall Park. Waterfront, Langley. Watch for whales and shorebirds while looking out over Saratoga Passage. Waterside parks with picnic tables complement the views. A bronze statue of a boy with his dog on the street level marks one of the access staircases. Open daily.

South Whidbey Historical Society Museum. 312 Second St., Langley; (360) 221-2101; southwhidbeyhistory.org. This small, free museum offers exhibits in a historic logger bunkhouse. Open weekends.

where to eat

The Braeburn. 197 Second St., Langley; (360) 221-3211; braeburnlangley.com. A cute cafe where you can dine on dishes made with quality, local ingredients as well as fantastic breakfasts. The casual vibe only enhances the joys of tucking into homey eats with a local flair like Penn Cove mussels or Dungeness crab fettuccini. Open Wed to Mon for breakfast and lunch; Thurs to Sat for dinner. $–$$.

Village Pizzeria. 106 First St., Langley; (360) 221-3363. A thin but substantial crust, slices big enough to fold in half, and freshness give Village Pizzeria its top reputation. The dining area is basic, but the waterfront location allows for a quick escape to stroll in the park. Open daily for lunch and dinner. $–$$.

where to stay

The Boatyard Inn. 200 Wharf St., Langley; (360) 221-5120; boatyardinn.com. Far more spacious than a yacht belowdecks but with all the same waterside appeal, the Boatyard Inn provides well-equipped suites and lofts. Feel the sea breeze from the deck, prepare local seafood in the kitchenette, or hunker down against a winter storm in front of the fireplace. A baker's dozen of units are independent and self-contained with the true romantic feel of a boathouse hideaway. $$$$.

worth more time

Earth Sanctuary. 2059 Newman Rd., Freeland; (360) 331-6667; earthsanctuary.org. Between Langley and Greenbank lies perhaps Whidbey's most unique attraction: a woodland pondscape of gardens and stone dedicated to inspiring peace and contemplation. The Cottonwood Stone Circle is one of many sculptures. Trace the labyrinth, walk beneath the tree canopy, and relax in a green environment that's in the first steps of a 500-year journey to become an old-growth forest. Open daily. $.

greenbank

The agricultural roots of Whidbey shine in Greenbank, and there's no hesitation about visiting the pie cafe, wine-tasting room, and market at Greenbank Farm. Then wander Meerkerk Rhododendron Gardens to enjoy vibrant blooms and woodland walks.

getting there

Travel 13 miles along SR 525 from the intersection with Langley Road to Greenbank.

where to go

Greenbank Farm. 765 Wonn Rd., Greenbank; (360) 222-3797 (wine shop); portoc.org/greenbank-farm and gbfwine.com. Long a focal point of the island and situated at one of its narrowest points, this historic farm has transformed from a large producer of loganberries (a raspberry-blackberry hybrid) into a community gathering point with shops and hiking trails. A wine-tasting room is the easiest way to sample wine from across Washington State ($1 per sample), but there are also galleries, a cheese shop, and an excellent pie cafe. Open daily.

Meerkerk Rhododendron Gardens. 3531 Meerkerk Ln. (off Resort Road), Greenbank; (360) 678-1912; meerkerkgardens.org. Of course the highlight of these gardens is the peak rhododendron bloom from late April to May, but with beds of daffodils (local deer eat any tulips) and woodland trails, the gardens are a year-round destination. A gatehouse reminiscent of fairy tales serves as the departure point for guided tours, botany hunts, and photography expeditions. Open daily. $.

where to eat

Whidbey Pies Cafe. 765 Wonn Rd., Greenbank; (360) 678-1288; whidbeypies.com. Come for the pies, stay for lunch. Loganberry, rhubarb, marionberry, and apple pies are some of the classic double-crust offerings at this small but often busy cafe. While the menu also offers sandwiches, soups, and quiches, I'm partial to simply indulging in a second slice. Open daily for lunch. $–$$.

coupeville

As the heart of Ebey's Landing National Historical Reserve, Coupeville and its historic charms may be the strongest pull of the island. Walk out on the pier to see Rosie—the skeleton of a male gray whale—or visit one of the many nearby state parks that feature army barracks and hillside batteries.

Stroll Front Street to find a downtown museum, restaurants with deliciously fresh seafood (including local Penn Cove mussels), and plenty of historic accommodations that make the town an excellent stopover.

getting there

From Greenbank, SR 525 continues for 5 miles before becoming SR 20. The route journeys another 5 miles before it intersects with Coupeville's Main Street.

where to go

Coupeville Chamber of Commerce. 905 NW Alexander St, Coupeville; (360) 678-5434; coupevillechamber.com. Stop in while exploring the wharf and shops in downtown. Open daily; closed Sun in spring and summer.

Ebey's Landing National Historical Reserve. Coupeville; (360) 678-6084; nps.gov/ebla. The expansive reserve encompasses the historic town of Coupeville, the battlements of Fort Casey and Fort Ebey State Parks, and an enduring farming community. Established in 1978, the historic reserve treasures working farmland and one of Washington's oldest towns. On summer weekends, add a visit to the 1856 Jacob & Sarah Ebey House or Ebey Blockhouse, which recalls conflicts with Whidbey's first Native American residents. Ebey's Landing State Park Heritage Site offers wild and sweeping water (and sunset!) views from the bluffs along Ebey's Landing Road. Open daily.

Fort Casey Historical State Park. 1280 Engle Rd., Coupeville; (360) 678-4519; parks .state.wa.us. The larger battery of the two coastal defense parks near Coupeville, Fort Casey is a fun and slightly eerie destination to explore with year-round camping. Roam along the coastline adjacent to Keystone ferry and view the Olympic Mountains in the distance. Visit

Admiralty Head Lighthouse (360-678-7475; open most weekends but schedule varies), the gun battery, or the underwater dive park. Open daily.

Fort Ebey State Park. 400 Hill Valley Dr., Coupeville; (360) 678-4636; parks.state.wa.us. The battery and concrete gun emplacements tell the story of the World War II coastal defense station. Trails snake along the bluffs with more options for hiking and biking inland. Walk, camp, surf, or simply admire the views of the Olympic Mountains. Open daily. $.

Island County Historical Society Museum. 908 NW Alexander St., Coupeville; (360) 678-3310; islandhistory.org. The warmth of carved cherrywood doors welcomes you to the museum and provides the first glimpses of Whidbey Island history. Venture inside to unearth the past of this agricultural and ocean-bound island. Open daily year-round.

Lavender Wind Farm. 2530 Darst Rd., Coupeville; (360) 544-4132 (shop) or (877) 242-7716; lavenderwind.com. Find out what the color purple smells like each summer at this lavender farm. The horizon teases with mountains and ocean, while the year-round gift shop in Coupeville offers the fragrant lavender in many forms including ice cream, soaps, and oils. Open daily mid-June to mid-Aug. $.

Rosie the Whale on Coupeville Wharf. 24 NW Front St., Coupeville; (360) 678-6379; portoc.org/coupeville-wharf. The skeleton of a nearly three-year-old male gray whale hangs from the rafters of the boat shed at the end of Coupeville wharf. Read the exhibits, grab a drink at the coffee shop, or watch the gulls circling overhead. Open daily.

where to eat

Currents Bistro. 103 NW Coveland St., Coupeville; (360) 678-5480; currentsbistro.com. A modern dining room serves seafood with tender care, including local Penn Cove mussels and wild salmon. Pasta dishes are a highlight and feature island grown produce. Open Wed to Mon for lunch and dinner. $$–$$$.

Knead & Feed Restaurant. 4 NW Front St., Coupeville; (360) 678-5431; kneadandfeed.com. Salads, soups, and sandwiches on homemade bread are served in the country-kitchen dining room that overlooks the water. It echoes the farming heritage of Ebey's Landing, and since 1974 this family-run restaurant has prepared baked goods with love. Open daily for breakfast and lunch. $–$$.

where to stay

Anchorage Inn. 807 N. Main St., Coupeville; (360) 678-5581; anchorage-inn.com. Seven rooms range from the attic Crow's Nest with a spacious layout and king-size bed to a main-floor budget room. All have private baths, and the floral decor adds a Victorian elegance without too much frill. $$–$$$.

Compass Rose Bed and Breakfast. 508 S. Main St., Coupeville; (360) 678-5318 or (800) 237-3881; compassrosebandb.com. Step inside the historic Victorian home and enter a world of curiosities and worldly treasures. Silver tea services, throne-like chairs, original art, and rescued wood carvings all add a distinct historical charm that is unmatchable. Two rooms each have a private bath. $$.

oak harbor

Best known for its naval base (watch for the planes zooming overhead and jet airplanes mounted alongside the highway), Oak Harbor also serves as a base from which to explore Washington's most popular state park: Deception Pass. Head to Deception Pass by land or approach by water—regardless, the views of the bridge spanning surging waters will delight.

The community also has a historic downtown, marina, and many accommodation options.

getting there

Oak Harbor sits 10 miles and about 20 minutes from Coupeville along SR 20.

where to go

Oak Harbor Chamber of Commerce. 32630 SR 20, Oak Harbor; (360) 675-3755; oak harborchamber.com. Learn about Whidbey's largest community, where you'll find the greatest number of services. Open Mon to Fri.

Deception Pass State Park. 41229 SR 20, Oak Harbor; (360) 675-3767; parks.state.wa .us. Rugged cliffs, plentiful (albeit sometimes noisy) camping, and photo-worthy views define this popular state park. The narrow passageways separating Whidbey, Pass, and Fidalgo Islands are the bottleneck for tidal surges. While outlooks offer picturesque vantages on both sides of the bridges, jet-boat rides with Deception Pass Tours provide more stunning pictures (888-909-8687; deceptionpasstours.com; $$$). There's also about 36 miles of trails, freshwater lakes, and shoreline access. The park is open daily. $.

PBY–Naval Air Museum. 270 SE Pioneer Way, Oak Harbor; (360) 240-9500; pbymf.org. Oak Harbor changed dramatically during WWII and this museum gives insight to naval air station operations through its best-known aircraft: the amphibious PBY-5A Catalina. Open Wed to Sun. $.

where to eat

Seabolt's Smokehouse. 31640 SR 20, Ste. 3, Oak Harbor; (360) 675-6485 or (800) 574-1120; seabolts.com. Wild seafood features in delectable fish-and-chips, sandwiches, and chowders. The atmosphere is straight-up, but the tried-and-tested recipes hold true as local favorites. Or, stash away some of the smoked delicacies for a picnic in a state park. They also have a location at Deception Pass. Open daily for lunch and dinner. $–$$.

worth more time

San Juan Islands. North of Oak Harbor lies Anacortes—the departure point for ferries to the San Juans, with three major islands in the group: San Juan, Orcas, and Lopez Islands. A one-way trip from Seattle takes 2.5 to 3 hours.

Take a weekend in this favorite summer destination to relax, whale watch, swim, kayak, bicycle, nap, bird watch, paint, and dine. The island time is truly yours. (888) 468-3701; visit sanjuans.com.

day trip 02

northwest

port towns:
port gamble, port townsend

From the New England streets of Port Gamble to the Victorian alleys of Port Townsend, this charming day trip boasts a civilized tour that spans northern Kitsap and the eastern tip of the Olympic Peninsula. Museums highlight everything from seashells to Art Deco light fixtures, while a state park provides the chance to explore a historic military base and visit the undersea world. Events, festivals, and adventures await in this lovely day trip from port to port.

port gamble

Built by New Englanders as a company town for lumber workers, Port Gamble is perhaps Washington's quaintest historic small town. A seashell museum and an insightful community museum both deliver surprisingly good exhibits. Rent a bicycle and explore a little further, perhaps through the huge network of trails in Port Gamble Forest Heritage Park.

Much of the town infrastructure is still used: from the church, a favorite for weddings, to the post office and huge general store. And if the Maine charm enchants you, the houses are still company owned and occasionally available for lease.

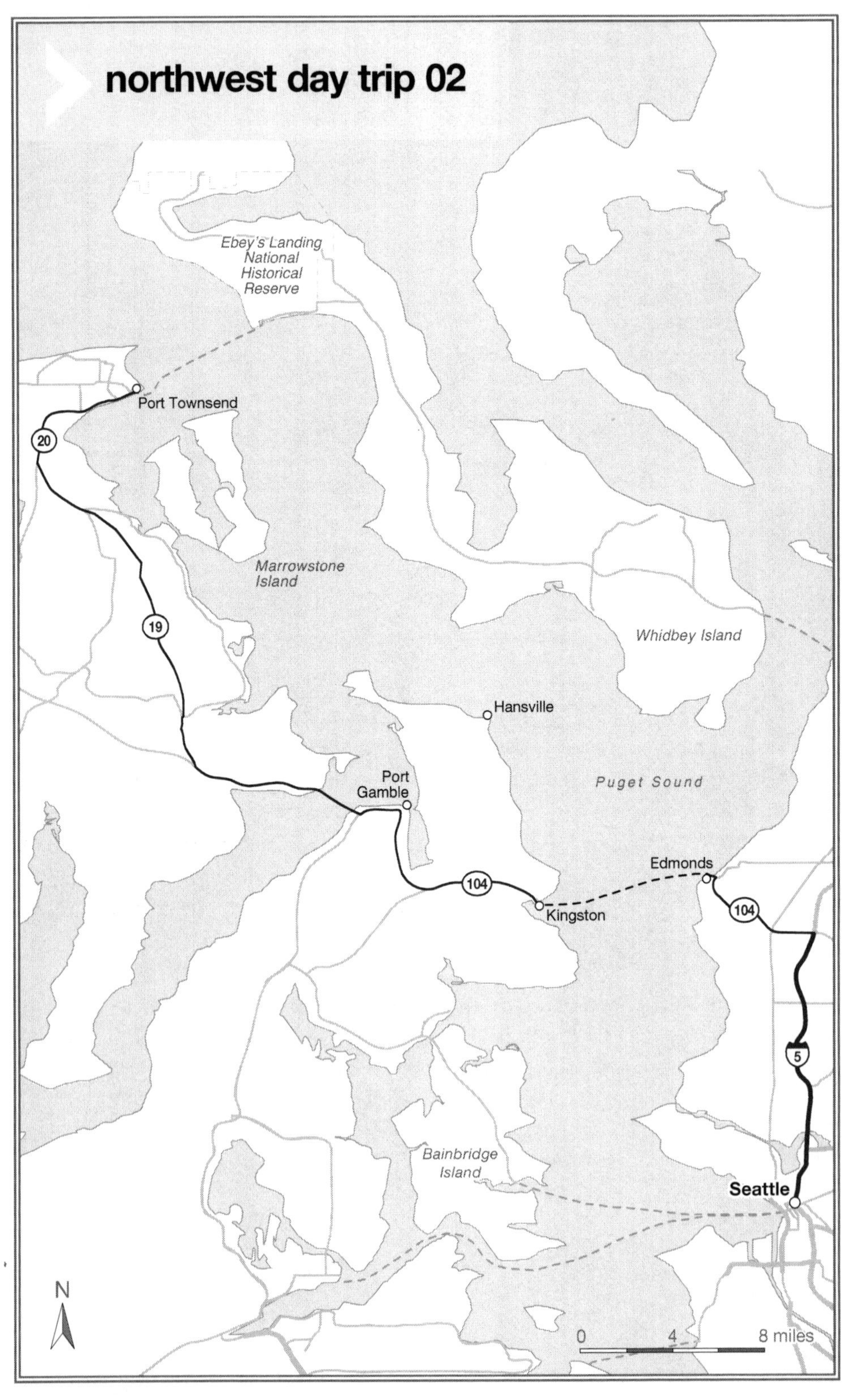
northwest day trip 02
Ebey's Landing National Historical Reserve
Port Townsend
20
Marrowstone Island
19
Whidbey Island
Hansville
Puget Sound
Port Gamble
Edmonds
104
Kingston
104
5
Bainbridge Island
Seattle
N
0
4
8 miles

getting there

Catch a ferry from Edmonds to Kingston, which is just southeast of Port Gamble. Follow SR 104 northwest for about 8 miles (15 minutes) into Port Gamble. From Port Gamble, Port Townsend lies further northwest.

where to go

Of Sea and Shore Museum. 32400 Rainier Ave. Northeast, Port Gamble; (360) 297-7637 (Port Gamble General Store). Whether it's the giant mollusks, thorny oysters, horseshoe crabs, Thailand land snails, or flowers dipped in a mineral spring, the treasures at this second-level museum delight and surprise. All the displays are informatively labeled, and the bright natural light creates a refreshing museum experience. By donation. Open daily.

Olympic Outdoor Center. 32379 Rainier Ave. Northeast, Port Gamble; (360) 297-4659; olympicoutdoorcenter.com. Explore by paddleboard, kayak, or bike—this provider has rentals and tours. Open Mon to Sat. $$$.

Port Gamble Historic Museum. 32400 Rainier Ave. Northeast, Port Gamble; (360) 297-8078; portgamble.com/museum. Retracing the journey of Maine businessmen Andrew Pope and William Talbot, who established a long-successful lumber mill at Port Gamble, the museum features excellent exhibits that succinctly tell the town's history. Discover why Port Gamble has a New England look, what happened before women arrived in town, or see Abraham Lincoln's signature on a land deed. Open Fri to Sun from May through Sept. $.

Port Gamble Forest Heritage Park. Town trailhead at South Teekalet Ave., Port Gamble; (360) 337-5350; kitsapgov.com. About 3,500 acres of forest offers wildlife viewing and 65 miles of trails, including the waterfront Bluff Trail. Open to bikes, hikers, and horses, the park does adjoin some private land and there may be some logging operations in progress.

where to eat

Butcher & Baker Provisions. 4719 NE SR 104, Port Gamble; (360) 297-9500; butcherandbakerprovisions.com. Fresh and inventive sandwiches as well as charcuterie boards and steak frites are more upscale than a typical counter-service eatery. It's housed in a heritage service station and perfectly fits with the pretty small town. You can also select from baked goods, cured meats, and cheeses to build a picnic. Open Wed to Sun. $$.

Port Gamble General Store & Café. (360) 297-7637; portgamblegeneralstore.com. Millworkers would stop in at this historic store for provisions, and you can do the same for ice cream, snacks, and coffee. Open Wed to Sun. $–$$.

where to stay

Port Gamble Guest Houses. 32440 Puget Ave. Northeast, Port Gamble; (360) 447-8473; portgambleguesthouses.com. Immerse yourself in New England charm with a room or entire house at one of the former mill company properties. The Port Gamble Guest Houses sit on a grassy meadow overlooking the water, and amenities include stocked kitchens, fireplaces, and patios. Best for groups as the houses sleep eight to ten. $$$–$$$$.

port townsend

This quaint Victorian seaport city combines a picturesque cliffside setting with historic buildings, a vibrant shopping district, and dining ranging from soda shops to bistros. Across the water from the defense forts on Whidbey Island, Fort Worden Historical State Park preserves historic buildings and barracks. Various former military buildings have seen reincarnations as museums, community centers, and accommodations—and the host to summer music festivals.

On the waterfront, get to know the maritime heritage and local wooden boat culture with the working woodshops and moored boats. Events embrace the waterside setting, including the late summer Wooden Boat Festival and the wacky Port Townsend Kinetic Race.

Washington Street provides incredible views and glimpses of heritage properties, while Water Street is a delight to explore on foot.

getting there

Traveling from Port Gamble, cross the Hood Canal Bridge via SR 104. There can be bridge traffic delays usually as a result of drawspan openings. Once on the Olympic Peninsula, turn onto SR 19 (Beaver Valley Road) until it merges with SR 20 for a short stretch before reaching Port Townsend—about 30 miles or 45 minutes from Port Gamble, or 60 miles and 2 hours from Seattle.

where to go

Visitor Information Center. 2409 Jefferson St., Ste. B, Port Townsend; (360) 385-2722; enjoypt.com. The info center is across the street from Kah Tai Lagoon Nature Park. Open daily.

Fort Worden Historical State Park. 200 Battery Way, Port Townsend; (360) 344-4400; fortworden.org or parks.state.wa.us. North of town, venture into a gated world of army barracks and waterfront batteries. A miscellany of museums, arts organizations, educational options, and accommodations are spread across the 100 historic buildings. Highlights include the **Commanding Officer's Quarters Museum** (under Jefferson County Historical

Society; jchsmuseum.org), **Coast Artillery Museum** (coastartillery.org), an aquarium and museum at the **Port Townsend Marine Science Center** (360-385-5582; ptmsc.org), and the views around **Point Wilson Lighthouse.** Open daily.

Jefferson Museum of Art & History. 540 Water St., Port Townsend; (360) 385-1003; jchsmuseum.org. In a grand downtown building that was the city hall (built in 1892), this museum relates the diverse history and artistic legacies of the Victorian port. The museum also operates Rothschild House Museum (418 Taylor St.) and the Commanding Officer's Quarters Museum at Fort Worden. Open Wed to Mon. $.

Kelly Art Deco Light Museum. 2000 Sims Way, Port Townsend; (360) 379-9030; kelly museum.org. The store Vintage Hardware is as much a museum as the exhibits are: Heavy wooden doors with brass plates (sourced from a Manhattan bank) lead to two floors of light fixtures, furniture, and miscellaneous décor. In the museum elegant light fixture displays demonstrate the distinct Art Deco style. Open Mon to Sat. $.

Northwest Maritime Center. 431 Water St., Port Townsend; (360) 385-3628; nwmaritime .org and woodenboat.org. From the polished brass of the chandlery to the smell of cedar shavings in the boat shop, the Northwest Maritime Center provides visitors an authentic and thrilling experience. Built in 2009 the polished complex offers water-focused education from sailing courses to boat building. Head to the third-floor observation area to look down on the boat shop's in-progress vessels. The center also runs the Wooden Boat Festival in early September. Open daily.

Port Townsend Aero Museum. 105 Airport Rd., Port Townsend; (360) 379-5244; ptaeromuseum.com. About two-dozen historic and restored aircraft are on display at this community-minded museum. Open Wed to Sun. $$.

where to eat

Nifty Fiftys. 817 Water St., Port Townsend; (360) 385-1931. Jukeboxes, Hamilton Beach milk-shake mixers, and syrupy cola create an iconic soda shop. Whether it's just a shake at the bar, a burger, or the halibut-and-chips, the friendly service and focus on authenticity will have you putting another quarter in the jukebox. Open daily in summer closed Tues during off-peak season. $–$$.

Point Hudson Cafe. 130 Hudson St., Port Townsend; (360) 379-0592. Breakfast is a specialty, with seafood dishes such as crab cakes or scrambled eggs with oysters to start the day. Cioppino, salmon burgers, and other simple eats are available for lunch. The dockside location provides access to the boardwalk for an after-meal stroll. Open for breakfast and lunch daily. $$.

Taps at the Guard House. 300 Eisenhower Ave., Port Townsend; (360) 344-4477. There's a small but interesting menu of bar bites, such as Dungeness crab cakes and flatbread pizza. The historic guardhouse is a welcoming spot to relax and occasionally hosts live musicians, plus there's a fantastic patio. Open daily for lunch and dinner. $$.

Vintage Wine Bar & Plaza. 725 Water St., Port Townsend; (360) 344-8271; porttownsend vineyards.com. Dishes showcasing fresh ingredients are planned to pair with award-winning house wines and incredible water views from the patio. This restored heritage building is connected with the large wine-tasting room of Port Townsend Vineyards (2640 W. Sims Way; 360-344-8155). Open afternoon and early evenings daily. $$–$$$.

where to stay

The Palace Hotel. 1004 Water St., Port Townsend; (360) 385-0773 or (800) 962-0741; palacehotelpt.com. It's best to be up front about these things: The Palace Hotel is not the place to stay if a few ghost stories rattle your chains. But if historic rooms with vaulted ceilings (most with en-suite baths) and the elegance of a Victorian-era hotel do tempt you, then by all means book a night's stay. The 1889 Captain Tibbals building has a storied history as a brothel, and the rooms are named after the girls. There's also a newer, mid-century wing of the hotel where rooms have kitchens and exposed brick—and some have cool loft sleeping quarters. $$–$$$$.

worth more time

Fort Flagler Historical State Park. 10541 Flagler Rd., Nordland; (360) 385-1259; parks .state.wa.us. The third coastal defense station in a trio with Fort Worden and Fort Casey, this now–state park offers wonderful shoreline access for swimming, boating, and fishing. Guided tours with the military museum give perspective on the 1907 military base, its gun emplacements, and the old Marrowstone Island hospital. Park open daily; tours run from the museum Wednesdays and weekends from May through Sept. $.

olympic discovery trail

With 130 miles of road and trails connecting Port Townsend to Sequim, Port Angeles, Forks, and the Pacific coast, the Olympic Discovery Trail is step-by-step becoming the recreational backbone of the region. Walkers, bikers, and equestrians enjoy the route near Olympic National Park, with its old railroad trestles, parks, and even a tunnel. McPhee Tunnel is a 450-foot-long span near Lake Crescent (olympicdiscoverytrail.org).

day trip 03

northwest

olympic rain shadow:
sequim, port angeles

In the rain shadow of 7,980-foot Mount Olympus, Sequim's dry agricultural fields are perfect for growing lavender. Oh, and add fruits, grains, and vegetables to the crop list too. Agriculture is so important to the town that there's an annual Irrigation Festival in May that celebrates harnessing the Dungeness River to water the fields more than a century ago. But despite the pastoral life, the wilds of the Pacific sit just north of town along Dungeness Spit—the longest natural sand spit in the United States.

West along the coast, Port Angeles mixes the modern with the natural, like the Pacific Northwest's largest unmanaged herd of Roosevelt elk in the vast, scenic, and wild territory of Olympic National Park. Add in the lore of the *Twilight* vampire book-and-movie series, and museums and quirky art parks that are perfect for families, and the town deserves more than a day trip. Port Angeles is the departure point for ferries to Victoria, Canada, and the views over the Strait of Juan de Fuca tease you to explore further.

For an intro when arriving in the region, stop by **Olympic Peninsula Gateway Visitors Center** (93 Beaver Valley Rd., Port Ludlow: 360-437-0120; olympicpeninsula.org; open daily), but know a day trip is only a taste of the peninsula.

sequim

Downtown Sequim (pronounced *S-qwim,* like *swim* with a *q* thrown in) offers a museum, small shopping district, and tasty dining. But the true magic of this nearly rainless town can

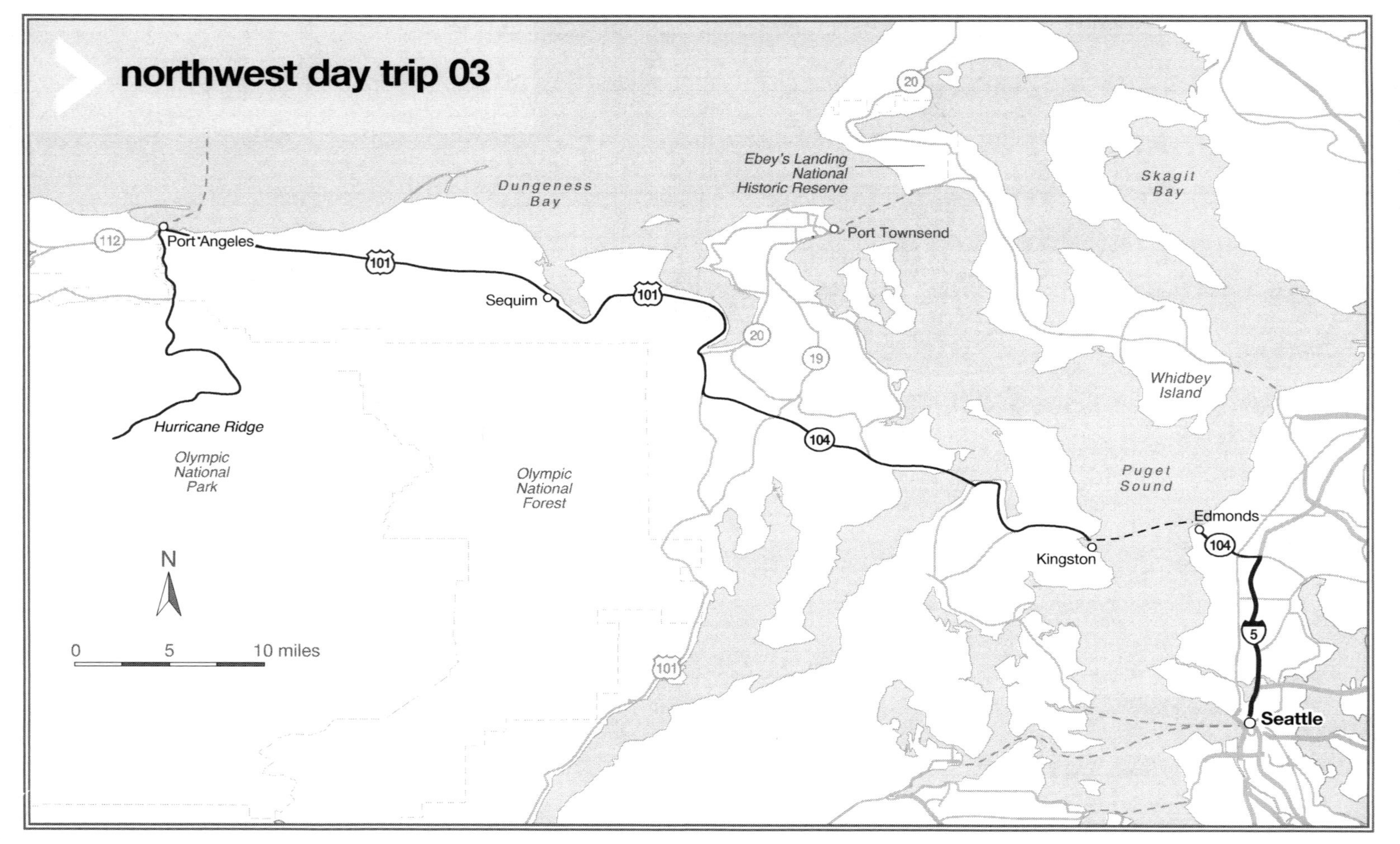
northwest day trip 03
Dungeness Bay
Ebey's Landing National Historic Reserve
Skagit Bay
Port Angeles
Port Townsend
112
101
20
19
104
5
Sequim
Whidbey Island
Hurricane Ridge
Olympic National Park
Olympic National Forest
Puget Sound
Edmonds
Kingston
Seattle
N
0
5
10 miles

be found in the fields and along the shore. Head north to the ocean where a lighthouse marks the arc of the country's longest natural sand spit. In the surrounding farmlands an animal park, more than a dozen lavender farms, and organic markets hold true to the area's agricultural heritage—and a herd of elk makes regular visits to the area.

The largest festival is Sequim Lavender Weekend, when the fields are at their most purple during the third weekend in July, but this heavenly blossom is a delight from spring through mid-summer. There is also a Saturday farmers' market.

getting there

Head north on I-5 and take the Edmonds-to-Kingston ferry, which makes about two dozen trips daily. SR 104 cuts across north Kitsap, crosses Hood Canal Floating Bridge, and connects with US 101. Also known as the Olympic Peninsula Loop, this route leads to Sequim for a total travel time of about 2 hours or 70 miles.

where to go

Sequim Visitor Information Center. 1192 E. Washington, Sequim; (360) 683-6197 or (800) 737-8462; visitsunnysequim.com. Close to US 101 and easy to find when arriving in town, this helpful center is open daily.

Dungeness River Audubon Center. Railroad Bridge Park, 2151 W. Hendrickson Rd., Sequim; (360) 681-4076; dungenessrivercenter.org. A railroad bridge is one of the Olympic Discovery Trail river crossings, and makes a great vantage for watching river birds in the 80-acre park. Inside the exhibit center, examples of local birds and other wildlife are on display.

Dungeness Wildlife Refuge. 554 Voice of America Rd., off Lotzgesell Road, Sequim; (360) 457-8451; fws.gov/refuge/dungeness. A shoelace of sand, beach cobbles, and grasses

become a lighthouse keeper

Becoming a volunteer lighthouse keeper at New Dungeness Lighthouse affords a unique opportunity. For a moderate weekly fee, live on the sand spit and complete the daily tasks that include polishing the brass, cleaning the restrooms, and raising the flag.

The lighthouse is open to tours daily so it won't be quite such a lonely task, and the keeper's quarters accommodate up to eight people. Visit newdungenesslighthouse.com for more details.

nearly closes off Dungeness Harbor. This area teems with birdlife and seals. A 5-mile hike (one way) trips to the end of the sand spit, while lookouts provide ocean and sandy views just 10 minutes down the trail. The reward for the longer journey is seeing the isolated New Dungeness Lighthouse, built in 1857. Open daily. $.

Lavender Farms. sequimlavender.org. A series of purple-hued farms with fields of the fragrant flowers, gift shops, accommodations, and activities form the Sequim lavender trail. Outside of Sequim Lavender Weekend in July, you can find the delightful bounty growing in the fields as well as at the Saturday farmers' markets, downtown boutiques, and local events.

Museum & Arts Center. 544 N. Sequim Ave., Sequim; (360) 681-2257; sequimmuseum .com. See the bones of the Manis Mastodon: the first (and initially greatly disputed) evidence that 14,000 years ago, humans hunted mastodons and lived on the Northern Olympic Peninsula—a timeline that put people in the region 4,000 years earlier than once thought. Digging a pond in his yard, Emanuel Manis discovered the tusks and bones of a mastodon that had a spear point lodged in its ribs. The museum delves into the mystery as well as local history. Open Tues to Sat.

Nash's Farm Store. 4681 Sequim-Dungeness Way, Sequim; (360) 683-4642; nashsor ganicproduce.com. This is the home turf for Nash's Organic Produce, and this packed market offers local veggies, picnic meats, and cheeses, plus snacks and drinks. Open daily.

Olympic Game Farm. 1423 Ward Rd., Sequim; (360) 683-4295 or (800) 778-4295; oly gamefarm.com. A driving tour takes visitors through the animal lands of the privately held park where feeding the animals whole-wheat bread prompts fun encounters with pastures of yak, grazing zebras, and munching llamas. After driving past the bears, bison, and elk, take a walking tour through the wolves, tigers, and cougars (summer only). The 84-acre farm was once connected with Walt Disney Studios and started out caring for animal actors during their off-set time. Open daily. $$.

where to eat

Alder Wood Bistro. 139 W. Alder St., Sequim; (360) 683-4321; alderwoodbistro.com. Lunch offers casual fare, but come at dinnertime for the wood-fired pizza and house-made desserts. Dishes draw on the local bounty of field greens, Pacific seafood, and quality meats. There's a lovely patio too, so plan ample time to indulge. Open Wed to Sat for lunch and dinner. $$–$$$.

Dockside Grill. 2577 W. Sequim Bay Rd., Sequim; (360) 683-7510; docksidegrill-sequim .com. Overlooking John Wayne Marina—named for the famous actor who used to visit the area on his yacht—this wharf-perched restaurant serves the area's bountiful seafood. Cedar planking is used to add subtle flavors to steaks and vegetables as well as the usual salmon. From Dungeness crab to local oysters, the ocean meets table at the Dockside. Open Wed to Sun for lunch and dinner. $$$–$$$$.

Rainshadow Café. 157 W. Cedar St., Sequim; (360) 797-1654; rainshadowcoffee.com. Hot breakfast dishes to start the day, pastries and coffee in the daytime, events and drinks in the evening—this small local cafe serves it all. Open daily.

where to stay

Red Caboose Getaway. 24 Old Coyote Way, Sequim; (360) 683-7350; redcabooseget away.com. From fine china in the dining car to individually themed cabooses, the station-masters roll out a truly fun overnight destination. "All it needs is a bullet hole!" I exclaimed about the Western-themed caboose. Lo and behold, the three layers of glass on the back door of caboose number four have spiderweb cracks where a bullet once hit—likely from a farm boy's gun during a cross-country trek. There's nothing else like it in the state, and it's also a certified wildlife habitat. $$$.

port angeles

Choose your version of Port Angeles: the *Twilight* locations of Bella Italia, Lincoln Theater, and Odyssey Bookshop; the accessibility of Olympic National Park with its mountain views and hot-springs hiking; or the wine tasting, fine dining, and storm watching at oceanside inns.

Port Angeles has a busy pier with fun family activities such as the aquarium at Feiro Marine Life Center. It's also where the ferry to Victoria, British Columbia, departs. There's lots of construction underway, and the city is a changing gateway to the national park.

The national park is of course the headliner, but the region teems with mountain, forest, and ocean activities, making it a delight to explore on a longer trip. Regular events celebrate music at the spring Juan de Fuca Festival of the Arts and seafood at the crowd-pleasing Dungeness Crab & Seafood Festival in fall.

getting there

The 16-mile journey from Sequim to Port Angeles takes about 25 minutes on US 101.

where to go

Port Angeles Visitor Center. 121 E. Railroad Ave., Port Angeles; (360) 452-2363; visit portangeles.com. Well-signposted when arriving in town from the east, the visitor center can provide maps and recommendations for Port Angeles as well as Victoria across the Strait of Juan de Fuca. Open daily.

The Carnegie Museum. 207 S. Lincoln St., Port Angeles; (360) 417-8545; elwha.org/departments/carnegie-museum. The Lower Elwha Klallam tribe took over this local museum that introduces the historical quilt of the Olympic Peninsula. Exhibits include artifacts from a 2,000-year-old village site near Ediz Hook. Open Tues to Sat. $.

Ediz Hook. Ediz Hook Rd. off Marine Dr., Port Angeles. About half of this 3-mile sand spit is drive-able. While the picnic areas are good for wildlife watching, it's more active than Dungeness Spit due to the coast guard station, harbor traffic, and log booms. Look back toward the city for views of the towering mountains.

olympic national park

Although it's longer than a day trip to venture to the Hoh Rain Forest, Forks, and the west coast of the Olympic Peninsula, the national park offers stunning destinations within an hour or so of Port Angeles. For further information on these destinations, check with the ***Olympic National Park Visitor Center*** *(3002 Mount Angeles Rd., Port Angeles; 360-565-3130; nps.gov/olym).*

- ***Elwah:*** *The park's largest watershed was dammed for more than a century. You can see the restoration in progress—salmon have now returned to the Elwha River. Due to large road washouts following the dam removal, as of 2020 there's access on Olympic Hot Springs Road only through to Madison Falls, a 60-foot cascade. (10 miles, 15 minutes from Port Angeles)*
- ***Hurricane Ridge:*** *Drive from Port Angeles up Hurricane Ridge Road to a popular visitor center, hiking trails, and viewpoint that's a mile high in the sky. Wildflower meadows and views of Mount Olympus are two of the top reasons to make the trip. Open daily during summer; reduced schedule in winter, with snow common in the colder months and necessitating winter weather preparations. (20 miles, 45 minutes from Port Angeles)*
- ***Lake Crescent:*** *West of Port Angeles, Lake Crescent is a summertime favorite for its clear water, stunning blue color, and spectacular views. The glacier-carved lake serves as a base for hikes to waterfalls (such as the 90-foot Marymere Falls) and other viewing points. Lodges and resorts like Log Cabin Resort (reservations: 888-896-3818) rent boats and offer accommodation. (20 miles, 30 minutes from Port Angeles)*
- ***Sol Duc Falls and Hot Springs:*** *The Sol Duc area offers resort hot springs, waterfalls, hiking in old-growth forest such as the Ancient Groves Trail, camping, and salmon watching during the fall run.* ***Sol Duc Hot Springs Resort*** *(360-327-3583; reservations: 888-896-3818; visitsolduc.com) offers cabins, pools, and dining, and is open late Mar to late Oct. (40 miles, 1 hour from Port Angeles)*

Feiro Marine Life Center. 315 N. Lincoln St., Port Angeles; (360) 417-6254; feiro marinelifecenter.org. On the Port Angeles pier, touch tanks and aquariums invite you into the ocean world with residents like a giant Pacific octopus. Open daily. $.

Olympic Cellars. 255410 US 101, Port Angeles; (360) 452-0160; olympiccellars.com. The gambrel roof of an 1890 barn shelters wine cellars and a gift shop. Whether it's for wine tasting or an event, the winery is a welcoming host. Open daily.

Olympic Coast Discovery Center. 115 E. Railroad Ave., Port Angeles; (360) 452-3255 in summer; (360) 406-2092 in the off-season; olympiccoast.noaa.gov. Get to know the wildlife of the Olympic Coast National Marine Sanctuary, which includes 65 miles of coastline. Located in waterfront mall The Landing, the info center has hands-on exhibits. Open daily Memorial Day to Labor Day; weekends only in fall; by appointment only mid-Oct to spring.

Olympic National Park Visitor Center. 3002 Mount Angeles Rd. (visitor center), Port Angeles; (360) 565-3130; nps.gov/olym. Maps, advice, and permits for Olympic National Park are available from this visitor center on the south edge of town. The road continues into the hills, leading to Hurricane Ridge. Open daily. Park admission is $30 per car. $$$.

Port Angeles Fine Arts Center and Webster's Woods Sculpture Park. 1203 E. Lauridsen Blvd., Port Angeles; (306) 457-3532; pafac.org. Alongside Port Angeles Fine Arts Center (which hosts gallery exhibits), Webster's Woods Sculpture Park creates a vibrant forest world to explore. The art pieces integrate with nature, and works can be spotted in trees, ponds, and brush. The art park is open daily; the arts center opens Thurs to Sun.

where to eat

Bella Italia. 118 E. First St., Port Angeles; (360) 457-5442; bellaitaliapa.com. Now best known as the location of Bella and Edward's first date in *Twilight,* Bella Italia also serves warming, classic dishes. Pizzas, pastas, seafood, and steaks shape a wide-reaching menu with a few surprises. While you can order up the *Twilight*-famous mushroom ravioli in the cozy dining room, the porterhouse chop with its roasted garlic potatoes may be best for warding off the vampires. Open daily for dinner. $$–$$$.

Michael's Seafood and Steak House. 117B E. First St., Port Angeles; (360) 417-6929; michaelsdining.com. The atmosphere is fun, intimate, and cozy. Look for the chanterelle mushroom dishes in season and regular happy-hour specials. Local seafood dishes include oysters, Dungeness crab cakes, and even fish-and-chips. Open daily for dinner. $$–$$$$.

Toga's Soup House. 122 W. Lauridsen Blvd., Port Angeles; (360) 452-1952; togassoup house.com. Emerging from the mountains of the national park, a home-simmered bowl of soup and perhaps a grilled sandwich are the ideal warm-up treats. Add friendly service, a casual country dining area, and efficient take-out service to quickly please hungry hikers. Open weekdays only for breakfast and lunch. $–$$.

port angeles twilight

If hunting for vampires, these Twilight *locations are popular haunts in Port Angeles: The site of Edward and Bella's first date,* **Bella Italia** *is at 118 E. First St., and the* **Lincoln Theater** *(132 E. First St.) is where Bella heads to watch a horror film in* New Moon. *Book shops are also pivotal to the* Twilight *plot, and Port Angeles has two:* **Port Book & News** *(104 E. First St.) and* **Odyssey Bookshop** *(114 W. Front St.).*

Want more titles for your Washington State reading list? How about Snow Falling on Cedars *by David Guterson,* The Egg and I *by Betty MacDonald,* Where'd You Go, Bernadette *by Maria Semple, or* Another Roadside Attraction *by Tom Robbins.*

where to stay

Domaine Madeleine. 146 Wildflower Ln., Port Angeles; (360) 457-4174; domainemadeleine.com. A cliffside bed-and-breakfast with lush gardens offers more privacy than most inns—plus decks or patios for all rooms. Fireplaces, ocean views, and décor inspired by the park all add to the appeal. Separate from the main house, cottages offer more privacy. All the rooms suggest the feeling of a secluded retreat. $$$$.

day trip 04

northwest

royal city:
victoria

victoria

As western Canada's royal city, Victoria features grand hotels, government houses, and legislature buildings. A long waterfront walk around Victoria's Inner Harbor bustles with performers, vacationers, and government employees on lunch during the summer.

But aside from its history—which includes coal barons, ghosts, and internationally famous artists—there are lush gardens, parks, and butterfly sanctuaries. For shopping, head to the character-filled shops that line Government and Lower Johnson Streets and fill Chinatown. This is a great spot to celebrate Canada Day on July 1.

getting there

A direct-from-Seattle passenger ferry makes the cross-border trip during the summer months for a total travel time of about 2 hours, 45 minutes. Contact Clipper Vacations for schedules (250-382-8100 in Victoria; 206-448-5000 in Seattle; clippervacations.com).

Alternately, if you'd rather travel with a vehicle (although the attractions listed in this chapter are almost exclusively accessible by walking or public transit), drive to Port Angeles (2.5 hours) and board the MV *Coho* ferry (250-386-2202 in Victoria; 360-457-4491 in Port Angeles; cohoferry.com) to cross the Strait of Juan de Fuca for a total travel time of about 4 hours.

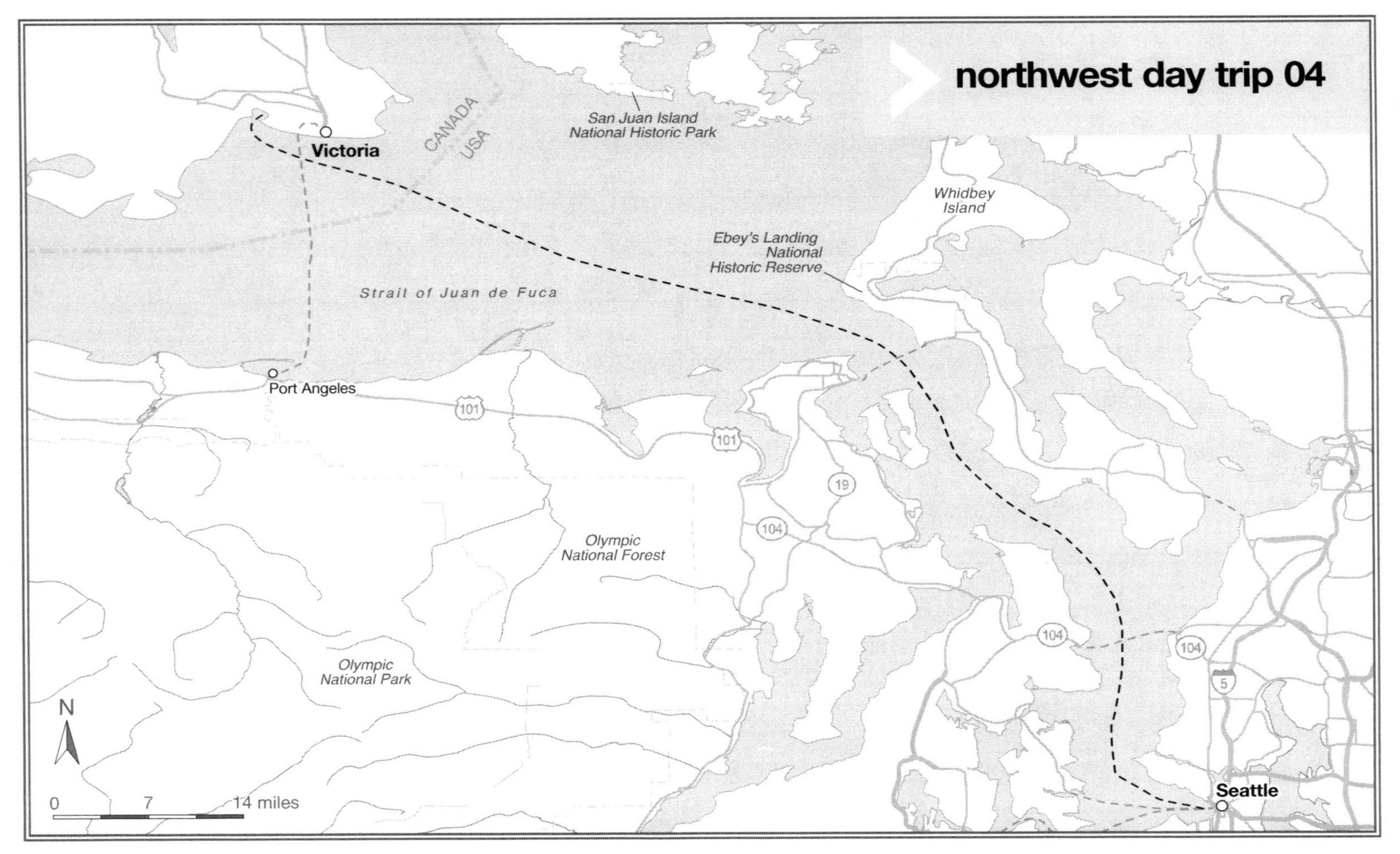

northwest day trip 04
San Juan Island
National Historic Park
Victoria
CANADA
USA
Whidbey
Island
Ebey's Landing
National
Historic Reserve
Strait of Juan de Fuca
Port Angeles
101
101
19
104
104
104
5
Olympic
National Forest
Olympic
National Park
N
0
7
14 miles
Seattle

where to go

Tourism Victoria. 812 Wharf St., Victoria; (250) 953-2033 or (800) 663-3883; tourismvictoria.com. A harborside information center provides maps, brochures, and details for local attractions, events, and accommodation. Plus, the location is handy to the ferry terminals and floatplane docks. Open daily.

Beacon Hill Park. Douglas St. at Southgate St., Victoria; victoria.ca. At its northwest end Beacon Hill Park lies close to the museums and attractions of downtown. But follow the paths deeper into the park to climb over rocky hillocks, past rare Garry oak ecosystems, and to a petting zoo. Victorian gardens and Northwest plants lace the grounds creating a lush land of discovery. Open daily.

Butchart Gardens. 800 Benvenuto Ave., Brentwood Bay; (250) 652-4422 or (866) 652-4422; butchartgardens.com. At Butchart Gardens Christmas is a season with dainty lights, ice-skating, and holiday garlands. But perhaps more magical is the Sunken Garden where ivies climb down the stone walls of an old quarry. Japanese, Italian, and rose gardens create outdoor banquet-like spaces—a feast for the senses. Open daily year-round with calendars available that detail the blooms, foliage, and special events. $$$.

Craigdarroch Castle. 1050 Joan Crescent, Victoria; (250) 592-5323; thecastle.ca. What would a royal city be without its castle? Craigdarroch Castle delivers the opulence of a palace but with a tumult of a history befitting Hamlet. Robert Dunsmuir, a man made wealthy from coal mining, commissioned construction on a new house in 1887, but he died in 1889 before the home was finished. Bitter disputes resulted from Dunsmuir's will, causing ongoing friction between his two sons, James and Alex, and their mother, Joan. When son Alex Dunsmuir died 10 years later, another inheritance dispute escalated into a lawsuit between Joan and James—who was then premier of British Columbia. A headline in the *New York Times* read: "Premier sued by his Mother." There's little wonder that with so much family turmoil, Robert Dunsmuir is said to haunt the halls of the castle. Open daily. $$.

Emily Carr House. 207 Government St., Victoria; (250) 383-5843; emilycarr.com. As an artist and anthropologist, Emily Carr painted First Nations villages throughout British Columbia. Her depictions of totems, longhouses, and BC's towering trees are iconic. This yellow home, built in 1863, was Carr's birthplace and now includes Victorian furnishings, artifacts from the artist's life, and work by Carr alongside that of local artists. Open Tues to Sat from May to Sept. $.

Government House. 1401 Rockland Ave., Victoria; (250) 387-2080; ltgov.bc.ca. Because Canada still retains the role of a Commonwealth nation and allegiance to the British monarchy, the lieutenant governor of British Columbia represents the head of state at the provincial level. Occasionally tours of the modern house are available while the gardens are open daily.

Legislative Assembly of British Columbia. 501 Belleville St., Victoria; (250) 387-3046; leg.bc.ca/learn-about-us. The waterfront stone building makes a favorite photo backdrop. Tour guides explain the role of the Legislative Assembly and provide history on the building and province. Free tours run daily from mid-May through Aug; weekdays only from Sept to mid-May.

Maritime Museum of British Columbia. 634 Humboldt St., Victoria; (250) 385-4222; mmbc.bc.ca. From pirates to fishing and shipwrecks, the museum brings the high seas to dry land. It's in a temporary location during renovation of the Bastion Square location, a historic jail and courthouse. Open Tues to Sat from mid-May through Aug; Thurs to Sat Sept to mid-May. $.

Royal BC Museum. 675 Belleville St., Victoria; (250) 356-7226 or (888) 447-7977; royalbcmuseum.bc.ca. This museum rates as the city's must-see attraction. From mystical towering totems to the house of a chief, the First Peoples Gallery tells the story of the Pacific Northwest's First Nations in living detail. Enter a Chinatown herbalist's shop, lock eyes with a grizzly, or admire a replica of Captain George Vancouver's ship. Open daily. $$$.

Victoria Butterfly Gardens. 1461 Benvenuto Ave., Brentwood Bay; (250) 652-3822 or (877) 722-0272; butterflygardens.com. Thousands of butterflies flit through the tropical conservatory, and while the colorful insects are the highlight at the gardens, iguanas, flamingos, and parrots also inhabit the animal house. Open daily. $$.

where to shop

For souvenirs a walk down Government Street will yield all the Canadian-flag T-shirts you'll ever need. Look for **Cowichan Trading Company** at 1328 Government St., featuring the original versions of the cozy woolens donned by the Canadian Winter Olympic team at the 2010 Games.

Off Government Street **Bastion Square** features vendors selling at an open-air market, Thurs to Sun and holidays from May through September. For boutique shopping, urban fashions, and cool finds, head to Yates Street, Johnson Street, and Market Square.

A small **Chinatown district** starts at the bold gateway at Fisgard and Government Streets. Shops selling broad selections of Asian goods are stocked to the roof, and prices are generally reasonable. Look for the narrow Fan Tan Alley that branches off Fisgard. The district is one of the oldest Chinatowns in North America and grew as a result of the gold rush.

where to eat

Bard & Banker. 1022 Government St., Victoria; (250) 953-9993; bardandbanker.com. This Scottish-style pub certainly rises above. The menu includes name-brand British fare including fish-and-chips as well as burgers, steaks, and west coast seafood. With a lovely streetside patio, the pub is worth visiting for more than a pint of stout. Open daily for breakfast, lunch, and dinner. $$–$$$.

ReBar Modern Food. 50 Bastion Sq., Victoria; (250) 361-9223; rebarmodernfood.com. With modern comfort food at its best and healthiest, this brightly decorated cafe has spawned cookbooks and an avid local following. The almond burger persists as a highlight while the salads and brunch items make excellent weekend fare. Open daily for breakfast, lunch, and dinner. $$.

Red Fish Blue Fish. 1006 Wharf St., Victoria; (250) 298-6877; redfish-bluefish.com. Tacones—"taco cones"—are the specialty here and the easiest thing to eat from a plate balanced on your knee. This bustling wharfside food stand serves fresh seafood, crisp fries, and immense sandwiches. Hours change with the seasons but expect the stand to be open most lunch and early dinner hours when the weather is nice. $$–$$$.

Teahouse at Abkhazi Garden. 1964 Fairfield Rd., Victoria; (778) 265-6466; abkhazitea house.com. Established as the gardens and home to a prince and princess, this unique property offers a tranquil escape. Reservations are recommended for this high tea dining experience amid the acre of lush landscapes, sculptures, and vistas. Open daily from Apr to Sept; Wed to Sun from Oct to Mar. $$$$.

Victoria Public Market at the Hudson. 1701 Douglas St., Victoria; (778) 433-2787; victoriapublicmarket.com. A variety of local-food vendors provide ready-to-eat meals and shopping options in this large market that was once a Hudson's Bay Company store. Hearty sandwiches, freshly baked meat pies, and waffles are among the tasty offerings. Open daily for lunch. $–$$.

where to stay

The Fairmont Empress. 721 Government St., Victoria; (250) 384-8111 or (866) 540-4429; fairmont.com/empress-victoria. The iconic building competes with the legislature for the title of most grandiose waterfront building. From the rich woodwork in the breakfast dining hall to the afternoon tea served on fine china, a stay at the Empress truly gives that regal feeling. Rooms range from standard to luxurious and there's an on-site spa. $$$$.

James Bay Inn. 270 Government St., Victoria; (250) 384-7151 or (800) 836-2649; james bayinn.com. Clean rooms with basic furnishings provide a budget option in town (with a little more space than the hostel listed below). Rooms vary in size and amenities and occasionally have a quirky feature, like a double-headed shower. There's also free parking. $–$$.

Ocean Island Backpackers Inn. 791 Pandora Ave., Victoria; (250) 385-1789 or (888) 888-4180; oceanisland.com. Although the private rooms are tiny, the central location, lots of advice on local day trips, and free eats and drinks make the hostel a fabulous budget deal. Rooms are clean. For increased privacy, opt for a pricier suite in the inn's off-site 1907 heritage house. $.

festivals and celebrations

january

Starting the new year, the **Skagit Eagle Festival** observes the majestic birds on January weekends in Concrete, Rockport, and Marblemount. Activities center on Rockport's Howard Miller Steelhead Park. concrete-wa.com/skagit-eagle-festival

In late January those searching for the elusive sasquatch gather in Longview at **sQuatch Fest.** kelsolongviewchamber.org

february

Well-timed to coincide with Valentine's Day (although officially on Presidents' Day weekend), Yakima Valley's annual **Red Wine and Chocolate Festival** pairs local fine wines with blends of dark chocolate. A tip from the festival: Taste the wine first then let the chocolate melt in your mouth. wineyakimavalley.org or redwineroute.com

Who wouldn't want to hang out with a group of cowboys? The **Spirit of the West Cowboy Gathering** in Ellensburg rounds up the folks in ten-gallon hats for a campfire sing-along of sorts in mid-February. Poets, musicians, and artists arrive in town to entertain. ellensburg cowboygathering.com

Langley Mystery Weekend takes over the Whidbey Island town in late February, with locals and visitors trying to solve a whodunnit mystery. visitlangley.com

Vancouver celebrates **Chinese New Year** with parades, costumes, food, and dances. The date changes annually and is based on the lunar calendar, although the date is usually in late Jan to mid-Feb. tourismvancouver.com

march

Things get steamy at the **Penn Cove Mussel Fest** in early March. Eating events, cooking contests, and demonstrations comprise the weekend festival in Coupeville, Whidbey Island. thepenncovemusselfestival.com

april

Skagit Valley Tulip Festival features a whole month of tulip, daffodil, and iris blooms as well as lively local events—although just when the flowers will bloom only Mother Nature knows. tulipfestival.org

In mid-April go birding at the **Olympic Peninsula BirdFest** when the Audubon community gathers to stake out the sand spits, tidal flats, and shoreline on the peninsula (olympicbird fest.org). Around the same time is **Grays Harbor Shorebird and Nature Festival** in Hoquiam, when returning migratory flocks gather on the mudflats of Grays Harbor (shorebird festival.com). Or, go see the whales off Whidbey and celebrate with the Welcome the Whales Parade in Langley (visitlangley.com).

Spring Barrel Tasting in Yakima is a preview event for that season's wines. Dozens and dozens of wineries participate in the late April event. wineyakimavalley.org

Running late Apr into early May, the **Washington State Apple Blossom Festival** in Wenatchee celebrates the spring blooms with parades, carnivals, and contests as well as square dancing, airplane flyovers, and a bocce ball tournament. appleblossom.org

may

Celebrating water and the agricultural life it brings to Sequim, the **Irrigation Festival** runs in early May. The festival is the oldest in the state, and you'll see everything from a strong-man competition to fireworks and a parade. irrigationfestival.com

The first two weekends in May—and again in Dec—there are **art studio tours** from Vashon Island Visual Artists. vivartists.com

May 17 is Norwegian Constitution Day and time to visit Poulsbo for **Viking Fest.** There's a lutefisk-eating contest, Norwegian entertainment, and road race. vikingfest.org

On May 18 **Mount St. Helens** remembers the lethal volcanic eruption that occurred in 1980. visitmtsthelens.com

Mid-May kicks off summer concert season with **Fisherman's Village Music Festival** in Everett—featuring music, a night market, food trucks, and more. thefishermansvillage.com

Canadian Victoria Day weekend (Monday on or before May 24) looks very tartan with the **Victoria Highland Games and Celtic Festival.** victoriahighlandgames.com

Memorial Day weekend in Port Angeles features live music concerts, a street fair, and activities for the **Juan de Fuca Festival of the Arts** (jffa.org). The holiday weekend is also an epic one for adventure racing, with the **Ski to Sea** relay from Mt. Baker to Bellingham (skitosea.com).

In late May/early June, the **Bellevue Jazz & Blues Festival** gathers exceptional artists to perform live on the Eastside. bellevuedowntown.com

june

Early June brings a variety of boats and ships to the waterfront for the **Port Angeles Maritime Festival**. portangelesmaritimefestival.org

Edmonds Arts Festival is a three-day family festival that makes a great destination for Father's Day weekend (edmondsartsfestival.com). Also on Dad's day is the roaring, soaring **Olympic Air Show** at Olympia Regional Airport (olympicairshow.com).

Head to Poulsbo around June 21 for **Skandia Midsommarfest.** Of course there's folk dancing, but this Swedish summer solstice celebration also features the traditional raising of the Midsommar pole. skandia-folkdance.org

First running in 1939, **Meeker Days Festival** is now the county's largest free street festival with entertainment, food, drink, and classic cars. Watch for it in the first days of summer. puyallupmainstreet.com

Sand-castle builders construct impressive sand structures beachside, while in the forest chainsaw carvers create cedar masterpieces. The **Sand and Sawdust Festival** runs in late June in Ocean Shores. sandandsawdust.org

All summer long **Olympic Music Festival** hosts classical musical acts at Fort Worden in Port Townsend. olympicmusicfestival.org

Wine country is another destination for summer concerts, with the free **Woodinville Summer Concerts** (celebratewoodinville.com), as well as well-known events at wineries such as Chateau Ste. Michelle (ste-michelle.com).

july

Defect north for **Canada Day** (July 1) and take in a parade, entertainment, and fireworks in downtown Victoria. canadadayvictoria.ca

Fourth of July weekend is big in most towns and cities around the state. Some that host the nation for a party include Leavenworth, Bainbridge Island, Everett, Port Orchard, Edmonds, Tacoma, and Bellevue, to name a handful. Unusual celebrations include chainsaw carving, a rodeo, and other demos for the **Loggerodeo** in Sedro-Woolley (loggerodeo.org) and Aberdeen's **Splash Festival,** when the tall ships are in home port (splash.aberdeenwa.gov).

Bellingham Festival of Music runs throughout much of July and welcomes artists for orchestral and chamber concerts. bellinghamfestival.org

For more than a century, Snohomish has hosted **Kla Ha Ya Days** festival—now including a street festival, cook-off, and more in mid-July. klahayadays.com

By mid-month the countryside is its most vibrant shade of purple during the **Sequim Lavender Festival.** Tour local lavender farms and then head to town for the party. lavenderfestival .com

Running for well over a century, the **Vashon Island Strawberry Festival** is just about the sweetest thing going—with two parades, music, and a pancake breakfast. vashonchamber .com

The **Bellevue Arts Museum's Artsfair** becomes a rich marketplace of art and craft from hundreds of artists. The juried arts show has been around since the 1940s and happens around the third week of July in conjunction with **6th Street Arts Fair.** bellevuearts.org/ artsfair and bellevuedowntown.com

Jazz in the Valley is a later-July collection of blues, jazz, swing, and Latin music in Ellensburg. jazzinthevalley.com

Late July there's more rodeo fun at **Cowlitz County Fair** with a carnival, music, and the **Thunder Mountain Pro Rodeo**. cowlitzcountyfair.com and thundermountainprorodeo .com

august

You won't find a more colorful parade in British Columbia than **Vancouver Pride Festival.** The first weekend in Aug, a week-long festival of events and a Sun parade take over Denman at Davie Sts. in Vancouver, British Columbia. vancouverpride.ca

In mid-Aug the Suquamish community hosts **Chief Seattle Days** with memorials, songs, dances, fireworks, canoe races, and salmon dinners. suquamish.nsn.us

The **Southwest Washington Fair** draws thousands to Chehalis for rides, contests, and concerts in the middle of Aug. southwestwashingtonfair.org

Mid-Aug is also the time for heritage aircraft to take to the skies for the **Arlington Fly-In** (arlingtonflyin.org). Meanwhile, find the tastiest of foods plus family activities and concerts on the shores north of Seattle with the annual **Taste Edmonds** (tasteedmonds.com).

More than 1,500 vintage vehicles are the draw for the **LeMay Marymount Car Show** in Tacoma, held in late August. lemaymarymount.org

september

The **Washington State Fair in Puyallup:** It's one of the largest fairs in the country with a carnival, rodeo, monster trucks, food, and entertainment. Running most of September, the fair attracts more than one million visitors each year. thefair.com

Olympia Harbor Days celebrates Labor Day wharfside in the state capital with tugboat races and ships on site. harbordays.com

The **Ellensburg Rodeo** gets rowdy over Labor Day weekend, along with the **Kittitas County Fair.** ellensburgrodeo.com and kittitascountyfair.com

In early/mid-September hundreds of wooden vessels launch in, sail to, and dock at Port Townsend for the **Wooden Boat Festival.** Expect sailing races, rowing competitions, and maritime music. woodenboat.org

Kilts fly at the **Kelso Highlander Festival** held in mid-Sept. It's Scottish-and-Celt everything with music, food, competitions, and activities. kelso.gov

30 Miles of Junque is an immense yard sale that takes over Westport and Grayland in mid-Sept. westportgrayland-chamber.org

Meanwhile in Yakima the grapes are coming off the vines for **Catch the Crush** weekend. wineyakimavalley.org

Maritime culture and delicious seafood are the highlights of **Bellingham's SeaFest,** the third weekend of Sept. bellinghamseafeast.org

There's lots of art, culture, and fashion afoot in late Sept with top-pick films and programming at the **Gig Harbor Film Festival** (gigharborfilm.org) and **Fashion Week** at The Bellevue Collection (fashionweekbellevue.com).

On the coast **Whidbey Island Kite Festival** fills the skies around Coupeville with colorful kites (whidbeykites.org) and Everett kicks off Oktoberfest early with the **Everett Sausage Festival** (everettsausagefest.com).

october

The **Festival of Family Farms** links Skagit Valley producers through farm tours, exhibits, mazes, pumpkin patches, and markets in early Oct. festivaloffamilyfarms.com

This event can only happen in a hop-growing region like Yakima: **Fresh Hop Beer Week** starts pouring for beer devotees in early Oct. freshhopalefestival.com

OysterFest is Shelton's major celebration with shucking competitions, marine exhibits, music, and lots of seafood. It takes place the first full weekend in Oct. oysterfest.org

Issaquah Salmon Days honors the annual return of the salmon to Issaquah Creek. salmon days.org

Port Townsend Kinetic Race features participants charting a course through town in human-powered vehicles that display engineering and artistic merit. Through mud, up hills, and around the course, the wacky race runs the first weekend in Oct. The town's race is the second-oldest version of worldwide kinetic race events—behind only the founding town of Ferndale, California. ptkineticrace.org

Apple Days offers no surprises but a delicious look at the locally grown fruit as well as entertainment. The Cashmere Museum, for which the event is a fundraiser, has the details on the early Oct event. cashmeremuseum.org

Whatcom Artist Studio Tour highlights the talented local artists at work in the county. During the first two weekends in Oct, admire, browse, and purchase the work of more than forty artists. studiotour.net

It's crab season in Oct and a fitting reason to celebrate with a festival in Port Angeles: enter the **Dungeness Crab & Seafood Festival.** crabfestival.org

Mid-Oct the **Cranberry Harvest Festival** coincides with the harvest of the tart berry. The Westport-Grayland Chamber of Commerce provides details on the event. westportgrayland-chamber.org

Leavenworth Oktoberfest means bottoms up the first three weekends in Oct. The keg-tapping ceremony is the center of the festivities, but there's also food, crafts, and entertainment. leavenworthoktoberfest.com

november

Thanksgiving in Wine Country centers on Yakima's wines and pairings with traditional and inspiring holiday cuisine. wineyakimavalley.org and yakimavalleywinecountry.com

Late Nov through the New Year, **Zoolights** brightens Point Defiance Zoo & Aquarium in Tacoma. The zoo even has a recycling program for old strings of holiday lights—so bring yours along. pdza.org

From Thanksgiving to late Jan, the **Bellevue Downtown Ice Rink** offers outdoor skating in the prettiest of settings. Other seasonal events include a parade as well as illuminations at the Bellevue Botanical Garden. magicseason.com

december

The **Leavenworth Christmas Lighting** is the town's iconic holiday festival. Over the first three weekends in Dec, carols, white lights, and Christmas cheer fill the Bavarian town. The local chamber will have the exact details. leavenworth.org

Hop aboard **Mt. Rainier Scenic Railroad** in Elbe for a holiday-themed train ride that ventures to the North Pole to visit Santa. mtrainierrailroad.com

index

C

G

H

I

O

P

Q

R

S

V

W

Y

Z